What the critics said

The Peculiar Case of the Electric Constable

'As gripping and readable as any crime novel, but all factual and based on remarkable research.'—*Sydney Morning Herald*

'Totally irresistible.'—*The Independent*, UK

'As lively and readable as a crime novel.'—*The Times*, UK

'A fascinating history, mystery and portrait of a complex, contradictory man.'—*Daily Mail*, UK

'A fascinating reconstruction of a real historical case . . . You can't beat a good courtroom scene, and the 50-page account of Tawell's trial is as good as any I've read in a crime novel.' —*Independent on Sunday*, UK

'A deftly woven tale.'—*Maclean's Magazine*, Canada

Captain Thunderbolt and His Lady: The true story of bushrangers Frederick Ward and Mary Ann Bugg

'This beautifully told story may change the way we see our history.'—*Good Reading*

'This compelling book is a valuable contribution to our colonial history.'—*Canberra Times*

'. . . a compelling yarn.'—*Sun-Herald*

Breaking the Bank: An extraordinary colonial robbery

'Colourful characters, daring deeds, crime and punishment, cruelty and compassion: Carol Baxter's meticulously researched book has it all.'—*The Australian*

'A story like [*Breaking the Bank*] is a mine of historical information but rather than a dry retelling of the facts, Baxter writes it like a crime thriller . . . riveting.'—*Adelaide Advertiser*

'A great story . . .'—*Launceston Examiner*

'. . . an accomplished story-teller.'—*Australian Historical Studies*

'. . . racy and packed with vivid descriptions and incidents that make for a compelling read and an incisive look into our brutal convict era.'—*Newcastle Herald*

An Irresistible Temptation: The true story of Jane New and a colonial scandal

'. . . with a fine eye for the complex motivations of characters, both political and personal, [Baxter] paints a vivid picture of Jane New's world.'—*Sydney Morning Herald*

'A vivid social history.'—*Canberra Times*

'[a] compelling work of popular narrative history.'—*Courier Mail*

'. . . a work that captures the reader . . . an excellent example of how a good story can illuminate the past.'—*Australian Literary Review*

'*An Irresistible Temptation* is just that—an irresistible mix of intrigue, scandal, crime, punishment tinged with romance and a dash of social history.'
—*Journal of the Royal Australian Historical Society*

BLACK
WIDOW

Other books by Carol Baxter

An Irresistible Temptation

Breaking the Bank

Captain Thunderbolt and His Lady

The Peculiar Case of the Electric Constable

The true story of Australia's first female serial killer

First published in 2015

This project has been assisted by the Australian Government through the Australia Council, its arts funding and advisory board.

Allen & Unwin
83 Alexander Street
Crows Nest NSW 2065
Australia
Phone: (61 2) 8425 0100
Email: info@allenandunwin.com
Web: www.allenandunwin.com

Cataloguing-in-Publication details are available from the National Library of Australia
www.trove.nla.gov.au

ISBN 978 1 74331 501 9

Internal design by Lisa White
Set in 11.5/17 pt Minion by Midland Typesetters, Australia
Printed and bound in Australia by Griffin Press

10 9 8 7 6 5 4 3 2 1

The paper in this book is FSC® certified. FSC® promotes environmentally responsible, socially beneficial and economically viable management of the world's forests.

Never before in the hundred years' history of Australia has a female criminal become so notorious as Louisa Collins.

Evening News

Contents

Louisa's favourite photograph, taken with her second husband, Michael Collins.

Part 1
SUSPICION

Suspicion cleaves to the dark side of things.

Publilius Syrus, *The Moral Sayings of Publilius Syrus*

Chapter 1

> Be extremely mysterious, even to the point of soundlessness. Thereby you can be the director of your opponent's fate.
>
> Sun Tzu, *The Art of War*

The newspapers sitting on Sydney's breakfast tables on Monday, 2 July 1888 contained little news from abroad. The two telegraph cables connecting Australia with the rest of the world—the umbilical cords that sated the public's appetite for 'instant' international news—had fallen silent the previous Friday evening. Tests showed that each cable had ruptured in the Bali Strait; however, 600 miles of ocean floor separated the breakages. Could a volcanic disturbance or other natural phenomenon simultaneously sever cables as far apart as Sydney and Melbourne?

The authorities were concerned. They knew that the Chinese government was unhappy about Australian responses to the 'Chinese question', notably the agitation to have the 'yellow hordes' banned from landing on colonial shores because they were taking jobs and profits and destroying Australia's Christian society. China was not the only nation of concern, however. The French had colonies in the Pacific, as did the Germans. And a Russian man-of-war had anchored in Sydney Harbour for the centenary celebrations only six months previously.

The Sydney newspapers reported that the Victorian and South Australian governments were taking precautionary measures to guard against a possible attack. Victoria had activated a war alert, sending its gunboat to patrol outside the Heads of Port Phillip Bay and ordering its fleet to put itself in fighting trim. Reinforcements had been sent to the Melbourne forts and submarine mines laid in the channels. If trouble was ploughing through the ocean towards Australia, Victoria was ready to defend itself.

The question preoccupying Sydneysiders on that rainy Monday morning was how their own premier, Sir Henry Parkes, would react. Were they too about to find themselves on a war footing?

• • •

Heavy rain pummelled Sydney throughout much of the miserable winter's day, and by five pm the streets were largely deserted. In the lamplight, a woman could be seen hurrying towards 241 Elizabeth Street, the home and surgery of Dr George Marshall.

When the doctor came to the door, she begged, 'Can you come and see my husband Michael Peter Collins at Botany? He is no better.'

Marshall frowned at the woman in confusion. Her plea suggested that her husband was a patient and had received recent medical treatment, yet the man's name sparked no memories. Nor was the woman herself familiar—a handsome woman, he observed, with heavy-lidded brown eyes and a sensual face framed by dark hair, although long past the bloom of youth.

'I do not recollect the case,' he replied cautiously.

'He was the man who came into the waiting room to get his fee.'

An image came to mind of a youngish man, much younger than the woman standing in front of him, a new patient who had entered his surgery four days previously without explaining his choice of physician. The man said that he had a bad cold and cough.

'How do you suffer?' Marshall had queried automatically, a question he'd asked thousands of times during his years practising medicine.

'I have a slight cough and no appetite and nothing will lie on my stomach. I also have a pain over my stomach and feel ill all over.'

'How long have you been feeling unwell?'

'I began to feel ill a few days ago. I felt a slight pain in my stomach upon coming home from work.'

Marshall had asked the patient to remove his shirt then listened to his lungs through a stethoscope. No suspicious rattles or bubbles or wheezes. His heart? No murmur or whooshing sound. Marshall reached for the man's hand and counted his pulse: slow and steady. Temperature: normal. He then told the fellow to open his mouth and poke out his tongue. It was clean and healthy-looking. Going by this quick general appraisal, he decided that the man's ailment was not serious. 'You are suffering from general malaise preceding an attack of fever,' he advised and wrote a prescription for expectorants to reduce the man's bronchial symptoms and diaphoretics to alleviate the coming fever. Then he asked for his fee.

Collins' response to that obvious request was the only odd note in the visit. He said that his wife was in the waiting room and that he would need to ask her for the money. It was duly produced.

Marshall had thought nothing more about the case between then and now. When Mrs Collins repeated her plea, he prevaricated, 'I did not think him very bad then.'

'He is very sick—worse than when you saw him before. He has been vomiting ever since and cannot keep the medicine down.'

'I saw nothing alarming about his condition,' the doctor assured her. 'Will it not do if I visit him tomorrow?' Botany was some eight miles to the south, so even a few minutes' attendance at Collins' bedside would take up hours of his time. 'I have an engagement this evening and scarcely have time to travel so far.'

'No!' she cried. 'I must have a doctor tonight! I am afraid my husband will die before morning.'

Faced with such desperation, he had little choice but to comply. He collected his medical bag and hurried with her through the rain to the nearby tram stop in Elizabeth Street.

Sydney was becoming increasingly familiar to the young Irish medical practitioner after six years beetling around the metropolis treating patients. The adventurous son of a County Tyrone medical family, he had gained his medical degrees from Dublin's Trinity College in 1882 and had sailed for New South Wales soon afterwards. Initially, he had joined his uncle's Liverpool Street medical practice before opening his own surgery on Elizabeth Street. Medical bags were a common sight here; indeed, medical practitioners had plaques on nine of the twelve properties lying between Marshall's and Liverpool Street. The luck of the draw, more often than not, determined which door a new patient would step through. However, as the doctor boarded the tram on this bitter winter's night, it seemed more like ill-luck that Michael Peter Collins had chosen his own doorway.

This particular tramline headed south to Botany Road, a lengthy thoroughfare that in its final stretch clung limpet-like to the north-eastern shoreline of Botany Bay. The history books said that Captain Cook had named Botany Bay after the wealth of plant-life collected by his botanists. A visionary, he had also wondered if the oyster-shaped bay might seed a future British settlement, another pearl in the necklace of the British Empire. Two decades later, the First Fleet had been 'bound for Botany Bay'—until Governor Phillip took one look at the area and abandoned the plan. Insufficient fresh water; an unhealthy swampiness. His decision proved wise. Later settlers found it hard to scratch out a living. The land surrounding the bay was better suited to industry than agriculture, businesses that drew male workers and their families to the area, people like Mrs Collins and her ailing husband.

The tram stopped at the Lower Botany terminus, where the pair alighted. Ignoring the allure of the lights welcoming them to George Amos's Botany Bay Hotel, they started walking through the darkness towards the Collins house. In daylight, the area might have seemed isolated. On a bleak winter's evening, it was desolate. To their right, a split-rail fence separated the road from an expanse of sandy scrub, beyond which lay the waters of Botany Bay. To their left, lights gleamed from the windows of scattered cottages, the homes of fellmongers and wool-washers who worked in the local industries.

They crossed a small bridge spanning a swamp. This section of flat, marshy scrubland bore the name Frog Hollow, and the frogs' mournful croaks filled the air.

Soon they reached Pople's Terrace, a collection of free-standing and semi-detached cottages paying tribute to their owner, Edward William Pople. Around six pm they stepped through the front door of 1 Pople's Terrace, a tiny cottage thrumming with the demands of children wanting their supper. Marshall found himself in a small sitting room with a window overlooking Botany Road. A fireplace featured on one wall, with glasses decorating its mantelpiece.

Mrs Collins pointed to a doorway and Marshall entered a small, grey-painted bedroom. A dressing table sat under the front window and the bed was pushed against the far corner. Collins lay on the bed, uncovered. Surprisingly, for someone reportedly on the verge of death, he was partially dressed, still wearing a shirt and trousers.

'How are you?' Marshall asked.

'The vomiting won't stop,' Collins complained.

Marshall asked if he had any other symptoms.

'I have diarrhoea and straining and am passing something like white of egg. I have a feeling of heaviness over my stomach, and I cannot get any sleep.'

Marshall cast a diagnostic eye over his patient and decided that Mrs Collins' fears were unwarranted; her husband didn't appear to be gravely ill. Commencing his physical examination, he noticed that Collins flinched slightly when his stomach was pressed but no more than the last time; otherwise, his pulse was still strong and regular and his tongue was clean. He asked Collins how his illness had begun.

'It came on while I was returning from work a few days before I first saw you.'

Marshall recollected from Collins' surgery visit that the fellow answered only the questions asked without volunteering any additional information. Needing more details, he probed, 'Had you eaten anything unusual in your supper the night before, like tinned fish or anything else likely to have disagreed with you?'

'No. I don't know of anything.'

That being the case, Marshall decided that Collins' continued illness without the onset of fever suggested that his initial diagnosis had been wrong. Seemingly, the fellow was suffering from a gastroduodenal catarrh, a congestion and soreness in the liver because of his body's failure to eliminate toxic waste. Just to make certain, he returned to the sitting room where Mrs Collins hovered and asked if her husband had eaten anything that might have caused the vomiting. When she too could think of nothing, he advised her to administer lots of fluids, especially soda water, barley water and milky tea, and to dose her husband with the new medicine he was prescribing. It included Grey Powder (mercury), which would serve as a laxative, and Dover's Powder, which included ipecacuanha and opium. Collins was to take the medicine night and morning to relieve the straining and lessen the pain. 'Let me know how he is tomorrow,' he added, then hastened to catch the returning tram.

• • •

Overnight, the rain abated. Sydney awoke to a bright winter sun beaming from a cloudless blue sky. News-wise, though, it was the blackest of nights. 'It is like a failure of the senses, a stoppage of hearing, an eclipse of sight,' moaned the *Sydney Morning Herald* as the fourth day of international silence began. 'We are cut off from that daily communication with the great world which has become to us something like a sixth sense. We are made to feel our isolated position.' Of course, some people felt the impact more than others, as the *Evening News* pointed out. Cricket fans were devastated. How could they learn the result of the Australia versus North of England match?

The New South Wales press also reported that Premier Parkes had dismissed the notion of an enemy invasion as alarmist nonsense. Like a sibling taking delight in salting his rival's wounds, he had boasted to Victoria's panicking politicians that Sydney's defences were more than sufficient to rebuff a surprise attack and that he would leave them to 'catch the enemy'. The *Sydney Morning Herald* also mocked the southerners, asking what they were planning to do if it were indeed a Chinese attack force. Levy the hefty poll tax now imposed on all Chinese landing on Australian shores and force the captains to pay the legislated fine for carrying more Chinese than their tonnage allowed?

Meanwhile, the probable cause of the two cable ruptures had been determined. Further tests had shown that the damage occurred at points lying 889 and 859 knots from Port Darwin, in the vicinity of neighbouring Sumbawa and Sandalwood islands. Volcanic activity rather than enemy action was the likely culprit.

Still, it was a reminder of the dangers of complacency, that enemies always lurked and that the advances of modern society could not always detect and protect.

• • •

That Tuesday afternoon, Dr Marshall received word that Mrs Collins had visited the surgery while he was out and had left a message saying that her husband was no better. His curiosity was piqued. While the message suggested that her husband was no worse—a promising sign, of sorts—it also indicated that the second medication had failed to take effect. Was his latest diagnosis also incorrect? Perhaps he should visit Collins again and check on his condition, if only to alleviate his own concerns.

The following day, just as he was about to leave for Botany, he received a visit from his brother-in-law, Dr Thomas Martin. Also Irish-born, Martin had joined Marshall's Elizabeth Street practice on his arrival in Sydney and had worked there until a few months previously, when he established his own practice in College Street.

'I'm just off to visit a patient,' Marshall apologised. Then, as Martin might have previously attended the man, he mentioned his name: Michael Peter Collins.

Martin said that he knew Collins and his wife, having attended their dead baby and Mrs Collins' first husband while working at Marshall's surgery. He began to describe his encounters with the family, one story that segued into a second. When he had finished, he left his brother-in-law alone to absorb the significance of his tale.

Before commencing his journey, Marshall decided to collect one last item for his medical bag—just in case.

Chapter 2

Where there is mystery, it is generally expected there must also be evil.

Lord Byron, *Fragment of a Novel*

Was Thomas Martin truly saying what Marshall thought? Had they both missed something vital? As the thoughts buzzed around Marshall's mind, the steam-driven tram carried him south to Botany, where he alighted around four o'clock that Wednesday afternoon. Finding Collins in bed looking no worse than before, he asked how he felt.

'The diarrhoea and straining have ceased,' Collins replied, 'and my motions are natural but the vomiting continues. I still have a slight pain over the stomach, although it is not very severe.'

Marshall reached down and pressed lightly on Collins' stomach. No reaction—a good sign. He made the usual examination, noticing only one new symptom: conjunctivitis, an inflammation of the eyelid covering. Otherwise, Collins' general condition seemed satisfactory and his symptoms consistent with the second diagnosis. There was still no cause for alarm.

While examining Collins, he had sidestepped a chamber-pot sitting on the floor near the bed. It contained foul-smelling vomit of an unpleasant greenish hue. He pointed to the pot and asked Collins: 'Did you vomit that?' Receiving confirmation, Marshall poured the lumpy liquid into the empty eight-ounce medicine bottle he had returned to his surgery to collect. He sealed it and slipped it inside his medical bag.

Glancing around the room, he saw a liquid-filled lemonade bottle sitting on an upturned box that served as a bedside table. He asked Collins if he knew what it contained. 'Brandy,' was the response. Continuing to look around the room, he spotted an empty bottle on the dressing table. Just what he needed. He poured some brandy into the bottle and tucked it into his medical bag. He then said that Collins would need to void some urine so it could be tested for kidney disease. Another empty bottle on the dressing table could be used for its storage—once it had been washed.

Marshall took the empty bottle to the kitchen, which lay at the back of the house behind the sitting room. Finding Mrs Collins there, he asked her to wash it, explaining that he would need to test a sample of Collins' urine as his condition wasn't improving.

While he waited, he wrote a prescription for a mixture that should relieve Collins' pain and vomiting. Among other ingredients, it contained bismuth subnitrate—a medical preparation widely used to treat gastric complaints—hydrocyanic acid (cyanide) to relieve coughing and gastric pain, and morphine hydrochloride for general pain relief.

As Mrs Collins washed and dried the bottle, she said: 'The powders you ordered before did not stop the vomiting. Will the new powders stop the vomiting at once or are they for the disease?'

'Not directly,' he replied.

'Could you give me something to stop the vomiting directly?'

'I will try.'

While they were talking, he noticed a three-quarters-full medicine bottle sitting on a kitchen shelf. 'Is that the medicine I prescribed first?' he asked. When she confirmed that it was, he put the bottle into his pocket.

After collecting the urine sample, he explained to them both that Collins was to have a half-ounce of the newly prescribed medicine every four hours. Mrs Collins was to let him know the next day how her husband fared. He then asked for his fee.

Mrs Collins said bluntly, 'I cannot give it.'

Marshall had heard this response many times before—usually after he had provided the requested treatment, of course. Impecunious patients were a hazard of the medical profession. For obvious reasons, the ailing often had difficulty earning the money they needed to pay for a doctor's treatment. Most tried to reimburse him once they were back in funds. Some didn't, and the bad debts accumulated. The doctor therefore told Mrs Collins that if her husband's condition worsened she should take him to the Coast Hospital at Little Bay as it was too far for him to come again. She made no reply.

• • •

Under the circumstances, Marshall was surprised to see Mrs Collins at his surgery the following day. Admittedly, he had asked her to report back—but that was before she had been unable to pay the fee.

'The medicine did not stop the vomiting,' she said. 'Collins was very bad last night and I thought he was unconscious. I thought he was going to die. And his throat is very sore.'

'Continue the mixture,' the doctor recommended, 'and have him gargle with alum and water.' He knew that the medicine he'd prescribed should ease the irritation and inhibit the vomiting—in ordinary cases, that was—so he was surprised that Collins still wasn't improving. All the more reason for him to test the collected samples.

'I cannot come again until you find my fee,' he warned. 'I advise you to send him to the hospital.'

'I am well known about Botany,' she reassured him. 'It will be all right.'

• • •

George Marshall's first opportunity to test the samples came the next day, Friday, at the dispensary of his cousin, Dr Hezlett Hamilton Marshall. Sydney had taken pride in the achievements of this colonial-born doctor, with the newspapers reporting in 1885 that young Hamilton had passed his second set of examinations for Edinburgh University's Bachelor of Medicine degree, gaining four first-class honours. Back in Sydney, Hamilton had taken over his late father's Liverpool Street surgery where George once worked. There in its little laboratory, surrounded by a rainbow of different-shaped glass carboys filled with herbs and chemicals, they would conduct their chemical investigation.

Only one test interested George Marshall. Although he hadn't mentioned it to the Collinses, he wanted to know if any of the samples showed traces of a certain sparkling white crystal, one that had long been nicknamed 'the inheritance maker'. Officially, it was labelled 'arsenious acid'; however, to the humble denizens of this century-old colony, the crystals had a shorter, more ominous name: arsenic.

The Reinsch test would serve his purpose. Chemists had used the simple procedure for half a century to detect arsenic and other heavy metals. It shouldn't be long before he had some answers.

As his cousin gathered the testing equipment, Marshall lifted the bottle of Collins' vomited matter from his medicine bag. He took out a small sample, about half an ounce, and tipped it into a glass test tube, adding enough water to cover the sample. Picking up a bottle of hydrochloric acid, he poured the required amount into the test tube and stirred the mixture. The acid would dissolve the vomit. He boiled the liquid over a Bunsen burner for some time, then picked up a strip of bright copper foil and inserted it into the test tube.

The test's inventor, the German chemist Hugo Reinsch, had determined that heat applied to the test-tube contents would convert the solid substance into a vapour. On cooling, the vapour would condense again into a solid state without becoming a liquid—that is, it would 'sublime' as a grey-to-black metallic coating on the foil. If such a discolouration appeared on the foil, it would signify the presence of arsenic.

Marshall pulled the copper foil from the test tube. He and his cousin peered at the foil. There was indeed a slight discolouration. But was it enough for them to be certain that arsenic was present? They conferred and peered again and conferred once more. They decided that it wasn't.

Perhaps they would obtain more definitive results from one of the other samples. They performed the same test on Collins' urine and also on the contents of the other bottles collected from his house. Again they found nothing noteworthy. Afterwards, they put all but the urine bottle on the top shelf of the dispensary and left them there for safe keeping.

George Marshall took the urine bottle back to his own surgery so he could conduct the necessary kidney-function tests. He tested the urine's albumin levels—increased levels indicated kidney damage—but the results were normal. He tested the urine's specific gravity and found that it too fell within the normal range. Clearly, his patient was not suffering from kidney disease. He poured the urine into a clean eight-ounce medicine bottle and stashed it away safely.

Having found no evidence of arsenic poisoning, his suspicions were allayed. Even so, he remained curious about the case. He decided to visit Collins once more to see how he was faring.

• • •

No one answered the door when he arrived at the Collins house around four that afternoon. Again he knocked and waited . . . and again. When Mrs Collins eventually opened the door, she said, 'Oh, it's the doctor. I had not expected you.' She welcomed him inside.

In the bedroom, he saw Collins leaning over the side of the bed as if he were about to vomit. He mused, 'It is strange that he is still vomiting.' Past experience had shown that his medicine usually suppressed the urge.

'I have just given him a vomiting powder I got from Waterloo,' Mrs Collins said.

Surprised, he queried, 'Why did you give him that?'

'I thought you weren't coming again and I didn't know what to do. A man told me Mick was suffering from biliousness and a vomit would do him good.'

Mick's friend Arthur Hamill had visited earlier in the day and had initially suggested a drink of hot beer and egg to sweat out Mick's cold. She'd prepared it for him but he hadn't liked it. When Hamill and his wife returned later in the day, they had suggested the vomiting powder.

As Louisa handed a liquid-filled glass to her husband, she explained to the doctor that she was giving him hot water to encourage vomiting.

Marshall didn't object. While perplexed that she should trust such unprofessional medical advice, he knew that the vomiting powder was unlikely to cause any harm. He waited until Collins had drunk the water before asking about his symptoms. Collins complained again of pain and of his continued inability to sleep. Marshall questioned him about his diarrhoea and learnt that the pendulum had swung the other way, to constipation.

He conducted another physical examination. Collins' pulse was still strong, that of a healthy man. His appearance remained satisfactory, little different to two days previously—certainly no worse. However, the continued eye inflammation led Marshall to ask Mrs Collins about it.

'The retching and vomiting have made his eyes sore,' she explained.

Marshall knew that the retching itself would not have caused conjunctivitis. It was, however, a symptom of a variety of other medical conditions, some that were of particular concern.

He wrote out another prescription, one containing five grains of calomel and two grains of powdered ginger. It would act as a purgative to relieve Collins' constipation.

By this time, the vomiting powder was taking effect. Collins spewed a large quantity of dark green matter into the chamber-pot—an ideal specimen, Marshall realised. He told Collins and his wife that he would need to collect a sample so he could conduct further tests. Helpfully, Mrs Collins went out to the kitchen and returned with a small cup. He didn't need it, though. Despite his failure to detect arsenic in the earlier samples, he still had a niggling concern. Moreover, he hadn't forgotten his brother-in-law's tales about his encounters with the family, so he had brought along another clean bottle.

'As you are not improving, you would be far better off in hospital,' Marshall told Collins in his wife's presence.

Collins made no reply.

After taking leave of his patient, Marshall paused at the front door to urge Collins' wife to heed his advice.

'People always die when sent to hospital,' she replied matter-of-factly. 'If he is going to die, it is better for him to die at home.'

Marshall had often encountered this attitude to hospital care. The public had known that hospitals were dangerous places long before Ignaz Semmelweis recognised the deadliness of a doctor's unwashed hands—made even more deadly when an earlier patient was an autopsied corpse. Unfortunately, with the arrogance of rank and conservatism, many doctors had dismissed Semmelweis's simple antiseptic solution and had continued with their unwashed practices. It would be a long time before the public lost its fear of hospitals.

'I see no reason to suppose he will die,' he reassured her. 'On the contrary, I think he will get better if he is well looked after. People are well-treated in hospitals.'

She didn't argue but nor did she look convinced.

'I will not and cannot call again,' he added firmly, having failed yet again to get his fee. 'Let me know tomorrow what you will do.'

He left the house, hoping she would take his advice and send her husband to the hospital. Meanwhile, he would undertake more tests on the new vomit sample.

• • •

The press continued to discuss possible threats from abroad even though concerns were easing about the cause of the cable ruptures. It was as if Australia had only now noticed its isolation, its vulnerability. The *Sydney Morning Herald* wryly observed that, when the country had been tied to grandmama's apron strings—that is, Britain—its people had been happy to thumb their noses at 'nasty, big boy Johnny', whichever country had had that honour at the time. Now that these apron strings had been cut, its citizens were wondering if Johnny was prowling nearby with the intention of whopping them at his leisure.

The *Herald* also opened the public's eyes to a potential threat that no one had reccognised. A derelict, bottom-up ship had recently been found anchored in front of New South Wales' chief coal port, Newcastle. What if this ship had been a Trojan horse with its entrails crammed with Russians—or, worse, Chinese? Thankfully, the government had at last recognised the danger and was planning to blow it up.

Some reminded the community that the press's alarmism was nothing more than fanciful nonsense. There were no threats from abroad, no bogeymen using stealth to attack and destroy. Clearly, even among adults, imaginations could run rife when confronted by the seemingly inexplicable.

Chapter 3

> It may seem a strange principle to enunciate as the very first requirement in a hospital that it should do the sick no harm.
>
> Florence Nightingale, *Notes on Hospitals*

Send Mick to the hospital? Not likely. Everyone knew that you might as well plan a funeral service as admit a loved one to the hospital—particularly the Little Bay hospital. It was the 'fever hospital', accepting patients with horrid diseases like smallpox and tuberculosis, diphtheria and scarlet fever. What hope had a sick person there? No, Louisa decided, she wouldn't send him to the hospital. But what could she do to help him? He was getting worse.

Mick had fallen ill while at work two weeks previously, on Saturday, 23 June. Since mid-April, he had been working for Botany fellmongers Elliott & Geddes, mainly as a carter in recent weeks. He would drive a lorry to either Glebe Island or Rookwood where he would load the 'green skins' of freshly slaughtered sheep then drive them back to the wool-washing site at Springvale, Botany. There the wool would be pulled off and dried and the skins prepared for leather-making.

That particular Saturday, he had been rostered to collect skins from Rookwood. Around three am, he had eaten bread and butter before heading off with his partner John Walker—the carters usually worked in pairs—to harness their teams and drive to Rookwood. He later said that, during the journey, his stomach had begun to churn, causing him to retch a couple of times. When they reached Rookwood, he had dashed into the bushes to vomit. He told Walker that he was too sick to load the skins, that Walker would have to do the work for him. He had managed to drive his own lorry back to Springvale, but since then his illness had prevented him from returning to work.

This meant that they were already short a fortnight of his £2 5s weekly wages. How could she pay the doctor when she had little income and limited savings? They no longer housed boarders, although her middle boys—Arthur and Frederick—added to the family's coffers. Arthur worked at the Botany glassworks and Fred at the woolwashers, but they were paid only a fraction of adults' wages. At least her two eldest sons weren't a financial burden: Herbert, now aged twenty-one, had moved to the Newcastle district four years earlier, before his own father died, while Reuben had recently joined him there. She still had three young mouths to feed, though: May, Edwin, and her youngest, Charles, aged five. Meanwhile, the cost of Mick's medical treatment had cut into their savings, and it hadn't helped him, anyway. Reluctantly, she sent Fred to Mick's boss, Mr Geddes, to ask for money to pay the doctor. It was a matter of pride to her that she always paid her bills, later if not sooner, no matter the circumstances. But she hated having to beg. Still, it was necessary in this instance. She wanted the very best treatment for her ailing husband.

• • •

Shortly before five on the morning following the doctor's third visit, Louisa slipped out of the house and hurried along Botany Road. The occasional square of light indicated that people were stirring. She wasn't alone in these darkest hours before the dawn.

No welcoming lights beamed from grocer Charles Sayers' house. She knocked gently on his front door, but he didn't respond. Not wanting to wake all the residents—Sayers had a wife and large family—she stood near his bedroom window and called out his name. A moment later, the door opened. A tousled head peered through.

'Can you come over?' she begged. 'Collins is bad.'

Sayers had been the most helpful of their visitors, dropping over multiple times each day, assisting Mick into a rocking chair, giving him sips from the drinks on the bedside box. Once or twice he had caught her crying. He was a kind man, the obvious person to turn to when Mick's condition suddenly deteriorated.

Mick was vomiting every minute or so when the grocer joined them. Asked how he was feeling, Mick said, 'I have been choking and feel like I have a lump in my throat. Can you look down my throat?'

Sayers looked but couldn't see anything. 'I think it's the vomiting causing the soreness,' he said. He remained for an hour, providing company for Louisa in her distress, then departed to open his store.

Grocery stores were focal points in every district. The lack of refrigeration and personal transportation meant that housewives made regular trips to the store, where they chatted with grocery staff and other shoppers. News of local happenings spread quickly—births and deaths, triumphs and tragedies. Word of Mick's illness soon got around, and as the day unfolded, a number of well-wishers made their way to the cottage.

Around four-thirty pm, Louisa asked her fourteen-year-old son, Arthur, to help her lift Mick onto the chamber-pot. Arthur hadn't assisted with Mick's care during his illness. In fact, he hadn't even spoken to or visited his ailing stepfather during the two weeks of his illness.

When Arthur entered the bedroom, he called out, 'Hullo, Bill'—Mick's nickname—in a bantering tone. 'How are you getting on?'

'All right, Coppers!' Mick replied, attempting a similarly jocular tone. 'I'll be right. I'll be up today or tomorrow.'

Louisa pulled back the covers. The trousers Mick was wearing created problems when they attempted to get him onto the chamber-pot. Somehow, though, they managed.

Not long afterwards, Mick tried to get up again. As Louisa and Arthur moved to assist him, he started shivering uncontrollably. Alarmed, they helped him lie down.

'Go to Dr Marshall,' Louisa urged her son. 'Tell him that Mick is no better, that I think he is dying.'

Arthur hurried out the door to catch the six pm tram.

Chapter 4

A wonderful fact to reflect upon, that every human creature is constituted to be that profound secret and mystery to every other.

Charles Dickens, *A Tale of Two Cities*

Dr Marshall had remained troubled about his Botany patient. The continued vomiting despite anti-emetic medications, the conjunctivitis—both hinted at arsenical poisoning, yet he'd found no traces of the deadly substance in the samples he had tested. It was perplexing.

That Saturday morning he had decided to experiment further, using Friday's vomited matter as his sample. Test tube . . . spoonful of dark green vomit . . . splash of water . . . dash of hydrochloric acid . . . a quick stir. He was more confident after carrying out the Reinsch Test four times the previous day. Bunsen burner . . . strip of bright copper foil . . . a close inspection. Nothing but a slight discolouration again. It was most perplexing indeed.

Early in the evening, a messenger arrived on his doorstep, a boy who identified himself as Mrs Collins' son Arthur. He said, 'My mother has sent me to say that her husband is dying.'

Mrs Collins had come herself on all previous occasions so her decision to send the lad lent credence to her claim that Collins' condition had deteriorated—and indicated that she had ignored his advice to send her husband to the hospital. He should probably attend Collins again but first he would discuss the case with Dr Martin. Perhaps it was time for a second opinion.

• • •

Among the visitors to the Collins house that same evening were neighbours Margaret Collis and Ellen Pettit, the latter accompanied by her son and an elderly friend. When they knocked at the door and asked how Collins was getting on, Louisa seemed unwilling for them to enter. She stepped onto the verandah and pulled the door partly closed behind her. One of the women said, 'We have come to see Mr Collins.' Only then did Louisa open the door—reluctantly, they noticed—and direct them to the bedroom.

Standing by Collins' bedside, they asked how he felt—a social nicety more than anything else as it was obvious he was suffering greatly. He responded politely, saying that he had a pain in his left shoulder and in his throat. Then he lapsed into silence.

As the women hovered, Louisa used the opportunity to send Ellen's thirteen-year-old son to the pub for beer. When he returned, she poured some of the beer into a glass and the remainder into a jug. She sipped from the glass throughout the evening. Her neighbours weren't surprised to see her drinking alcohol. She had a reputation for enjoying a tipple.

Then Collins asked for a drink. Louisa lifted a large, almost empty tumbler from the bedside box and gave him a sip of its milky contents. Soon, he asked for another drink, indicating that he wanted milk. Louisa collected the big tumbler and went out to the kitchen.

While she was absent, a confused Collins asked where she was. He seemed desperately thirsty so Margaret Collis offered him a drink of tea. He rejected the offer, saying he didn't want any. 'It makes me sick,' he explained. 'I want milk.'

Louisa returned a moment later, carrying the big tumbler. It was now three-quarters filled with milk. She raised his head and let him drink from the glass.

Not long afterwards, he began to convulse. His eyes rolled into the back of his head leaving only the whites showing. His body arched as if stretched taut around a bowstring then began to shudder. For minutes his body waged a battle against itself until the spasms eased and his body relaxed to a state of limpness. When he came to his senses, he said, 'Oh, look at all the lights and stars. Blue lights. I can see one that is green.'

Around ten-fifteen pm, more visitors arrived. Two gentlemen strode into the bedroom as if they owned the house. The Collinses' friends and neighbours didn't recognise the pair. Who could these men be?

• • •

The crowd of visitors at the cottage served as confirmation that Collins had indeed taken a turn for the worse. Still, the two doctors were startled by the extent of his deterioration. He was in a stupor, taking little notice of the goings-on around him. His eyelids were still inflamed, but his eyes were now sunken and his cheeks hollow. His lips were covered with sores and his breathing was laboured.

Dr Martin stood to the side watching while Dr Marshall took his patient's pulse. Collins' skin was cold and clammy and his pulse weak, almost imperceptible; however, he wasn't unconscious. He was still capable of being roused to answer questions.

Marshall asked if he had any pain.

'Yes,' Collins answered slowly, 'in my stomach and in my left shoulder. And I have a feeling of tightness in my throat.'

'This morning he vomited a lot of dark brown matter,' Mrs Collins reported, 'but the vomiting has ceased and since then he has kept everything down that I have given him.'

Marshall said that he didn't think there was any connection between the cessation of vomiting and the collapse. Collins might simply be too weak to vomit.

'I would like you to see him raised up in bed,' Mrs Collins continued, trying to lift her husband into a sitting position, 'as you will see that he trembles all over and is unconscious-like.'

Marshall stopped her. It was clear that Collins was too weak to raise himself. He probably couldn't even turn himself over or reach the items on the bedside box without assistance. Under the circumstances, it was unnecessary to make him suffer any further.

'How did your illness commence?' Marshall asked again, curious to know if Collins would answer differently. He didn't.

There was no point in prescribing any further medication. Instead, Marshall told Mrs Collins to mix some eggs and brandy and give her husband frequent sips. 'He is dying,' the doctor said gravely. 'He will not live many more hours.'

She seemed agitated but offered no response.

'Let me know in the morning how he is,' were the doctor's final words as he and Dr Martin departed.

As the doctors walked back to the tram stop, they discussed the case. They agreed that Collins' symptoms were common to many diseases. They also agreed that, if they took his symptoms only as they saw them, they could come from a gastric complaint and a concurrent attack of conjunctivitis. But that didn't explain the suddenness of his collapse. Moreover, there was more to this medical puzzle than these pieces alone, as Dr Martin could attest.

It wasn't long before one of them aired what both were thinking, 'He is dying under very suspicious circumstances.'

They decided to make a detour—to the Botany police station.

• • •

Peeping through the Collins' bedroom doorway, Ellen Pettit and her companions had watched the two gentlemen inspecting the room as if the items on display were part of a job lot being sold at auction. One man had opened the dressing-table drawer and peered into it, while the other had picked up a bottle and smelt it.

After the pair departed, Margaret Collis asked Louisa who they were. Louisa said that they were doctors. 'I do not know why they came out,' she added. 'I sent the boy in to see if I could get anything to make Mick sleep and the doctor did not send anything. I do not know why they followed the boy out in the next tram when they sent word that they could do no more for him and to send him to the hospital. I cannot send a dying man to the hospital.'

Collins' voice broke through with a request for another drink. Louisa looked at Ellen, who was standing near the bedroom door, and said, 'Would you mind handing me a glass off the mantelpiece in the front room?' Ellen went into the sitting room and picked up a small, plain tumbler—a nobbler glass—that was sitting upside down on the mantelpiece. Lifting her apron, she wiped the tumbler carefully, both inside and out, then held it up to the light to make certain it was clean. Satisfied, she passed it to Louisa.

Louisa turned to Margaret Collis. 'The jug of milk is on the kitchen table. Can you hand it over?'

Margaret went into the kitchen and found the requested jug. It was filled with milk, about a pint's worth, and was yellowish in colour like condensed milk. As she reached to pick it up, little May said: 'Do not take the milk. It is only for Mick.' Margaret explained that she was collecting it at Louisa's request.

Louisa took the jug from Margaret and poured some of the contents into the glass tumbler, adding a dash of brandy. She lifted it to Collins' lips and he drank half the contents. A short time later, he asked for more milk and drank that glassful as well. All that remained were some dregs at the bottom of the tumbler.

Chapter 5

When clouds appear, wise men put on their cloaks.

William Shakespeare, *Richard III*

Poisoning?

The two police officers who manned the Botany station were startled by the doctors' suspicions. Of course, crime was not unknown in their district, particularly in recent times. Businesses were struggling and families suffering, so theft, drunkenness and violence were not uncommon. Still, the doctors were alluding to something much more serious: to murder—or at least attempted murder, since Collins was still alive.

Both officers knew the Collinses. Constable George Jeffes had served at Botany for three of his six years as a policeman. He regularly encountered members of the Collins household while tramping his beat. In fact, he had spotted them waiting at the tram stop only twelve days before, on the morning of Monday, 25 June. Pausing for a moment to make conversation, he had asked if they were heading to the city. Mrs Collins said that they were, that Collins needed medical attention. When Jeffes asked what was wrong with him, she again spoke for her husband, saying that he had a cold.

As Jeffes and his superior made their way to Pople's Terrace to investigate the doctors' allegation, Jeffes remarked that he hadn't been surprised to hear that Collins was seeking medical attention. He had often noticed, over the past two or three months, that the man seemed to have a sore throat.

Jeffes' superior, Senior Constable Abraham Sherwood, had served at Botany for a similar period, although his own rise through the police ranks had been faster because of his previous service with the Irish constabulary. He wasn't as familiar with the Collins family; nevertheless, he knew that Mick Collins was a quiet, inoffensive man. As for Mrs Collins, he had heard the gossip but had no reason to notice anything . . . officially.

Sherwood had also encountered the Collinses in recent times—on Thursday, 28 June, to be precise, the day Marshall said the pair first visited his surgery. He remembered seeing them on the tram from Sydney. Collins had been lying on a seat, clearly unwell. Which raised the curious question: if the Collinses had first visited Dr Marshall on Thursday, 28 June, what doctor had they seen the previous Monday when Jeffes met them? Perhaps they hadn't made it as far as the city for some reason.

Jeffes reported that he'd also spoken to the Collinses in the past few days. Mrs Collins had been standing in her front doorway when he passed the house, so he had stopped to ask how her husband was faring. 'Very bad,' was her reply. A voice had rung out, Collins' voice, inviting him in. After venturing inside, Jeffes had asked the patient how he was getting on.

'All right,' was the valiant response. 'I will be up in a day or two.'

Jeffes recalled this ill-founded optimism as the two policeman regarded the man in the bed. Collins did indeed look dreadful, on the verge of death, as the doctors had reported. Nevertheless, that mustn't deter them from their investigation. It was better to question him while they could.

'What is the matter with you?' asked the forthright senior constable.

There was a long pause as Collins struggled to answer. 'I have a bad cold,' he finally said. 'I can keep nothing in my stomach.'

'Do you have any pain?'

'I feel a joint pain in my left shoulder.' He slowly moved his right hand to point to the spot. Then he began picking at the bedclothes.

Neighbours thronged the bedroom doorway, eager to know why the law was making a late-night appearance. The small bedroom was so crowded that Jeffes eased back through the doorway, leaving Sherwood to continue his questioning alone.

'Have you had any other medicine but what the doctor ordered?' Sherwood asked.

'No.'

'No,' repeated Louisa. 'I gave him the medicine and I know what he has taken. He could not have taken anything without my knowledge.'

Sherwood turned to Collins again and asked bluntly: 'Do you suspect that anyone has given you anything to make you ill?'

'No,' the sick man said, adding with attempted firmness, 'I'll be up and all right in a few days.' Then he indicated that he wanted another drink.

'Why don't you give him some brandy?' suggested neighbour Johannah Bartington.

'Give him as much brandy as he likes,' ordered Sherwood. 'It will do no harm.'

Louisa left the room and came back with a half-filled tumbler of white liquid, saying that it contained milk. She added half a teaspoonful of brandy. Johannah raised Collins' head while Louisa put the glass to his lips. Afterwards, she placed the glass on the bedside box.

Soon, Sherwood signalled that they were departing. As he and Jeffes left the house, he said to Louisa, 'If he dies before morning, you had better let me know.'

• • •

A visit from two policemen late at night? Louisa was troubled. 'Why do they want me to let them know when Mick dies?' she asked. She slumped onto the bed, her gaze unfocused.

Ellen Pettit attempted an answer. 'It is very likely the doctors sent them in.'

'I do not know the cause of that,' was her bewildered response.

'Don't be uneasy,' Ellen soothed. 'It may be for the best that they came.'

'I cannot understand them coming here at all,' Louisa countered. 'They must have felt suspicious of me or they would not have come into the house.' She paused again, seemingly lost in her thoughts. Then she added fervently, 'I have done my duty by him, God knows. They need not suspect me of giving him anything.'

Gradually, the neighbours drifted away. By the witching hour, only Ellen Pettit remained. She sat with Louisa during the eerie silence of the early-morning hours, leaving around two-thirty am to return to her home. Only one other person seemed to be awake: Louisa's son, Arthur, who was hovering in the kitchen.

Chapter 6

> We see death coming into our midst like black smoke . . . a rootless phantom which has no mercy.
>
> Ieuan Gethin

Across Sydney and its suburbs, church bells summoned their flocks. Fathers prepared to enjoy their only full day of leisure. Mothers, who had none at all, tweaked skirts and bows and used a dab of lick-and-spit to restrain unruly locks. As the peals grew more demanding, families ventured into the warm winter sunshine and trooped to their local place of worship—perhaps a spire-topped wooden box or a majestic cathedral or some other structure that provided the spiritual comfort or social engagement they craved.

The less devout, who found the services boring and the collection plates an affront, knew more enjoyable ways of spending their time and money, like picnicking at the Sir Joseph Banks Pleasure Gardens at Botany.

The Botany police rarely had a day off, either. There were only two officers manning the station and they had to be available whenever the public needed them. The wicked saw no need to rest on the Sabbath while the starving had no choice. And the doctors' concerns about

Michael Peter Collins meant that this particular Sabbath might prove busier than most.

• • •

When Sherwood returned to the Collins cottage just after eleven am, he noticed that Louisa was looking distressed. She was sitting on the side of Collins' bed saying, 'Poor Mick! Poor Mick!' as she curled his moustache and rubbed his face and hair.

Collins seemed not to notice his visitor until Sherwood asked how he was feeling. Focusing his gaze on the senior constable, he said, 'I am bad, but I expect to be all right in a couple of days.'

'Have you taken any medicine other than that given by the doctor, or anything that could make you sick?'

'No.'

Louisa spoke up, repeating her comments of the night before. 'I am the only one that gives him medicine and drinks. He could not have taken anything without my knowledge.'

Sherwood ignored her intrusion and directed another question at Collins: 'Do you suspect any person might have given you something to make you sick?'

'No,' was the simple response.

Again, Louisa said that Mick couldn't have taken anything unknown to her. Picking up his hands, she rubbed them as if to warm them.

'Are the doctors coming again today?' Sherwood asked.

Collins had lapsed into a stupor, but he roused himself at the sound of Sherwood's voice and asked Louisa: 'What is Sherwood saying?' After she repeated the question, he replied, 'No, the doctor is not coming anymore.'

'The doctor did not say that, Mick,' she chided gently.

'Yes he did,' came the irritated response. 'The doctor said so last night. He said he need not and would not come anymore.' Collins then stretched out an arm and shakily lifted a small teacup from the bedside box. After taking a sip, he put it down again.

'What does the cup contain?' Sherwood asked.

'Cold tea,' said Louisa.

Sherwood looked back at the bedside box. He saw a tumbler half full of a milky-white liquid, one that was probably too far away for Collins to reach. Among the other items was a box of matches. Gesturing to the half-burnt matches scattered on the floor near the bed, he asked Louisa what they had been used for.

'I had to light them for Mick a short time before you came in because he complained that the whole place was in darkness.'

After ten or fifteen minutes, Sherwood headed home. There he was told that Mrs Collins had left a message earlier that morning saying that she wanted to see him. He wondered why she hadn't mentioned this summons while he was at the cottage. What had she wanted to communicate?

• • •

Dr Marshall wasn't surprised when Louisa didn't send word of Collins' condition. She must have realised he was responsible for the late-night visit from the police. Still, he was curious to know how the case was unfolding. Payment of his fee no longer mattered. With Dr Martin in tow, he returned to Botany at noon to see his patient.

Louisa was alone with Collins. He was still alive, although in a state of collapse. His breathing was heavy and laboured, his pulse weak. His extremities were cold and his core temperature only 96 degrees instead of 98 or 99. Death was imminent.

'Why didn't you send him to the hospital as I urged?' Marshall censured Louisa.

'If you were sick yourself, you wouldn't care to go into a hospital,' was her indignant reply.

He didn't respond. What could he say? Instead, he asked if she had been giving her husband the recommended egg-and-brandy mixture to keep up his strength. She said nothing. He repeated his question.

'I suppose you think I would not give it to him?' she replied bitterly. 'Mick knows I would, don't you, Mick?' She went over to the bed and put her arm around his neck. He took no notice, having lapsed again into a stupor.

Calling his name, Marshall managed to rouse him. He asked how his illness had begun and whether he had taken anything likely to make him ill. Collins replied as before.

The doctors remained for only a short time. When they departed, they knew they would not be returning.

• • •

Around two-thirty pm, Louisa sent a message to her next-door neighbour, Catherine Mudge, asking if she would come over as Collins was dying. Catherine arrived a short time later, accompanied by Johannah Bartington. They joined Louisa and two of her children, who were maintaining a bedside vigil. Looking at Collins, they could see that his time had come.

'Mrs Collins, his mouth looks awfully dry,' said Johannah. 'You might get something and wet it.' Louisa agreed that it was a sound idea. Johannah suggested brandy and water. Louisa left the bedroom and returned with some brandy in a little cup and water in a dipper. She poured the water into the cup and held it to his lips. He was too weak to drink it.

'Perhaps you should get a quill and wet his lips with some brandy through it,' Johannah suggested helpfully.

Louisa collected a quill and brought it back to the bedroom. Johannah dripped some of the brandy-and-water mixture into it, then used it to moisten Collins' lips. A moment later, without saying another word, he took his last breath.

Chapter 7

Suspicion is far more to be wrong than right; more often unjust than just.

Hosea Ballou, *Treasury of Thought*

Clouds were mushrooming as Constable Jeffes made his way to the Collinses' place around three o'clock that afternoon, heralding an ominous change in the previously fine weather. Arriving at the cottage, he saw Louisa standing at the front door. He asked after her husband.

'He is dead,' she said baldly.

Jeffes pushed past her into the bedroom. He saw Collins lying on the bed with silver coins over his eyes—the customary mourning tradition. Few remembered its pagan origins: the ancient Greeks had believed that the souls of the dead must cross the river Styx to reach the underworld and needed two silver coins to pay the ferryman.

'When did he die?' he asked.

'About ten minutes to three this afternoon.'

'Have you sent for the doctor?'

'Yes, I have sent my son by the tram just gone.'

Immediately after Mick had passed away, she had dispatched Arthur to the city to obtain a death certificate from the doctor. She had also sent May to request the services of local grocer and midwife Ellen Price, who supplemented her income by washing the dead.

'Put a sheet over his face,' Jeffes ordered. He stood there for a moment, thinking about what he should do next. He decided to stay at the cottage until Arthur returned to see if he would bring back a death certificate. At this point, the responsibility for initiating an investigation lay with the attending physician. If Dr Marshall signed a death certificate, it would signify his satisfaction that Collins had died of natural causes. But if he refused . . .

• • •

The crowd hanging around the Collins cottage had increased by the time Mrs Price arrived. Louisa's neighbour Rosetta Mapstone offered to assist the body washer. The two women cleared the odds and ends from the bedside box to make room for the water container. Louisa, dry-eyed, stood at the foot of the bed watching them.

Mrs Price removed Collins' shirt and washed the upper portion of his body. As she pulled off his dark brown trousers, she noticed they were filthy, only partly because of his post-death secretions. She passed them to Louisa, who dropped them on the floor near the foot of the bed. Tugging down Collins' socks, Mrs Price saw a six-inch wound on his leg. Although unprotected by bandage or plaster, the wound was dry enough that his sock hadn't stuck to it.

The two women tried to wash the lower half of Collins' body but found Louisa's vantage point an inconvenience. Rosetta asked her to move but she ignored the request, forcing the women to work around her. When they finished, Louisa gave Mrs Price a pair of new white stockings and told her where to find a shirt so they could dress him.

Afterwards, Louisa asked some of her neighbours to put together two tables in the sitting room. They carried Collins' body from the bedroom and laid it on the makeshift bench. Louisa stared at her husband's corpse for a while then looked at Mrs Price in despair. 'I'll not stop here tonight,' she said. 'I'll go for a walk.'

'If I thought you were going to talk like that, I would not have come to you,' Mrs Price responded.

'Don't you think it would do me good to go for a walk?'

'Don't do anything of the kind,' Mrs Price said firmly. 'If you do, the police will lock you up.'

She knew her suspicions were correct when Louisa said bleakly, 'I don't want to live any longer.'

• • •

Constable Jeffes was still waiting outside the Collins cottage when Sherwood joined him. He told his superior that the local clergyman was attending Louisa and that Arthur hadn't yet returned from the city. As it was teatime, the two policemen decided to return to their homes and to leave questioning Louisa until later that evening.

Jeffes was nearing the police station, where he lived, when he spied Arthur alighting from the tram. He asked the lad if the doctor had signed a death certificate.

'No, he won't give one,' was the response. 'He told me to report the matter to the police.'

Jeffes sent Arthur on his way and hurried to Sherwood's home with the news. Sherwood said that he would alert head office but, meanwhile, Jeffes was to return to the Collins house and take possession of all the bottles he could find.

Neighbours Johannah Bartington and Charles Sayers crowded Jeffes when he arrived back at the cottage around six pm, saying that they were worried about Louisa. Johannah had remained at the cottage after Collins' death to comfort his heartbroken widow. She had noticed that Louisa seemed even more upset—indeed angry—after Arthur reported that the doctor wouldn't provide a death certificate and wanted the matter reported to the police. Louisa had spat, 'If I had sixty sovereigns in my pocket, he would not get a penny of it.'

'You had better stop at the house,' the neighbours urged the constable. 'She wants to get out. We're afraid that she will do some harm to herself.'

Jeffes saw that Louisa's face was red and her manner excited, the result, no doubt, of the alcohol he could smell. He sidestepped the neighbours and made his way to the Collinses' bedroom. Louisa followed, seating herself on the bedside box so she could watch him. Sayers and Johannah also slipped through the door while others thronged behind them, wondering why the police were so interested in this particular death.

Jeffes began searching the bedroom, looking for anything that might contain poison, medicine bottles included. He opened all the drawers and peered into the corners to see if anything was hidden. He looked at the items on the dressing table, recognising that some had previously been sitting on the bedside box. He picked up a small tea cup about half full of a brown liquid.

'That's brandy and water,' Louisa said. It was the drink Johannah Bartington had given Mick just before he died.

Jeffes poured the cup's contents into the brandy flask then placed the flask and cup on the dressing table, ready to be taken away. He added to his stash a chipped box containing a white ointment. As he lifted a small glass tumbler that was about three-quarters full of white liquid, Louisa leapt up from her seat and caught his arm, nearly tipping the glass over. 'That's milk,' she said. 'I have been giving it to Mick. It is nothing.'

'Sit down and keep quiet!' he admonished. 'I want everything in the place. I must take it.'

'There is no medicine here. Dr Marshall has taken all the medicines away, hasn't he?' she said, as if appealing for support from the neighbours milling around the bedroom door. She fell silent again as Jeffes continued searching.

Pushing aside a looking-glass, he reached for a small paper package lying underneath. It contained a white powder.

Louisa jumped up again. 'That's a powder I got for him. It's all right.'

'Sit down and keep quiet!' Jeffes ordered again. 'I want everything.'

He picked up a square medicine bottle and looked at Louisa. 'I thought you told me that Dr Marshall had taken all the medicine away.'

'That's a bottle of medicine which was ordered by the doctor,' she said. 'I got it at Mr Hamilton's.'

As Jeffes added it to his pile, he realised that he had too many items to stuff into his pockets. The ever-helpful Charles Sayers left the room and came back with a small cigar box.

After Jeffes indicated that he had completed his search, Louisa left the bedroom and slipped through the front door clutching her purse. The clouds had dissipated and the night sky was brilliant with stars—a beautiful night for a walk. Before she could go far, Jeffes stopped her, demanding to know where she was heading.

'I want to go down to the beach for a walk—or to the brickyards.'

Jeffes knew that the brickyards contained waterholes. 'What for?' he asked.

'It's where Mick and I used to walk,' she said, adding sadly, 'I don't care about living now that he is dead.'

'Go inside and keep quiet or I will take you down to the police station!'

Meekly, Louisa returned to the sitting room and sat near Mick's corpse. After a while, she turned to Arthur and asked him to fetch Mick's vest and trousers from the bedroom. Arthur collected the clothing and handed it over. She pulled Mick's watch and chain from his vest pocket then dropped the clothes onto the floor. Clutching the much-loved item, she headed towards the door again, saying firmly, 'I want to go out!'

Before Jeffes could say anything, Arthur planted himself in front of her, asking: 'What do you want to go out for?'

'I want to go to the brickyards! I want to go to the beach!' she cried.

'What for?'

'I love the ground Collins put his feet on.'

Arthur grabbed his mother's arm and urged her towards her seat. As she sat down again, she said: 'I'm tired of life. I shall not live after tomorrow.'

'You did not seem to get so excited on Father's death,' Arthur said. 'What are you to do with the children?'

'What do I care for the children now?' But she subsided once more.

Jeffes remained at the cottage throughout the evening to guard against Louisa's endeavours to leave the house. He mentioned her state of mind to Sherwood when the officer returned around eleven pm.

Sherwood turned to her and asked, 'What do you mean by wanting to go out?'

She ignored his question, acting as if he didn't exist.

He too could smell the alcohol seeping from her pores. He organised for another constable to remain at the cottage overnight so that Jeffes could be relieved.

Jeffes returned to the police station carrying the cigar box. He inscribed a number on each collected item and tucked them away safely. If the doctors' suspicions were correct, one of them might provide a clue to the cause of Collins' death.

Chapter 8

Life and death are one thread, the same line viewed from different sides.

Lao-Tzu

Still no telegrams from abroad—and *more* cricket games had been played in the intervening week. To offset his readers' frustration, the *Evening News*' editor decided to treat Sydney to some tongue-in-cheek offerings from his pressmen's mischievous imaginations. Supposedly, the Australian eleven had triumphed, so much so that marriage offers were flooding in. Its six-foot six-inch star, George Bonnor, had declared that nothing less than a duke's daughter and a £100,000 dowry would secure his affections; however, the remainder of the team would be content with commoners and £50,000. As for blowing up the derelict ship off Newcastle, the exercise had proven so difficult that British naval experts were recommending that, in the event of war, Australia should devote a portion of its naval budget to buying derelicts and mooring them outside Port Jackson, Newcastle and Port Phillip. Evidently, a properly fitted-out derelict would have defied all efforts to destroy it, making it more beneficial for defence purposes than the vessels of war financed by the British Admiralty.

Soon, though, the blanket of international silence would be lifted. A ship sailing to Banjoewangie in Java was under orders to collect all the international cablegrams and transport them to Port Darwin. From there, the continental telegraph would transmit the news around Australia. No longer would its citizens feel so blind and vulnerable, uncertain if something might have happened in the interim that meant that life would never be quite the same again.

• • •

For Dr Marshall, the cycle of life and death continued on the Monday morning: new patients to meet, new illnesses to diagnose—or old ones to continue treating. One face he didn't expect to see in his waiting room was that of Louisa Collins. He asked why she had come.

'The constables told me to meet you here at ten o'clock. My husband is dead, and I need a certificate.'

'I will not give a certificate,' he said bluntly. 'I have reported the matter to the coroner and he must give the certificate.'

Mrs Collins seemed unable or unwilling to understand. She said she would wait for the police. He gave up trying to explain the situation and allowed her to bide her time at his premises.

She was a puzzling woman—quite odd, in fact. During their previous encounters, he had noticed that she often seemed apathetic. Instead of meeting his eyes when he spoke to her, she looked down as if she wasn't listening. Sometimes, she ignored his questions altogether as she was now doing. Of course, this might reflect absence of mind rather than apathy. Yet this morning she seemed different, as if she was buoyed by excitement—or, more likely, the alcohol he could smell on her breath. Everyone coped with death in different ways, of course. For some, a few stiff drinks were necessary to endure the pain.

An hour later, when the police hadn't arrived, he told her to go home. She didn't argue the point. She just stood up and left.

• • •

Once a doctor reported a suspicious death, it was the coroner's responsibility to decide whether to initiate an investigation. Sometimes he would begin by questioning the physician. If further investigation seemed unnecessary, he would officially return the responsibility for providing a death certificate to the physician.

Unfortunately, Dr Marshall's report ticked all the right—or wrong—boxes. City Coroner Henry Shiell decided that further investigation would indeed be necessary. He signed the paperwork ordering Collins' corpse to be collected and delivered to the South Sydney Morgue.

Sherwood and Jeffes arrived at Louisa's cottage shortly before midday. The front door was wide open as if to welcome mourners yet nobody was inside—except her dead husband, of course.

Not knowing where Louisa had gone or when she would return, the officers decided that they couldn't wait for her to say her final goodbyes. Jeffes headed off with the body to the morgue, leaving Sherwood to search the premises.

Soon, Sherwood was joined by Sub-Inspector George Hyem. A twenty-year veteran, Hyem had risen steadily through the police ranks and was stationed at Darlinghurst, a major police station near the Darlinghurst gaol and courthouse. With more seniority and experience in murder cases, Hyem had been ordered to take charge of the investigation.

The two policemen searched the house, looking for anything that might contain poison, especially arsenic. Although Marshall had failed to detect its presence, the doctors still thought that these crystals were the most likely cause of Collins' death. Arsenic could be found in many places—in flypapers, for example. Indeed, history told tales of enterprising murderers who had soaked them in water to release the deadly poison. Criminals could often be admired for their ingenuity if not their malevolent intent.

Sherwood found a jar of hair dye—presumably Louisa's rather than her youthful husband's. He stuck it in his pocket to take away for testing. He and Hyem felt through every piece of clothing, turning out the pockets to make sure they hadn't missed anything. They pulled back the bedding and separated the layers as if peeling an onion. When they had finished inside, they searched the yard and outhouse. They even looked under the house.

Afterwards, Hyem returned to Sydney while Sherwood waited for Louisa; he didn't want the grieving widow to think that her husband's body had been stolen. When she still hadn't returned by one pm, he began walking back to the Botany police station. By chance, he crossed paths with her as she headed home from the tram stop. He asked where she had been.

'I have been to the doctor's,' she told him, 'and had expected to meet either you or Constable Jeffes there for the purpose of getting a certificate.'

'I gave no such instructions,' said the surprised officer. While she might have been to the doctor's, Jeffes sensed another destination as well. She seemed sober enough, though, able to look after herself at any rate.

'I have had the body removed from the house to the South Sydney Morgue,' he informed her. 'It is by order of the coroner for the purpose of a post-mortem examination.'

She seemed uninterested in the revelation. Instead, she mused, 'Isn't it curious that Dr Marshall refuses to give me a certificate of the cause of his death? He said he would not be much of a doctor if he gave me a certificate at once.'

• • •

At seven pm that same evening, four doctors gathered at the morgue to perform an autopsy on Collins' body. George Marshall and his relatives

Hamilton Marshall and Thomas Martin were joined by Frederick Milford, a revered figure in Sydney medical circles. Milford was one of the founders of St Vincent's Hospital and the first lecturer in the Principles and Practices of Medicine at Sydney University. It would be his responsibility to ensure that the post-mortem examination was efficient and exhaustive.

The men gathered around the autopsy table where Collins' body was lying. They manipulated his limbs and determined that rigor mortis was still present in his legs but had passed off in his arms, which was to be expected as death had occurred twenty-eight hours ago. They continued their visual examination, noting that the body was fairly well-nourished and was wiry rather than muscular. They could see two abrasions on the right side of the thorax—the upper part of the torso extending from the neck to the abdomen—and another two on the right buttock. Midway between the right knee and ankle was a six-inch long cavity that was about half an inch wide and half an inch deep. It was a necrosis, an area of dead tissue and bone. They all agreed that it wasn't severe enough to be fatal.

They began the internal examination. First, they sawed through the skull bone and examined the brain. It showed signs of congestion. Then they sliced through the flesh of the corpse and lifted out the organs. The tonsils were slightly enlarged and the thyroid gland considerably enlarged but the heart and lungs were healthy. The spleen was abnormally large—weighing ten-and-a-half ounces compared to the average five to eight ounces. The liver too, weighing four-and-a-half pounds instead of three or four. The serous surface—the covering on the outside of the intestine—was darker than usual and congested, and the stomach was significantly distended. The other organs, though, looked normal.

Cutting open the stomach, they found that it contained about twelve ounces of dark greenish-brown fluid, which they tipped into a clean glass jar. With the stomach's mucous coat uncovered, they could see that it was considerably inflamed. Red patches dotted the surface. A sizeable patch lay near the pyloric orifice, the area of the stomach that connects with the small intestines. These were signs of peritoneal inflammation, although they couldn't determine its cause. To answer that question, chemical tests would need to be conducted.

Milford picked up the stomach and tipped it and its contents into a glass jar. He added portions cut from the kidney, liver and jejunum—the middle section of the small intestine. Carefully, he corked and sealed the jar then locked it in a tin case. He would hand it to the relevant authorities when the inquest was convened.

Court procedure dictated that the physical evidence in a criminal trial should be appropriately secured and the chain of custody kept intact. In the event of any noteworthy discoveries, the jury needed to be able to feel confident that nothing untoward had happened to the evidence. It could mean the difference between life and death for the accused in a murder trial.

Chapter 9

How eloquently must the symptoms have spoken to the doctor.

Regina v. Louisa Collins

The pressman for John Fairfax & Son's evening newspaper, the *Echo*, stepped through the large iron gates in Belmore Road and headed towards the garden surrounding the caretaker's cottage. Behind the cottage squatted the South Sydney Morgue, where hundreds of bodies were deposited each year for investigation. The morgue's location was appropriate: in a corner of the old Church of England section of the now closed Elizabeth and Devonshire Streets Cemetery. Such a location might provide reassurance for family members, a reminder of the natural cycle of birth and death, except that there was nothing natural about the demise of many of the morgue's inmates. Sometimes misfortune inked the nib recording an admission; sometimes suspicion. Before discharge details could be added, explanations must be sought.

Adjoining the caretaker's cottage was the small coroner's courtroom where inquests were conducted. There the relevant questions would be asked and perhaps answered. It was the pressman's job to record the witnesses' responses for the benefit of *Echo* readers and also for the morning newspaper, the *Sydney Morning Herald*. Crime and misfortune helped sell newspapers. Indeed, courtroom dramas were among the pleasures of modern society. The largely verbatim reports transformed the black-and-white print into graphic scenes as if the witnesses had stepped from the courtroom stage and were performing their monologues in the colony's parlours.

In general, only a score of people traipsed along the path to the coroner's courtroom, mainly the deceased's family and close friends as well as witnesses and jurors. Sometimes, hundreds milled around the iron gates, even thousands in the aftermath of a tragedy or gruesome murder. On Tuesday, 10 July, the numbers were small. The pressman wasn't surprised. Few knew about this particular death. 'This case is one in which the police refused to give any information whatever,' he wrote, 'as they were of the opinion that the matter ought not to be published until after the inquest.' Naturally, such reticence piqued his interest. What tales was the courtroom about to hear?

Coroner Henry Shiell took his seat. He was a well-known figure to members of Sydney's fourth estate, having sat in the coroner's chair for two decades. He had overseen inquests into natural deaths as well as those caused by murder and misadventure. He knew that inquests were inquisitional rather than adversarial, intended to find answers rather than cast blame. Accordingly, defence lawyers were rarely present and prosecutors never. If, however, the jurors decided that a death was caused by malicious intent, they could point their official finger at a particular person or persons. The accused would then be committed to stand trial, beginning a process that could end in the law's legislated punishment of death.

Before the witnesses could be called, it was necessary for the coroner and jurors, along with Louisa Collins, Constable Jeffes and Dr Marshall, to view and officially identify the corpse. They trooped across to the morgue where Collins' corpse was displayed. Death was a familiar sight to most of the populace, although few had seen the rows of ragged autopsy stitches that held a body together after an autopsy. A draped sheet hid most of the ugliness, but what confronted them, what almost assaulted them, was the stench of death that seeped from the pores of the building itself.

'About a fortnight back,' continued the coroner after they had seated themselves in the courtroom again, 'the deceased became ill, and Dr Marshall was called in to attend upon him. He continued so to do until his death, which took place on Sunday afternoon last. In consideration of the circumstances surrounding the case, Dr Marshall declined to give a certificate for the cause of death. He is of the opinion that the circumstances of the case are of a very suspicious character. The medical evidence will be taken and then the inquiry will be adjourned to allow a chemical analysis of the deceased's stomach and contents.'

Having explained why the case had been brought to his attention, Shiell looked down at his notes to remind himself of the necessary background information. 'Mrs Collins lost a husband about thirteen months ago, a man by the name of Andrews, and the illness in his case was identical with the illness of the present deceased. A few days after the death of the first husband, she married the deceased, and now he has died under almost the same circumstances as the former one.'

No wonder Collins' death was being investigated. The *Echo* journalist turned his gaze towards Louisa Collins, who had just been called to testify. She appeared overly excited—not that emotional widows were an unusual sight in a coroner's courtroom. In truth, her manner would have been more noteworthy if, after such an insinuating introduction, she had shown no emotional response at all.

Louisa stepped into the witness box and swore to tell the truth, the whole truth. Then the questions began: name, address, relationship to the deceased, personal information about the deceased . . . date of marriage?

'We were married on 9 April 1887,' she stated.

She confirmed that Collins was her second husband and that her first husband had also died. 'On 5 February 1887,' she said, although other sources would later reveal that his death had occurred on the second of the month.

Meanwhile, those with an aptitude for arithmetic were making some calculations. Obviously, her first husband hadn't died thirteen months previously as the coroner had stated, but seventeen months ago. And she hadn't remarried only a few days after his death; it was two months later. True, two months was a brief mourning period, but it wasn't scandalously short. For poor widows with young children and little income, a speedy remarriage was often an economic necessity. Attractive widows like Mrs Collins rarely stayed in the marriage market for long.

The coroner asked about her second husband's illness. Louisa reported that he had been ill for a couple of months and that Dr Marshall had attended him for the latter part of his illness. 'He told my husband he was suffering from a "feverish cold",' she told the court. She mentioned that Dr Martin, the surgeon who had attended her first husband, had also visited her second husband a couple of times before he died. At that point she hesitated, seemingly unable to remember when her husband had died even though it was only two days previously. 'The afternoon of Sunday last,' she finally recollected.

And then came the question alluding to motive. Had he life insurance?

'No,' she said. 'His life was not insured.'

No obvious motive then. But what about her previous husband?

'My former husband's life was insured. I got the insurance. He willed it to me,' she replied defensively.

After the coroner indicated that he had no further questions, the clerk wrote out Louisa's deposition and read it back to her, asking her to sign it. She began writing then paused and looked up at the coroner: 'I have made a mistake. I put down *Louisa Andrews*.'

The coroner advised her to sign her name correctly. But what did this odd slip-up say about her relationship with her second husband?

• • •

Her exhaustion was catching up with her. She'd had little sleep in the past couple of weeks, having attended Mick night after night as he moaned and vomited. During the daylight hours, she'd had her family to feed and the usual chores to do. On a number of occasions, she had also travelled into the city to seek the doctor's assistance. Was it surprising that she could barely keep her head up when people spoke to her? As for forgetting to sign her correct surname, twenty-two years of writing *Louisa Andrews*—on the rare occasions she had needed to—had overridden fifteen months of *Louisa Collins*.

To make matters worse, the coroner had now pointed the finger at *her* as if the fact that she had married Mick so soon after Charlie's death was grounds for thinking that she might have killed him—if not both of them.

• • •

'A man who gave his name as "Collins" came to my consulting room,' said Dr Marshall in his lilting Irish brogue when he was called to the witness box. He described his dealings with the Collinses and the conversation with Dr Martin that had aroused his suspicions. He added that he had failed to find anything untoward when he tested Collins' vomit and urine, yet Collins' rapid deterioration and death had left him deeply troubled. 'Under the circumstances,' he concluded, 'I declined to give a certificate of the cause of death, not being satisfied what the cause was.'

As the *Echo* reporter scribbled his detailed notes, he recognised that Marshall had suspicions but no evidence of foul play. Of course, it was the inquest's role to determine if Collins had died of unnatural causes.

Would the next witness, Dr Frederick Milford, be able to provide any evidence? Milford conducted post-mortem examinations every two or three weeks so he was a regular in the coroner's courtroom. His was the hand that reached beneath the surface of the human body, his the eyes that saw what others couldn't see. What could he tell the jury?

Milford described in gruesome detail the results of the autopsy examination, concluding, 'From the appearances here described, I am of the opinion that the death was lingering and protracted, that the cause of death was peritonitis of a low form, and that this may have been caused by the use internally of some noxious drug, or probably may have arisen from natural causes.'

The coroner recalled Dr Marshall, who agreed with Milford's opinion. Asked what natural causes could produce such an effect, Marshall said that alcoholism was a well-known cause, although this was unlikely in Collins' case because of the man's seeming temperance. While treating Collins, he had assumed that another natural cause was responsible until Dr Martin had mentioned his own involvement with the family. Even then, he had remained unconcerned about Collins' condition until the night before his death.

As Dr Marshall left the witness stand, the coroner brought the proceedings to a temporary close. 'The inquiry is adjourned until Tuesday next,' he informed the jurors, 'to allow the deceased's stomach and contents to undergo a chemical analysis by the government analyst.'

• • •

SUSPICIOUS DEATH OF A MAN AT BOTANY was the headline in that afternoon's edition of the *Echo*. The report itself contained little more than a verbatim account of each witness's testimony, with few personal details and no speculation. Still, the number of column inches devoted to the topic served as speculation in itself. With allusions to the possibility of infidelity as well as murder—one committed by a woman, no less—the case was already nudging the boundary between the merely interesting and the sensational. And 'sensation' was a financial windfall, as any successful newspaper proprietor could attest.

Chapter 10

The poetry of homicide belongs in a special degree to poisoning.

The Times

The role of a government analyst—the man responsible for investigating poisoning deaths—was only a recently established occupation for the simple reason that forensic toxicology, indeed toxicology itself, was only a recently established science. But it was a much-needed one in these 'civilised' times, many would declare grimly.

In times gone by, crimes had generally been of a cruder nature—physical expressions of rage or passion or cold calculation that left visible traces on the victim. Civilised times spawned more sophisticated crimes, as the Italian courts could attest. No classical Roman or Renaissance statesman—no Borgia—would openly stab a rival when poison was at hand. An inscrutable mask; an unseen hand; an invisible but nonetheless deadly violation. Suspicion might arise, but certainty?

By Victorian times, the dark art of poisoning was sweeping through all classes of society like a fashion filtering down the social ranks. Poisoning homicides were increasing, although, as experts tried to point out, improvements in the ability to identify specific poisons in the human body were partly responsible for the seeming upsurge. Doctors were advised to watch out for the well-known symptoms. When they aired their suspicions, the toxicologists—the poison detectives—could begin their hunt. They were the foe the poisoner feared the most.

Ironically, men of science had once been feared because of the threat their discoveries posed to entrenched religious views and cultural beliefs; however, the pendulum was beginning to swing the other way. Science itself was coming to be seen as society's saviour, as the means for determining the truth about subjects as vast as the origins of the universe and as small as the goings-on beneath the human exterior, both physiological and psychological. Yet while scientific knowledge was growing exponentially, the technology of discovery still had its limitations. Thus, toxicological evidence-analysis wasn't just a craft but an art. And therein lay one of its dangers. The craftsman might be skilled, but was he skilful enough to uncover the truth? It was of little benefit to society—and particularly to the executed—if a 'murderer' was later proven innocent because no 'crime' had been committed in the first place.

• • •

New South Wales Government Analyst William Hamlet knew that he had to be meticulous and methodical when conducting his investigations because the question of guilt or innocence might hinge on his evidence. The official transfer of the Collinses' items had occurred at and after the inquest: from Dr Milford to Constable Jeffes, then to himself. Upon receipt he had noted the date and time—Tuesday, 10 July 1888 at eleven forty-five am—before carrying the items back to his laboratory.

Opening the locked tin case, he unsealed the glass jar and began extracting its contents: a human stomach and portions of liver, kidney, bowel and intestines. Liquid spilled from the stomach. He collected it and poured it back into the jar. It was essential that he test all the liquid in addition to the physical remains.

First, he examined the stomach. It was noticeably discoloured, showing signs of inflammation and extensive bruising. The pyloric aperture—the opening that allowed food to move from the stomach into the duodenum—revealed a severe stricture along with parallel bands of discolouration, as if some powerful irritant had passed through at the time of the stricture. Such striations and discolourations were well-known signs of arsenical poisoning.

He washed the stomach so as to gather any poison that might be clinging to it and added the washings to the liquid already in the jar. His preparations completed, he was ready to begin the chemical tests. The coroner had recommended that he begin with the arsenic test. From the sight of the remains, he agreed that arsenic was the most likely cause of death—if the man had indeed died from poisoning.

Instead of using the Reinsch test, he employed the widely accepted Marsh test. It was the brainchild of chemist James Marsh who in 1833 had recognised the need for a definitive arsenic test after a jury failed to convict a suspected and later self-confessed arsenic poisoner. Marsh knew that he had to find some way of isolating the pure element ('As', the thirty-third element on the periodic table) from human and animal tissue as well as from the food or drink that served as its vehicle of ingestion. He also needed to establish a method that would reveal the element's presence by means of its reaction with other chemicals. It took three years. Chemists had already determined that arsenic and hydrogen combined to form the toxic gas 'arsine' (AsH_3). This knowledge provided the foundation for his testing procedure. The resulting Marsh test could detect arsenic traces as small as two parts per million and would become the standard arsenic test for the next 140 years.

Hamlet poured some of the liquid from Collins' remains into a glass container and added dashes of acid and zinc. If arsenic were present, arsine gas would soon bubble from the solution. Quickly, he attached a glass tube to the container. The tube had a fine nozzle at its other end, which he trained on a sheet of glass. In the gap between nozzle and glass, he lit an open flame to ignite any escaping arsine gas. When the gas ignited, any metallic arsenic that was present would coat the sheet of glass with a black film.

He needed to be careful, though. If the glass was too near the flame, it could explode into dangerous shards. Even worse was the threat posed by the arsine gas itself. It was so deadly that half-a-dozen chemists had already died from inhaling the gas while performing the Marsh test.

Indeed, arsenic was so deadly that it was called the 'poison of poisons'. Less than one five-thousandth of an ounce (150 milligrams) could kill an adult. Moreover, not only was it poisonous to humans, it could kill any being with a central nervous system and many plants as well. And it didn't have to be ingested to be deadly. Inhalation or skin contact could also cause poisoning. It could even be absorbed through the urethra, the vagina or the rectum. A French servant who had failed to kill his mistress with arsenic-laced soup succeeded when he added arsenic to her enema liquid. A German farmer bumped off his wives by inserting arsenic-coated fingers into their vaginas.

Yet in its elemental form it wasn't dangerous at all, which was fortunate since the shiny steel-grey substance was the twentieth most common element in the earth's crust. It was also found in spring water and sea water, volcanic emissions and meteorites. It only became toxic when it formed compounds with other elements. One such compound was the original arsenic, the yellow-hued orpiment used as a pigment. The Greeks called it *arsenikon*, probably from the Persian word for 'yellow'.

What Hamlet was attempting to find was the arsenic-oxygen compound As_2O_3. It was generated when ores like gold, copper, zinc, lead and tin were smelted. The elemental arsenic escaped from the hot ore in gaseous form and combined with oxygen in the atmosphere to produce the white crystals known as 'arsenious acid' or 'arsenic'. So much of this deadly poison was produced in the smelting process that alarmed government inspectors had reported in the 1870s that the output of one month's smelting in a single Cornish factory could produce enough arsenic to destroy every creature on the face of the earth.

Most of the arsenic output ended up in the world's oceans. As for the rest, it tainted fruit and vegetables, wine, beer and cigarettes, confectionery, candles, cookware and cosmetics, fabrics and furnishings, ornaments, toys and, in some instances, the money used to purchase these goods. Even the air people breathed could contain arsenic as it was released from the coal that heated homes and fired factories. One writer lamented that, through arsenic's deadly intrusion, homes had been transformed from places of health and happiness into sepulchres.

The amount of arsenic absorbed through these forms of toxic pollution was usually so small that it had little or no medical impact. Of course, sometimes the toxin was introduced intentionally rather than being absorbed unwittingly—not that it was Hamlet's job to determine intention even if he could detect arsenic in the first place. That was up to the coroner.

As the liquid bubbled, Hamlet watched the glass sheet closely. There. He could see a black film appearing on the sheet of glass. The test was conclusive. Collins did indeed have arsenic in his body.

Hamlet calculated the amount then turned to the other remains. Stomach, kidneys, liver: all showed traces of arsenic. No arsenic crystals could be seen on the stomach coat itself, which was significant. It suggested that the arsenic had been ingested in a liquid solution.

He began testing the other items. The small brandy flask collected by Jeffes contained only brandy and water. The ointment proved to be regular zinc ointment, a simple remedy to dry up a wound or sore.

The packet of powder was regular Grey Powder (mercury); he put that aside for later testing as he knew that medical preparations sometimes contained arsenic adulteration. The square medicine bottle contained bismuth, peppermint and traces of hydrocyanic acid (cyanide); he also put that aside for later testing. The bottle of hair dye was composed of nitrate of silver and water. The small nobbler glass was about half-full of a turbid liquid comprising milk and a thickening agent like starch or arrowroot—and something else, as he soon discovered.

Hamlet knew that he need not wait until the inquest's resumption to report the results of his investigation. Two days after the inquest's adjournment, he contacted the coroner.

Shiell sent a message to Inspector Hyem, advising that arsenic had been found in Collins' remains and also in the small glass tumbler collected from the Collinses' bedroom. Since Mrs Collins had repeatedly stated that she alone had given her husband his drinks and medicine, she was the obvious suspect in this apparent poisoning. 'Arrest her,' the coroner ordered.

Chapter 11

Suspicion is . . . always an enemy to happiness.

Hosea Ballou, *Treasury of Thought*

Louisa and her five children were eating their tea in the kitchen when Sherwood and Jeffes arrived at ten to six that evening. Louisa was red-faced and bright-eyed, her usual passivity replaced by the aura of excitement that alcohol seemed to stimulate.

Sherwood called her into the front room where they could talk out of earshot of the children. 'I want you to accompany me to the police station,' he said.

'When am I coming back again?' she asked innocently, without enquiring why she was wanted at the police station.

Sherwood said nothing. What could he say?

She sank into a chair and covered her face with her hands. 'I know,' she said despairingly. 'I am not coming back again.'

He couldn't assure her otherwise. Trying to forestall an emotional disintegration, he told her it was time to depart. She would need to dress warmly. The clouds from earlier in the day had drifted away and without their protective barrier the night was chilly.

Silently, she pulled on her outdoor clothing. As she showed no signs of resisting, Sherwood told Jeffes to return home, that he would escort Mrs Collins to Sydney alone.

They trudged past Louisa's favourite drinking hole, the Botany Bay Hotel, to the tram stop. They were heading to Darlinghurst police station, which sat on a triangular-shaped block at the intersection of Forbes and Bourke streets. As they walked the final short distance from the tram to the police station, Sherwood saw her stagger a few times; however, the chilly air seemed to have a sobering effect.

Reaching the station, he took her into the charging room to question her. He began by asking if she had given anything to Collins. With her defences lowered by alcohol's mellowing influence, she might tell him everything he needed to know.

'Yes,' she replied, appearing ready and willing to discuss Collins' death.

'What did you give him?'

'What the doctor ordered him.'

'What was that?'

'Medicine, brandy and egg, milk and eggs,' she said, then added, 'I gave him the milk out of a glass.'

'What became of that glass?'

'Constable Jeffes took it away.'

This, the policeman presumed, was the glass in which Hamlet had found the arsenic. He asked if she had given her husband anything else.

'A man named Arthur Hamill prescribed some beer and egg for him and a vomiting powder,' she said.

'Who gave him the vomiting powder?'

'I sent my boy Fred to Evan Thomas' chemist shop at Waterloo for it, and Hamill gave it to Mick.'

Sherwood made a note to question Hamill, then asked, 'Did anyone else attend your husband or give anything to him?'

'Charles Sayers gave him a drink. Mrs Bartington gave him a drink off a quill. Also, Mrs Mudge and Mrs Hamill.'

He returned to the subject of the glass tumbler Constable Jeffes had taken away and asked about its contents.

'It contained egg and milk which I mixed,' she reported.

Sherwood decided that he had asked enough questions. She hadn't confessed to poisoning Collins, yet she hadn't suggested another likely culprit. The casual interviewer disappeared, replaced by the officious lawman. He said that he was charging her on suspicion of having caused the death of her husband Michael Peter Collins at Botany on or about 8 July.

She made no reply.

He filled in the necessary paperwork then took her to the female cell in the Darlinghurst lock-up.

• • •

Night-time's broom swept up prostitutes and petty thieves, drunks and vagrants, and deposited them in the lock-up. The stench of unwashed poverty crowded in with them. For some, the lock-up had the familiarity of a second home, no less uncomfortable and a bit warmer than a bed on the streets. For Louisa, however, these companions-in-crime added a new level of horror to the day's experiences.

Sherwood arrived the following morning to take her to the police court. The magistrate ordered that she be remanded to the women's ward of neighbouring Darlinghurst Gaol until the inquest reconvened the following Tuesday.

Sydney's only gaol lay next door to Darlinghurst Courthouse, where the city's criminal trials were held. These buildings formed their own walled city, with prisoners travelling between the police station, the gaol and the courthouse through convict-hewn underground tunnels. If the inquest jury committed Louisa Collins to stand trial for murder, she would remain locked within these forbidding walls until the trial was concluded—and possibly forever. The unconsecrated soil within the gaol walls contained the skeletons of many an executed murderer.

Chapter 12

Murder most foul.

William Shakespeare, *Hamlet*

The reports of Louisa's arrest stoked the flames of what had been only a middling fire. Sydney's leading newspapers sent their own pressmen to attend the second day of the inquest. The authorities, expecting a sizeable crowd, had moved the inquest to the larger coroner's courtroom in the grandly renamed Chancery Square in Macquarie Street—once the less auspicious Hyde Park Barracks, home of Sydney's convicts.

Constable Jeffes was the first to testify. He described his encounters with the Collinses and his search of their bedroom. He listed the items he had taken away, including the small glass tumbler of milk. 'When I got hold of that tumbler,' he told the jury, 'Mrs Collins rose from her seat, got hold of my right arm—the tumbler was in my right hand—and said, "That is nothing."'

He had everyone's attention. This was the first evidence of odd behaviour from Louisa. Did the tumbler contain something she didn't want the police to know about?

Jeffes reported that she had reacted similarly when he picked up a packet of white powder from the dressing table. He described her attempts to leave the house in the hours after Collins' death, and he sombrely repeated her remarks that she didn't want to continue living.

Heads swivelled towards Louisa. Everyone knew that suicide was a mortal sin in the eyes of the church, that God chose when to give life and when to take it away. The law thought similarly, perceiving an act of self-murder—*felo de se*—as little different to murder itself. As suicide was therefore a crime, an unsuccessful attempt at killing oneself could be punished by confinement in a prison or madhouse rather than expressions of sympathy and support.

Jeffes continued, 'Her son Arthur Andrews said to her: "What are you talking about? What's going to become of the children?" She said, "I don't care about them"—or words to that effect.'

When the coroner asked Louisa if she had any questions to ask the witness, she knew that she had to defend herself against these character-destroying charges. She didn't want the jurors to think she was a bad mother, one who would choose death over caring for her own children. Worse, if they thought she was a bad mother, they'd be more likely to believe she was a bad wife, the type who might be inclined to poison her husband. She challenged Jeffes about his recollections.

'You did say you were tired of your life,' the constable retorted. 'Twice!'

She lapsed into silence again.

The coroner called the government analyst, the witness everyone was eager to hear. No doubt his testimony would explain why Louisa Collins had been arrested.

Hamlet reported that he'd found nearly two and three-quarter grains of arsenic in Collins' stomach contents and one-sixth of a grain in the liver portion.[1] He then picked up the small glass tumbler that sat among the exhibits, the tumbler that Jeffes said Mrs Collins had tried to stop him taking. 'This, upon analysis,' he told the court, 'was found to contain the tenth part of a grain of arsenic.' He added that the bottle of urine yielded a faint trace of arsenic while the bottle containing vomited matter handed him by the constable contained two-thirds of a grain of arsenic.

As it happened, the latter two were the samples that Dr Marshall had tested for arsenic traces without success.

Hamlet's testimony was a bald and unemotional recitation of the facts as he believed them to be. He made no allusions to the testimonies of others. He offered no speculations as to how or when the arsenic might have entered Collins' body or who might have administered it. He didn't even specify what constituted a fatal dose. That was not his responsibility. It was up to the doctors to determine when a substance turned from tonic to toxin.

The coroner recalled Dr Marshall and asked the critical question: how much constituted a lethal dose?

'From two to three grains of arsenic is a fatal dose for an adult.'

It wasn't hard for the jurors to make the calculation: there was enough poison in Collins' stomach contents alone to have killed him.

Just to make sure that the jury didn't miss this crucial point, the coroner declared: 'We have now demonstrated that Collins died from arsenical poisoning. The question now is: by whom was it administered?'

The question was largely rhetorical. When Sherwood took the stand and testified that Coroner Shiell's was the voice of authority ordering Louisa's arrest, it was clear that the coroner had answered the administration question to his own satisfaction. Still, the inquest continued. Sherwood reported that Louisa had told him multiple times before Collins' death that she alone was responsible for giving Collins his drink and medicines. Yet later, while being interviewed at Darlinghurst police station, she had mentioned that others had also given Collins drinks.

Those she had named were called to testify. All declared that they had only given Collins drinks that were already in the room, not ones they had prepared themselves. Eventually, the late hour and the still-lengthy witness list forced Shiell to adjourn the inquest.

The attendees stepped from the warmth of the courtroom cocoon into a dismal winter's evening with bouts of heavy rain. Exposed to a sudden downpour, the sixty-two-year-old coroner caught a severe chill, forcing a delay in the inquest's resumption until Tuesday, 26 July, two weeks from its original adjournment. Shiell remained unwell when that bitterly cold morning dawned, but duty called. He rose from his sickbed and headed to the coroner's court, a decision that he—and his wife even more so—would later regret.

One after another, the Collinses' neighbours entered the witness box and spoke about their relationships with the couple. As Rosetta Mapstone finished her testimony, the coroner asked Louisa if she had any questions. She had—a curious one. She asked Mrs Mapstone if she had noticed Collins' clothing when she visited him on the Saturday evening before his death. Was he wearing trousers at that time?

'Collins did not have any trousers on when I was there,' Mrs Mapstone replied.

More witnesses followed. Charles Sayers reported seeing Jeffes take the items from Louisa's house; however, his own recollection differed from the constable's. 'I did not see her get up and catch hold of him by the arm when he took up that glass tumbler,' he declared.

What was he suggesting—that the constable had lied?

Louisa indicated that she wanted to ask Sayers a question. Surprisingly, she didn't refer to the discrepancy between his and Jeffes' testimonies. Instead, she repeated her earlier question about Collins' attire.

Sayers replied, 'When I was at your house on Sunday morning, I noticed that the deceased had his trousers on him in bed.'

Coroner Shiell couldn't help noticing Louisa's interest in the subject of Collins' clothing. He asked Sayers if this had been Collins' habit.

'That was the first time I noticed his trousers on,' Sayers said.

Neighbour Catherine Mudge also testified to being present when Jeffes searched the bedroom. She too told the jury that she hadn't seen Louisa grab Jeffes' arm.

Again Louisa failed to use her right to ask questions to expose the critical discrepancies between the testimonies of these witnesses, even though the coroner was clearly building a case against her and was using Jeffes' claims as the strongest piece of incriminating evidence. Without legal training, how could she be expected to understand how to defend herself?

Chapter 13

Keep your eyes wide open before marriage, half shut afterwards.

Benjamin Franklin, *Poor Richard's Almanack*

When Louisa first testified, she was not under arrest. Now, with the murder charges laid against her, she was called to the stand again. Coroner Shiell indicated to his clerk that she would need to be sworn again on the Bible. He then advised her of her rights: 'You are not bound to answer any questions that you think might incriminate you. You may decline on that ground. You yourself are to determine whether you think they might produce that result.'

Louisa acknowledged the coroner's words then began to speak. 'When we left Johnson's Lane to go to Botany in February last, we were clear of debt. I had £25 in gold. Collins got two or three half-days' work at Botany. He got the sack and was eight weeks idle. One Saturday during that eight weeks he said, "Louie, will you give me £1? I'll find a way of making money," naming a certain gambling-house in George Street. I told him I had a great horror of gambling; however, I gave him the £1. He came home that night at half past eleven. He fetched me £4 10s. He was very pleased. He said it was better than hard work. He said, "If I had had £20 tonight, I could have fetched you £100 just as easy as I did that." He said, "Will you give me £20 next Saturday?" I told him it was a great risk. He said he felt sure that he could get me £100 or more with it.

'I gave him the £20 on the following Saturday. He did not come home till the last tram. I was in bed but not asleep. I said, "Mick, is that you?" He made me no answer, but struck a match and lit the candle. I never shall forget his look. He sat down on the side of the bed. He said: "Louie, I have lost all the money." He commenced to cry and I did too. I couldn't help it. He said, "Here I am out of work, and I have lost all the money." I told him I would forgive him when I saw he was in such a dreadful state of anxiety and misery. He said, "What will I do to get work?" There was no work about Botany at the time. He came to bed but could not sleep.

'He got up the next morning and only had a cup of tea. He said, "I wonder where I could go for work?" He sat thinking for some time on the chair. At last he said, "I think I'll go up the Illawarra line." I gave him a pound. He said if he got work he would be away a week.

'He went up the Illawarra line, and not knowing the stations, being a stranger on that line, I did not expect him back for a week, but he came back the same night. I was surprised to see him. He was perfectly speechless. I asked him what was the matter? He said, "Don't ask me." Then he said, "I have ruined myself and you too." I said, "Tell me what has happened."

'He said, "I went six miles further than the station my ticket was for. The guard asked me for my ticket and when he saw the distance it was for, he caught hold of me and pulled me out of the carriage onto the platform, and I struck him. He gave me in charge and fetched me back to Sydney. When I got to the railway station in Sydney, the guard said, 'I'll let you off if you give me £3 10s.' I had no money on me but the remainder of the pound, and I said to the guard, 'I have no money on me but if you wait till I pawn my watch, I'll give you the money.' "

'He said he pawned it and took the money back to the station and the guard let him come home. He was thoroughly broken-hearted, and said, "Louie, I wish you had got someone else besides me; I have dragged you down to ruin." I told him not to mind, that I would put up with it.

'He got work at last in Botany at 36 shillings per week. He had just worked two weeks when the baby died. That sent us further into debt and trouble. I had no money. I borrowed £1 2s 6d off Mrs Bullock, the draper at Botany, to pay for the ground to bury the child. I have never been able to pay it back. I owe Dr Martin a guinea for his visits. I have never been able to pay him.

'After the funeral of the child, he went to work. He used to say, "There is no use of me working, my wages will never pay the back-debts and redeem the watch." I tried to cheer him all I could, but it was no use. He had a broken-hearted look.

'A month ago last Monday I was brushing his overcoat, and in the heart pocket I found a package of white paper. It had no writing on it. I opened it. There was a large teaspoonful of white stuff, like salts, only much finer. It had a bright and sparkling appearance. It had no smell, but I put my tongue to it, and it made my tongue hot and my mouth watery during the rest of the day. I could not help spitting all the day.

'When he came home, between seven and eight o'clock that night, I said, "Mick, what little package is that in your coat pocket?" He said, "Have you been at my pockets?" I told him I was brushing the coat and saw it there. He said, "I'll search your pocket after tea, and see what's in it." After supper, he went to bed . . .

'Oh, I'm going too fast,' she then said to the coroner and backtracked for a moment. 'I said, "Tell me what it is that's in your pocket." He said, "I'm damned if I know what's the name of it. A man in Waterloo gave it to me to take in a little water for a lump I have in my groin." From what I knew he suffered, I believed him, and we went to bed. I said, "Will you take some of that tonight then?" He said, "No, not tonight, then it's too cold."

'The next morning, he got up at four o'clock as usual, lit the candle, and dressed himself, put his hat on and turned and looked at me in the bed. He put his hand up to the coat I spoke of before, and took this package out, and put it into his trousers pocket—in the trousers he had on. I said, "Will you take some of that now?" "No," he said, "I'll take it over at the stables."

'He came home at seven o'clock to his breakfast. He pushed the meat which he was always very fond of to one side and said he would have some milksops. I gave him a clean basin and he made some sops himself. He went down the yard and commenced retching dreadful after eating the sops, the first time I have ever seen him retch. I said, "Whatever is the matter with you? Did you take some of that medicine?" meaning the stuff he took away. He said, "No, I did not." I said, "Will you have some more breakfast?" He said, "No, give me sixpence." I had not a sixpence and gave him a shilling.

'He was away all day as usual and came home to his supper and ate very little and went into the room to go to bed. When in the room a few minutes—I was in the kitchen—he called me by name to fetch him the small glass, which he had never done before. I said, "Will a cup do?" He said, "No, fetch me in a glass."

'I got half a dipper of water from the kitchen and went into the front room and got the glass and went into the bedroom. I was surprised to see him sitting on the side of the bed with his new trousers on. I said, "Are you going out?" He said, "No, you won't mind me sleeping in these trousers?" a thing he never did before. I said, "No, if you are comfortable I am satisfied." I then said, "Whatever do you want this glass for?' He replied, "I want it just to rinse my mouth out with a little water, that's all." I believed him and went to bed.

'I was awoke in the middle of the night by him retching dreadful. I said, "There is something strange the matter with you." He said, "It's only the cold I have." He had a very bad cold at the time and used to cough very much.

'He kept getting worse and worse but remained at his work up till the Sunday dinner time a fortnight before his death. From the time I saw the powder till the time he was laid up was one week. On the Monday, he sent word over to say he could not go to his stables. I asked him to go with me to see a doctor one day that week and we went to Dr Marshall. When we came home that night, Collins took a spoonful of the medicine and said he was sure it would do him no good, it was throwing money away. He said, "The bailiffs will be in the house, there's nothing surer." Every knock during the second week of his illness, he turned as pale as death and would say, "Oh Christ . . ."

Louisa paused and looked apologetically at the coroner. 'He used to swear a bit,' she said. Then she continued, '"Oh Christ, I thought that was the bailiff."

'There was two unfortunate things I done during his illness,' Louisa concluded, 'and that was to take over that glass he had used so often without having once washed it out, and to put the trousers in water which were taken off his back after his death.'

The coroner asked if Collins had any life insurance.

'His life was not insured,' she said. 'He was in no lodge or any society whatever. He has left me penniless and in debt.'

'When did you redeem the watch?' the coroner asked, having remembered the previous remarks about Collins' watch being taken out of his vest pocket after his death.

'I will tell you all about that after dinner,' Louisa replied.

It was a reminder that it was time for the midday break. Afterwards, Coroner Shiell decided not to return Louisa to the witness box.

Instead, he recalled the government analyst and asked him about the powder found on the Collins' dressing table.

'That powder consisted of mercury and chalk,' said Hamlet. 'It's what is known as common Grey Powder. It contained no arsenic.'

Coroner Shiell decided that he had interviewed enough witnesses. It was time to begin his summation. 'You have heard the long rambling statement made today by the widow,' he began, 'and doubtless you have seen what the object of that statement was, which was to make it appear as if the deceased had poisoned himself, having taken small doses of arsenic, and thereby caused his own death.' He asked the jurors to consider whether a man would be likely to poison himself slowly and thereby prolong his own agony or whether it was more likely that the poison was administered by some other person, someone who, naturally, wouldn't confide in others. Who might that person be?

After running through the evidence, he told the jurors that if they thought Collins had given himself small doses of arsenic, they would have to return a verdict that he had died from self-administered arsenical poison. If, however, they decided that the case was sufficient to go to a jury, they must vote to convict.

With such a clear direction from the coroner, no one was surprised at the speed of the jury's decision or the nature of its verdict: death by arsenical poisoning administered by Collins' wife.

'I concur entirely with the verdict found by the jury,' Coroner Shiell told Louisa, 'and commit you to stand your trial at the Quarter Sessions for the wilful murder of your husband, Michael Peter Collins.'

Chapter 14

The very dead shall be drawn up out of the grave to bear witness.

Pharmaceutical Journal and Transactions

'The extraordinary and mysterious circumstances surrounding the death of a man named Michael Peter Collins at Botany have now assumed alarming aspects,' the *Echo* had declared two weeks previously, on Friday, 13 July, when the news broke that arsenic had been found in Collins' body. The *Echo*'s pressman knew that this discovery was momentous, yet more sensational news was to come. 'This morning,' he continued, 'Inspector Hyem waited upon the coroner, where he was supplied with the requisite warrants for the exhumation of the body of Mrs Collins' first husband and also a child (of which Collins is the father). If practicable, exhumation will take place today.'

The newspaper provided some basic information about the two deaths, reporting that both death certificates had been signed by Dr Thomas Martin, the surgeon who had joined Dr Marshall on his visits to the Collins house. 'Be it mentioned,' the paper concluded tantalisingly, 'the symptoms preceding the death of all three were similar in all respects, and the suspicions go to show that all met their death by poisoning.'

• • •

John Wallters remembered both cases. He had first encountered the woman at the centre of this drama when she came to his place of employment, Charles Kinsela's funeral parlour, following Charles Andrews' death. She had said that her name was Mrs Andrews and that she wished to order a coffin and funeral for her husband. He had engraved her husband's death details in gilt letters on a metal plate and later attached it to the lid of the cheap pine coffin she had ordered.

In the days after her first visit, he had made two journeys to her house. The first was to measure her husband so his body fitted comfortably into his coffin; there was an art to creating a pleasant viewing experience for relatives. The second time, he collected the coffin and took it to its final resting place in Sydney's main cemetery, the government-owned Rookwood Necropolis. He hadn't made a note of Andrews' plot number. He saw no need to retain such information.

He hadn't noted the plot number when he buried her infant son fourteen months later, either. He had even less reason for doing so. It was in fact a pauper's grave.

• • •

Inspector Hyem was carrying the two exhumation warrants when he joined John Wallters in the funeral cart to begin the journey to Rookwood cemetery. As the senior officer in the Collins investigation, his duties had been broadened to include the exhumation of these other possible murder victims.

The cemetery office provided the necessary plot numbers and the assistance of gravediggers. Following the signposts, they made their way to Charles Andrews' grave. Wallters looked around the site and reported that it seemed undisturbed. The gravediggers thumped their spades into the ground and began the time-consuming operation of removing the hard-packed earth from the grave site. When they reached the coffin, Wallters brushed the soil from its lid and found the metal plate bearing Charles Andrews' details.

The coffin was sitting in water although not entirely covered by it. Its wood was spongy, as if the waters of the Styx were gradually rising from the netherworld to embrace it. The soil's weight had depressed the cheap lid, causing a split that extended from its upper left to its lower right corners. The portion to the right of the split was beginning to break away.

The men attached ropes to the coffin and began pulling it up and out of the grave. The foot lifted first, shedding some water. Carefully, the men tugged on the ropes, trying to balance it evenly. The last thing they wanted was for the flimsy casket to fall apart and tip Andrews' partly decomposed remains into the muddy hole.

When the intact coffin reached the surface, the men loaded it into the cedar shell that Wallters had brought with him. The shell would protect the coffin and its contents during the journey to the South Sydney Morgue.

The men then drove to the paupers' section, where the gravediggers dug up the tiny casket bearing the Collinses' infant son. They placed this inside a rough pine shell that Wallters had also brought with him.

The exhumations complete, Wallters ferried the two unopened coffins back to the morgue and deposited them in the autopsy room.

• • •

The following morning, when John Wallters opened the cedar shell protecting Charles Andrews' coffin and peered inside, he was relieved to find that the jolting of the previous day's eleven-mile journey hadn't caused any visible damage, although he would only know for certain when the coffin was lifted from the shell. He asked for some assistance from the other men in the room. Inspector Hyem, Coroner Shiell, and William Hamlet were gathered in the autopsy room, along with Dr Samuel Knaggs, who would conduct the post-mortem examination, and Dr Martin, who would assist him. As the men lifted the coffin, water seeped from it and settled into the bottom of the cedar shell.

Wallters and Hyem made a cursory inspection then announced that the coffin appeared to be in the same state as previously. Knaggs examined it more closely, concluding that, despite the damage, there was no evidence of tampering. He gave the signal that the lid be removed. Moments later, the odour of decaying flesh assailed them.

The men looked inside the open coffin. The body lay in a shallow pool of muddy water, although the water didn't appear to have reached the critical central region of its torso. Knaggs inspected the body, noticing that its grave clothes were rotted but seemingly undisturbed. He took hold of some fabric and tugged gently. It tore, exposing the remains. He pulled away the remainder of the fabric until the naked body was revealed. Parts were significantly decomposed and the whole mass had subsided, giving the coffin a half-filled appearance.

Knaggs began his visual examination, noticing that the head, upper thorax, legs and arms had disintegrated. Helpfully, the torso bones remained intact. This would make it easier to identify the different parts of the body and the probable locations of the organs needing to be extracted for chemical analysis. Surprisingly, the lower section of the thorax and abdomen were fairly well-preserved. Indeed, the contour of the abdomen down to the navel depression was discernible. Their coverings had only partly undergone the soapy change that produced the wax-like covering known as adipocere.

Nothing further could be done until the inquest jury had seen the body, so the men turned to the infant's coffin. Wallters removed the little casket from its pine shell and unwrapped its blue cloth covering. On the lid was a metal coffin plate with an inscription containing the infant's name and death details. He lifted the lid and looked at the remains. Neither the coffin itself nor the body showed any signs of interference.

Knaggs took over again. He removed the infant's linen robes and exposed the remains. The integuments covering the face were well preserved; however, the soft tissues of the nose, eyes and lips had disappeared and the rest of the body showed considerable decomposition.

By this time, the inquest jury had assembled. As the doctors stepped away from the coffins, the jurors filed into the autopsy room, handkerchiefs raised to noses, eyes mostly averted. Buckets were on hand for those unable to endure the stench—or the gruesome sight. Hasty footsteps spoke of their relief when the order was given for their return to the courtroom.

With the jurors' departure, the doctors were able to continue the autopsy. Dr Knaggs made an incision through the covering of Charles Andrews' torso, allowing them to see the structure of the integuments and muscular tissue. The lungs were merely a dark brown mass, while a muddy substance occupied the position where the liver would have been. A thin white membrane stained by a dark yellow fluid seemingly represented the stomach, and a greyish soapy mass the intestines. Curiously, the left kidney was in a good state of preservation and could easily be identified. The right kidney was also recognisable, although it wasn't as well preserved.

Hamlet was watching the autopsy doctors. He needed to make sure that Knaggs collected the anatomical sections that would most likely reveal traces of arsenic—if any had been administered. He told Knaggs that he was most interested in the gastrointestinal region.

Knaggs carefully washed and dried three glass jars. Into one, he placed the two kidneys; into the second, what he and Martin believed to be the stomach and intestines; into the third, the remains of the lungs and of the tissue that covered Andrews' abdomen. He closed and sealed the jars, labelling them with their contents, then handed them to Inspector Hyem.

There was little Knaggs could do with John Collins' tiny body. Although buried for a considerably shorter period than Andrews', it had decomposed faster. All its tissue resembled the greyish soapiness of adipocere. Nonetheless, he removed several ounces of matter from the thorax and abdomen regions and placed it in a clean glass jar that he sealed, labelled and handed to Hyem. It would be Hyem's responsibility to officially hand the container to Hamlet, but not until the autopsy results had been reported to the coroner at the newly convened inquest.

Chapter 15

In the midst of life we are in death.

Book of Common Prayer

In the morgue's courtroom, Dr Martin had been called to testify. Not only had he assisted at the post-mortem examinations that morning, he had signed the two death certificates reporting that each death had resulted from natural causes. The coener wanted to know why he had reached such a conclusion.

'About the twenty-seventh of January 1887, I was called to see a man named Charles Andrews . . .' he began.

• • •

Actually, it was 29 January 1887 when the drama began, as he would later advise the court. Around eight o'clock that evening, a man named George Osborne came to the Elizabeth Street surgery and begged him to visit a sick friend, Charles Andrews. Osborne said that he was a boarder residing in the house of the ailing man.

Martin accompanied him to the Andrewses' home at 10 Pople's Paddock, Botany, which lay on the other side of the paddock from the house he would later visit with Dr Marshall. Mrs Louisa Andrews—later

Mrs Collins—opened the door and ushered him into the bedroom, then remained in the room throughout his visit.

Lying in bed was a man aged about fifty. He was of an average size, more lanky than robust, and appeared exhausted and worried. He complained of severe pain in his stomach and of constant vomiting and diarrhoea.

Martin examined his new patient and concluded that his health was generally good with no signs of serious illness or constitutional disease. He found tenderness over the epigastrium (the upper central part of the abdomen) and also over the right hypochondrium, just under the ribs. As he placed his hands on the various parts of Andrews' body, he asked about the history of his illness. Andrews said that he had been ill about a week with the same symptoms.

Deciding that Andrews was suffering from a gastrointestinal disorder, Martin wrote a prescription for a medical preparation that would relieve the pain and vomiting, one that included bismuth and carbonate of magnesia, which were commonly used to treat gastric complaints. He also prescribed a pill that contained Dover's Powder (ipecacuanha and opium) to relieve straining and pain. As he handed the prescription to Mrs Andrews, he provided instructions about her husband's food and general treatment and asked her to let him know the following day how her husband was faring.

George Osborne served as the messenger again, journeying into the city that Sunday to tell Martin that his landlord was still vomiting. As Andrews hadn't seemed seriously ill, Martin felt it unnecessary to visit him again. Instead, he wrote another prescription, this time for a medicine that rarely failed to curb vomiting. He told Osborne that Andrews was to take a tablespoon every two hours.

Two days later, on 1 February, Osborne came to his door begging him to visit Andrews again. When Martin reached the cottage around four pm, he could see that Andrews' condition had deteriorated.

His cheeks were hollow and sunken and his lips and gums pitted with sores—a sign of his body's distress. He also complained that the vomiting was still incessant, and that the severe burning feeling in his stomach continued although the diarrhoea had eased.

Martin was perplexed to hear that the vomiting hadn't ceased. He asked Andrews if he had been taking the prescribed medicine. The man confirmed that he had. That being the case, the doctor wondered whether he had correctly diagnosed the man's complaint. He examined him again and noticed that his pulse was weak, another worrying sign. He looked around the room and saw some greenish vomited matter in the chamber-pot next to the bed. Turning to Andrews' wife, he asked, 'What has Andrews been taking?'

'He has had some beer,' she replied.

Beer? He was surprised and annoyed. He had specifically told her not to give her husband beer. Perhaps she had forgotten. It might have contributed to her husband's deterioration as alcohol could prevent the medicine from working properly. He decided not to write another prescription. Instead, he provided further instructions about the quality of food her husband should consume, mentioning milk and boiled water. He explained that her husband was seriously ill, although his condition should not be life-threatening.

He was wrong. On 3 February, Osborne returned to the surgery to report that Andrews had died the previous day. The doctor would need to sign a death certificate.

As Martin would later tell the inquest, he was surprised at the suddenness of Andrews' death. Still, he provided the necessary death certificate which noted that Andrews had died from 'acute gastro-enteritis'. He had no reason—at that time—for thinking that his diagnosis might be incorrect.

• • •

Dr Martin was reminded of the case a year later, on 20 April 1888, when he received a visit from Andrews' wife, who was now calling herself Mrs Collins.

'Will you come and see my child?' she said. 'It died during the night. I want a certificate.'

Thirty years after New South Wales legislated the civil registration of births, deaths and marriages, the public knew that a doctor needed to sign a death certificate. If medical care had not been requested prior to death, a doctor needed to examine the patient to ensure there were no suspicious circumstances associated with the death.

'What were the symptoms?' Martin asked.

'It woke up crying late at night and died in half an hour.'

He went with her to her Botany residence, the same property he would later visit with Dr Marshall. Her new husband was there, a much younger man than the first. The pair took him into the bedroom to see the child.

'How old?' he asked.

'Five months,' she said.

Five months? He made some mental calculations then asked, 'Did the child go all its time?' When she indicated that it was indeed a full-term pregnancy, he made another quick calculation. It suggested conception in February 1887, the same month—according to his recollection—that her first husband had died.

He examined the infant and noticed signs of teething and constitutional delicacy. He asked Mrs Collins for more details about her son's last few days. She said that the baby had been suffering from a sick stomach for a couple of days prior to his death, although they hadn't thought his condition serious enough to seek medical attention. At about one pm on the day of his death, they had given him castor oil. Around ten pm, he had awoken crying. Mick had lit the lamp and cuddled him and his crying eased. Soon, he was laughing at the light.

Mick had given him to her and she fed him and they all fell asleep. About eleven-twenty pm he had awoken screaming, clearly in great pain. He had died less than twenty minutes later.

Martin told her that he wouldn't provide a death certificate, that she was to report the matter to the police and that he would send a memo to the coroner. In his memo, he merely recounted the circumstances of the child's death, as told to him by the parents, and reported that the baby's general appearance and condition gave him no reason to disbelieve their account. The coroner responded, 'As there are no grounds for supposing this child died from any but natural causes, an inquest may be dispensed with.'

• • •

When Martin later told the jury about the deaths of Andrews and the infant, he said that he'd had no suspicion of poisoning at the time of Andrews' death. When asked about the infant's death, he said that he hadn't seen anything in the boy's appearance that would lead him to think that death resulted from anything other than natural causes. At no time did he explain why he had thought it necessary to report the infant's death to the coroner. No doubt he felt that it was now the jury's responsibility to decide whether there was anything untoward about the two deaths.

Chapter 16

> On account of the facility with which [arsenic] may be procured in this country, even by the lowest of the vulgar, and the ease with which it may be secretly administered, it is the poison most frequently chosen for the purpose of committing murder.
>
> Robert Christison, *Treatise on Poisons*

Sydney was on tenterhooks. The resumption of the second inquest had also been delayed by Coroner Shiell's illness. When would they hear if Louisa Collins was to be indicted for a second murder . . . or even a third? Could she be a baby-killer in addition to a husband-killer?

When the inquest resumed on 3 August, Dr Knaggs described the results of his post-mortem examinations. His testimony about the decomposed state of the two exhumed bodies created concern among some jurors, who wondered if poison could really be found under such conditions. Knaggs reassured them. 'I think it is quite possible, notwithstanding the condition of the bodies, to find traces of poison if any existed.'

It was the cue for the government analyst, William Hamlet, to return to the witness box. He had completed his chemical analysis nearly three weeks earlier and had made some interesting discoveries.

Hamlet had decided to investigate the infant's death first as it would be faster to test a single jar. Again he chose the Marsh test to tease out any deadly morsels. He poured and stirred and burnt and peered at the sheet of glass. No sign of any precipitate. He conducted a battery of tests for other well known or easily accessible poisons. Again, he found nothing.

Charles Andrews' remains were stored in three jars. Hamlet tested the first jar—the kidneys—but the precipitate glass remained clear. In the second jar, which contained what appeared to be the stomach and sections of intestines, he found a tiny trace of arsenic: one five-hundredth of a grain. He also found one and a quarter grains of bismuth, an ingredient used in the medicine Dr Martin had prescribed. In the third jar he found another five-hundredth of a grain of arsenic.

To confirm that these measurements were correct, he conducted a second arsenic test and obtained the same result. He also undertook a control experiment involving arsenic and water alone, and found that the reaction was equivalent to the results of the viscera tests. Clearly, arsenic was not only present in the remains of Louisa Collins' second husband; it was in her first husband's body as well.

• • •

When Hamlet was called to testify in this second inquest, Coroner Shiell began by questioning him about the infant's death. Hamlet told the jury that he couldn't find poison of any description in the infant's remains.

The coroner asked about Charles Andrews' remains. Hamlet reported that he had discovered a minute trace of arsenic.

The atmosphere tensed as the courtroom attendees waited for him to elaborate. The *Echo* had previously reported that Hamlet had found a 'faint trace of arsenic' in Charles Andrews' remains. Yet the newspaper had added a disclaimer—from Hamlet himself—stating that the evidence was not enough to indicate deliberate poisoning because arsenic was sometimes found in the earth and in metallic coffins. Did he have any new information to impart?

Hamlet continued with his explanation, so coldly scientific that it seemed as if the testing procedure was automatic and unequivocal rather than subject to perceptual fallibilities. Finally, he told the jury that he estimated the amount of arsenic found in Andrews' body to be about one five-hundredth of a grain.

Those who had read the reports from the earlier inquest—or the newspaper reports of the dozens of other arsenic deaths—knew that a fatal arsenic dose for an adult was two to three grains. A quick calculation determined that it would take at least a thousand times more arsenic to kill a man than had been found in Andrews' remains. It could hardly be considered evidence of murderous intent.

As if he had heard these courtroom surmises, Hamlet added an important qualification: 'The fact that arsenic is not found in a body after death is no evidence that the deceased person did not die from arsenical poisoning.'

A juror asked if the water found in the Andrews coffin might have washed most of the arsenic away.

'If water was to get into the coffin in which a person was buried who had died from arsenical poisoning, the water might dissolve the arsenic,' Hamlet confirmed.

The coroner authorised Inspector Hyem to take a sample of the earth surrounding the grave area and to pass it to Hamlet for testing.

• • •

Instead of calling a doctor to clarify how the absence of arsenic traces was not proof that it hadn't been administered, the coroner switched gear: from means to motive. He called Meyrick Fitzpatrick Rainsford to the stand.

An accountant employed by the Mutual Life Association of Australia, Rainsford began his testimony by reporting that Charles Andrews had purchased a life insurance policy for himself in March 1877 and that the policy was still in force at the time of his death. On 7 April 1887, the policy's death benefit had been paid to the office of solicitor James Arthur Dowling on the order of Andrews' widow, to whom Andrews had bequeathed the money in his will.

When Rainsford was asked who had prepared the will and who now held the original, Louisa piped up, 'The will is now at the office of Mr Dowling as good as ever, I should think. It was made out by my husband and showed that he was a sensible and sober man.'

There was still one question to be answered: the circumstances under which the will in Louisa's favour had been signed. Her neighbour William Farrar was called to answer that question.

Farrar told the court that, late in January 1887, he had received a message from Mrs Andrews asking if he would come over and witness her husband's will. Arriving at the house, he had found Andrews lying on a sofa in the sitting room, feeble but not seemingly at death's door. Another neighbour, John Stephen, was waiting nearby. Mrs Andrews said to him, 'Andrews wants you to witness his will.' Andrews was more gracious. Rising from the sofa, he said politely: 'Will you be kind enough to sign the will in the presence of John Stephen? I think my time has come.' He read out the will, his strong, clear voice belying the import of the document. It contained one bequest only, leaving everything to his wife.

As Farrar and Stephen signed their names, Andrews added, 'I won't like to have to endure another night's sickness like I had last night.' His voice might still have been strong, but his body seemed to be fighting a losing battle.

• • •

Arthur Andrews was the first family member to testify at the inquest. 'Charles Andrews was my father,' said the fourteen-year-old, a picture of robust health like his siblings. 'The woman before the court, Louisa Collins, I have always looked upon as my mother.'

Brows furrowed at his remark. This strange statement suggested that he was willing to accept his relationship with his father yet was distancing himself from his mother—which perhaps wasn't surprising under the circumstances. Was he trying to wash his hands of the whole affair or was his odd response an indicator of revelations to come?

'My father first became sick about Christmas 1886,' Arthur told the jury. He reported that his father had taken to his bed when the vomiting commenced about a week before his death. His father had repeatedly complained of pain across his shoulders and of vomiting and purging—not that his father needed to mention the vomiting and purging; their house was too small for it to pass unnoticed.

The prosecutor asked about his parents' relationship.

'My father and mother did not live very happily together,' Arthur admitted. 'They were always picking rows with each other.' And a sorry tale began to emerge . . .

• • •

Arthur's father was much older than his mother. British-born Charles Andrews was thirty-two years of age when he married Louisa Hall on 28 August 1865 at Merriwa, New South Wales. Louisa had just turned eighteen at the time. She was the fourth of nine children in the family of emancipated English convict, Henry Hall, and his Irish-born immigrant wife, Catherine Ring, and was born on 11 August 1847 in the Scone district, 130 miles north-west of Sydney. Her parents had been living at the Belltrees pastoral property near Scone in May 1845 but had moved into the town of Scone itself at some stage between that date and Louisa's baptism in November 1847.[2] The Halls rarely stayed in one place for long. Henry worked as a shepherd at a number of different properties in the Hunter Valley district over the next twenty years but the family eventually moved back to the Scone district, where Henry died in 1880.[3]

When it was time for Louisa to seek employment, she found work as a domestic servant in Merriwa. That's where she met Charles Andrews—*Charlie*, she called him—who was working as a butcher in the town.

Kind, genial and hard-working, he was considered by her mother to be an ideal husband. She succumbed to her mother's pressure and married him two weeks after her eighteenth birthday. Children arrived in regular succession: first Herbert (1867), then Ernest (1869), although her second-born died of convulsions when aged only three. By the time Reuben was born (1871), they had moved to Muswellbrook, a more central place for Andrews' new job as a carrier. There Arthur was born (1873) and Frederick William (1875) and their only daughter, May (1877). In 1876, Andrews decided to return to butchering and applied for a slaughtering licence; but the competition was tough and he was forced into liquidation with debts that surpassed his assets by nearly £80. The couple made the decision to take the family back to Sydney, where Andrews had lived after he and his birth family arrived from England in 1848.

They settled in Botany, where Andrews found work in the wool-washing and fellmongering industries. He was a healthy, hardy man who worked long hours to support his family and was well respected in the Botany community. Another three children were born: Edwin (1880), David (1881), who also suffered convulsions from birth and lived only twelve days, and Charles (1883).[4]

Times were difficult, though, so boarders were welcomed into their home. In 1886, a man in his early twenties named Michael Peter Collins joined the household. And that's when the trouble began.

Arthur couldn't help noticing the change in his home's atmosphere in the spring of that year. Most days his father was at work; however, when he was home, his parents bickered. As Christmas approached, the rows became worse. His father seemed to be jealous of his mother's friendship with Collins. On 16 December, matters came to a head—and Arthur knew that he was to blame.

During the day, he had seen his mother and Collins walking side by side towards the tram stop. A short time later, he'd spotted them together on the Sydney tram. He had casually mentioned the sightings to his father. When the pair came home, his father began shouting at his mother. She didn't shout back, replying instead in a low tone. Then his father turned to Collins and screamed at him to get out of the house . . . permanently.

'What are you doing that for?' Arthur asked his father after Collins departed.

'I don't want him in this 'ere house,' his father raged.

'Why?' asked the confused lad.

'Oh, I don't want to tell you what for,' was the surprisingly evasive response. Then his father ejected the other boarders as well.

• • •

'My father became ill about three weeks after he put Collins out of the house,' Arthur Andrews continued in his testimony to the inquest jury on 3 August. 'As soon as my father died, Collins returned to the house. He married my mother about three weeks after my father's death.'

It was a devastating testimony, particularly as it came from Louisa's own son. As the coroner adjourned the inquest for the night, the jurors were left to dwell on the day's testimonies—on the evidence that confirmed the presence of two of the quintessential motives for murder: lust and greed.

Chapter 17

> The preparations of arsenic are, of all the poisonous substances in the mineral kingdom, the most fatal; and are those, the properties of which the physician ought to be best acquainted with.
>
> Mathieu Orfila, *A Treatise on Poisons*

When the inquest resumed the following day, the coroner returned to the subject of the money trail. He called Alfred Newman, the assistant custodian of wills in the prothonotary's department of the Supreme Court, who reported that he had brought along a copy of Andrews' will.

The coroner asked to see it. After scanning the contents, he announced to the courtroom, 'It is evident that the will was not prepared by Andrews. The only part in the handwriting of the deceased is the signature.'

Louisa didn't miss the implication. She called out, 'A man in the insurance office filled the will up.'

Recognising that this man would need to be found if the subject was to be pursued any further, the coroner dismissed Newman and called Constable Jeffes to testify.

The coroner asked Jeffes if he'd had much contact with the family in the months leading up to Andrews' death. Jeffes reported that he had seen Andrews nearly every day. He was also aware that Andrews had ejected Collins from the house because Mrs Andrews had come to the police station in the aftermath to tell him that her husband was fighting with the boarders.

Jeffes knew that Andrews wasn't the type of man to turn on his boarders, particularly as he needed their payments to supplement his own income. And while he liked his beer, he wasn't one to drink to excess.

'Can you call at my house?' Mrs Andrews had then begged.

The constable agreed to do so but didn't get the opportunity until that evening. When he reached the Andrews house, all seemed quiet. He knocked but no one answered, so he checked the neighbours' houses and found James Law at home. He explained why he was there.

'You arrived too late,' Law told him. 'Collins has been put out.'

Like everyone else, James and his wife, Mary, had noticed the goings-on at the Andrews house. They were curious to know why Andrews had turfed Collins out—although it wasn't hard to guess the reason.

When Mary talked to Louisa a few days after Jeffes' visit, she decided to ask the question. Louisa's answer was surprisingly frank: 'He was jealous of me and Mick.'

The Laws knew that the cause of Andrews' jealousy hadn't vanished when he was booted from the house. Collins had taken lodgings at the Stephens house on the opposite side of Pople's Paddock only fifty yards away and had continued to sneak over to Louisa's when her husband was at work. One day Andrews came home early and found Collins there. He was beside himself with rage. 'You have brought trouble on me and my family,' he screamed, so loudly that Mary could hear him as she walked past. 'I don't want to see you in the house again. Go away!'

• • •

Jeffes told the court that he knew nothing about Andrews' illness or death although he had seen Mrs Andrews not long afterwards and had realised that she wasn't prostrate with grief. Far from it.

A report of loud noise from an empty house in Pople's Terrace had brought him to the neighbourhood at eight o'clock one evening, two weeks after Andrews' death. Looking into a cottage a few doors from the Andrews house, he saw some of the locals dancing and singing, Collins among them. Mrs Andrews was also there.

'Why the merrymaking?' Jeffes asked someone standing nearby.

'It's to commemorate the wedding of Mr Collins and Mrs Andrews,' the person answered. Yet no one seemed to know anyone who had attended the ceremony or when or where it had taken place.

James Law said that he was the organiser, having decided that an empty house was too good an opportunity to waste. When word of the Collins' nuptials spread, he had realised that it was the perfect excuse for a party—not that the happy couple would be spared from contributing to the evening's costs. During the festivities, he had made a point of asking Collins if he would put up some money for the spree since he was now wedded. Collins obtained half a crown from Louisa and gave it to the host. Law then asked Louisa for a dance.

Collins replied possessively, 'My old woman does not dance.'

• • •

Those in the courtroom who had listened closely at the previous inquest remembered that Louisa had said they were married in April 1887, two months after Andrews' death. So why did her own family and neighbours think they were married two months earlier? It was a curious discrepancy.

As the courtroom attendees pondered the significance of these testimonies, the coroner recalled Dr Martin and asked his opinion about Charles Andrews' cause of death. Martin said that he had changed his mind since signing the death certificate. In view of Andrews' symptoms and the fact that arsenic had been found in his remains, he now thought that death was probably caused by an irritant poison. He explained, 'Gastritis is one of the results of arsenical poisoning, and even if no arsenic had been found in his remains, I would still have the same opinion as to the cause of his death, from the symptoms and from the well-known fact that no arsenic may be found in the bodies of those who have died from poisoning by that drug.'

To some in the courtroom, it seemed an odd argument. Why hadn't he thought of arsenic poisoning during Andrews' illness when eighteen months later he was prepared to testify that, even if traces of arsenic had *not* been found in Andrews' body, he would still think it the likely cause of death?

Then Dr Martin added, 'During my attendance on Charles Andrews, it struck me that his wife Louisa Andrews had her eye on a second husband. From her manner, she seemed to be indifferent to Andrews' fate.'

• • •

Coroner Shiell turned to the jury. 'You must exclude from your thoughts the child John Collins,' he said as he began his summation. 'He clearly died from natural causes. There was no suspicion in the first instance, but it was necessary in exhuming the body of Andrews to do the same with the child to set any doubt at rest. At the same time, I had very little doubt when I ordered the exhumation that the child died from natural causes. The chemical analysis demonstrated the fact that not a trace of poison was found in the body.'

Considering Dr Martin's recent statement, some found Shiell's conclusion to be strangely contradictory. Despite the fact that the child had died in the aftermath of a vomiting condition, the absence of arsenic post-death was being accepted in this instance as evidence of its absence pre-death.

'In the case of the deceased Charles Andrews, it was different,' the coroner continued. He reminded the jury that it was Collins' death and the discovery of nearly three grains of arsenic in his body that had led to the opening of the current inquest. 'That Charles Andrews died from arsenical poisoning very few could doubt,' he stated firmly. 'The symptoms were those of arsenical poisoning. The fact that a small trace of arsenic only was found in his remains affords no evidence whatever that he did not die from arsenical poisoning.'

He directed the jury's attention to Louisa's actions, mentioning her relationship with the boarder, the fact that Andrews had fallen ill and died soon after evicting Collins, and that a wedding feast had followed a short time later. 'Was there no suspicion in all that?' he asked incredulously. 'You must consider whether the woman had transferred her affections to Collins and was interested in getting her first husband out of the way.'

Having made it clear to the jury that lust was a clear motive for murder, he turned his focus to greed. He repeated the evidence showing that Mrs Collins had known she was the sole beneficiary under Andrews' will.

This brought him to the jury's role. The jurors were being asked to determine if Andrews' death was caused by arsenical poisoning. If they believed it was not, their verdict should be 'death by natural causes'; if so, they had to ask themselves by whom it was administered. If they thought Louisa was responsible, they should return a verdict of murder against her; if not, they should exonerate her. He concluded pointedly, 'The symptoms in this case were those of arsenical poisoning, and from the fact that arsenic has been found in the remains, how could you arrive at any conclusion other than that arsenic was the cause of his death?'

Again, with such a strong direction from the coroner, the jury's verdict was speedy and unsurprising. The foreman announced that the child died from natural causes whereas Andrews died from arsenical poisoning, the poison having been administered by his wife.

Louisa's countenance remained unmoved as she listened to the jury's verdict. A short time later, as the police officers ushered her from the courtroom, her expression changed—but not to shock or fear, as would be expected. Instead, a secretive smile tugged at her lips.

What sort of woman would remain so strangely unconcerned when committed to stand trial for murder—indeed, not just one murder, but two—particularly when the mandated punishment was to be hanged by the neck until she was dead?

• • •

The discovery of a 'Louisa Collins' in society inevitably served as the catalyst for a discussion—or diatribe—about the nature of women. 'When she is good, she is very, very good, but when she is bad, she is horrid,' Longfellow had lamented, reflecting society's dichotomous attitude towards women. Indeed, the notion of the 'good/bad' woman lay at the heart of the Victorian perception of women, a perception that could have serious ramifications for Louisa when she faced a jury of twelve men charged with deciding her fate.

'We know that woman, when she yields to crime, is stayed by no consideration,' Premier Parkes declared in parliament that year—and Parkes was more progressive than most on the subject of women. 'The worst of crimes in the worst of times have been perpetrated by women. In that fearful period when France ran riot in blood, those who were most guilty in the very ferocious delight in blood were women—young women and tender girls. The creatures who hoisted the heads of their fellow creatures on pikes were women. At all times, and under all circumstances, when woman once forgets the character of her sex, there is no barrier to the lengths she will go to in crime.'

The shrill voice of moral panic resounded from the press, pulpit and political podium whenever the 'woman question' raised its determined head. At a time when many members of the community were demanding gender equality in terms of education and the vote, misbehaving women like Louisa became the proof of whatever anti-emancipation point the conservatives wanted to make. They declared that, if women were granted political, social and financial independence, the marriage bond would be destroyed, the family would disintegrate, the wrong sort of people would be bred and the effect on society would be disastrous.

As so often happens, the attacks soon turned from the political to the personal, aimed at the suffragists themselves. Bitter, ugly, man-hating spinsters was the derisive cry, for all that the ranks of these 'spinsters' included married women and, indeed, men. They were the visible proof of what happens to women who venture outside the home and demand a role in society's affairs. Did our women really want to become like them: unfeminine, unmarried, unfulfilled . . . unbalanced?

The feminine dichotomy—good or bad—was in fact a triptych: good, bad or mad. It was easier for the gainsayers to pigeonhole women like the suffragists as mentally unbalanced because, in doing so, they denied them any control over their actions and, thereby, any validity in their arguments. The same pigeonholing occurred when women like Louisa breached any of the other female norms, including the criminal laws. In society's view, men could do 'bad' things without being 'bad', but women could not. When a woman broke the law, society asked if she was a 'good' woman forced into criminality—for example, a mother who stole food to feed her children or a wife coerced by her husband into committing a crime. Or, conversely, was her 'badness' caused by 'madness', making her incapable of controlling her wicked impulses? It was a question the community would continue to ask about Louisa, particularly those who had seen her unruffled countenance when two inquest juries had committed her to stand trial for murder.

'When she is good, she is very, very good, but when she is bad . . .'

Could a jury of twelve men reach a verdict based on evidence alone or would their political and social views about women and their moral judgements about Louisa's behaviour and manner influence their decision?

Part 2
CONFUSION

A clear and innocent conscience fears nothing.

Elizabeth I

Chapter 18

> The case is one in which the elements of criminal romance and guilt are strangely blended with those of the commonplace and of the prosaic.
>
> *Daily Telegraph*

One week, that's all he had: one week to prepare a defence in a murder trial. The prosecution had had a month. And they'd had the government's coffers to draw upon and the witnesses' depositions to peruse. What did he have? A request from Justice Foster that he, Hugh Hart Lusk, should conduct the case pro bono, which meant no fee, no assistance and no money to search for witnesses. He had little else to work with, just Louisa Collins herself and the newspaper reports of the inquest testimonies. The deck was stacked against him—and against Louisa, of course. Still, he had agreed to take on the case. Although he had practised law for two decades in New Zealand, he was only a recent settler in Sydney and a junior barrister at that, so this sensational case might help to drum up future business.

How should he proceed?

Obviously, a criminal trial was different to a coronial inquest. Ideally, its aim was to bring the perpetrator to account so as to gain justice for the victim, for men like Mick Collins—if Collins had indeed been murdered. In practice, by virtue of the adversarial nature of the courtroom, these lofty principles often fell victim to pragmatics. Barristers needed to prove their legal skills or accused criminals—and the Crown itself, for that matter—wouldn't want to pay them to defend or prosecute cases. Accordingly, the focus was on winning. A trial was a battle of wits as much as evidence, a theatrical spectacle rather than a laboratory investigation. And in these winner-takes-all games, the accused could become piggies-in-the-middle: necessary, yet in a strange way almost invisible. Or, worse, irrelevant. Could he make sure that this didn't happen?

• • •

A clear sky had seen the overnight temperature drop to near freezing point, but it didn't deter the crowds bustling along Oxford Street on Monday, 6 August. Most were heading towards the large sandstone building perched atop Darlinghurst Hill. Once, this elegant tribute to classical Greek architecture could be seen for miles around, its imposing pediment and sturdy pillars a declaration of the law's majesty and authority. The lengthy stone wall behind the courthouse, jutting like wings from either side, served as a testament to its wrath—it fenced the gaol accommodating those who had violated the law. Recent extensions, however, had hidden the intimidating wall. The western wing was not yet completed. The eastern wing housed the courtroom in which Louisa's case was about to commence.

As the hoi polloi pushed through the courthouse door, they were directed up the stairs to a large gallery overlooking the courtroom, the theatre box of the poor. Journalists, magistrates and potential jurors gathered at the main courtroom door to show their passes to the constable guarding the entrance. Once past the sentry, the journalists made their way to the two comfortable press boxes where they pulled out their pads and pencils. The jurors were ushered towards the adjacent jurors-in-waiting boxes. The magistrates and other respectable citizens—those who held a ticket from the sheriff or could cadge one from the constable himself—sat in the gallery at the back of the courtroom or in spare seats in the jurors-in-waiting box.

As they looked around, they saw a room modelled on the Grecian-Doric style. The judge's imposing throne—the bench—was positioned in the centre of the wall opposite the gallery. The jury box partly filled the right side of the wall, while the press box was on the left. Bewigged barristers sat at a large table in the open area between the bench and the raised wooden dock. Both the prosecution and defence sat on the same side of the table so they could face the jury, with the Crown sitting near the judge and the defence near the dock.

Soon, Louisa's head could be seen bobbing up the stairs at the back of the dock. She had been brought through the tunnel from the gaol and locked in one of the underground cells until the court was ready. Reaching the top of the stairs, she walked a further few steps to the front of the dock. She removed her crepe-trimmed hat and dark grey cloak, revealing a blue print dress. Then she sat in the dock chair.

From their prime position, the pressmen saw a countenance that looked less becoming than that of the handsome matron whose face had graced the pages of many an illustrated newspaper. Strangely, though, that was the only sign of the stress she must be feeling. She didn't look fearful or cowed as might be expected. Rather, she seemed unconcerned, as if she herself were a spectator settling in to watch the drama that was about to unfold.

• • •

Louisa sat facing the dock's spike-topped bars, positioned there to prevent fearful prisoners from attempting to flee their fate.

'Innocent until proven guilty': that was the legal presumption underpinning the charges against her. But were the scales of justice truly weighted in favour of her innocence? Just standing in the dock was intimidating, as if every pound of that weighty faceless authority known as 'the establishment' was piled on top of her. It would be easy for the fear spawned by that overwhelming sense of intimidation to be interpreted as guilt. She would not give the gawping faces the satisfaction of seeing anything that could be interpreted in such a damaging way.

Just standing in the dock was also prejudicial. How easily could the jurors slough off the burden of suggestion—'she must be guilty because the law officers have put her there'—and assess her case as if she were truly innocent?

And what about the witnesses? As soon as they knew she was to stand trial for murder, the prism of their viewpoint must inevitably have changed. The events they were describing would no longer be seen through eyes that automatically presumed innocence, eyes that recognised that unexpected death was simply a part of everyday life. Instead, by virtue of her committal for murder, those eyes would now see the same events through a glaze of suspicion. That difference in perspective could easily influence what they said—a subtle word here, an inflection there. Inference could become implication; suggestion, fact.

Nonetheless, she was so sure of her acquittal that she handed one of the court officials a veil, saying she would wear it when she left the court so the public would not recognise her.

• • •

The judge's clerk called out for silence. Justice William John Foster entered the courtroom dressed in the magisterial authority of horsehair and bombazine.

Many of his contemporaries would not forget the words of a letter-writer to the Catholic *Freeman's Journal* who mocked Foster as 'the most singularly striking and original specimen of the modern Puritan prig'. Recently appointed to the Supreme Court bench, Foster had been praised by Chief Justice Sir Frederick Darley as a man of upright character and unblemished honour and by the conservative press as a sound lawyer and fair prosecutor. All the same, he had his detractors. Anglo-Irish by birth, he was an evangelist with such rigidly sectarian views that he believed that Orangeism—the Orange Institution was Protestant Ireland's militant defender of its liberties—had done more for religious freedom in New South Wales than the combined efforts of lawyers, barristers and judges. He was also such an active temperance—nay, abstinence—advocate that his initials, W.J., had spawned the derogatory nickname 'Water Jug Foster'. From Louisa's perspective, he was not the ideal judge to be hearing a case involving a drunken adulteress charged with poisoning two husbands.

Twelve men were ushered into the jury box and remained there, unchallenged. The Crown's case could begin.

Crown Prosecutor William Coffey looked at the jurors from under his own imperious wig. He commenced his case by summarising the facts brought out at the inquest, then he called Dr George Marshall to the witness box and asked for his medical opinion as to the cause of Collins' death. Marshall replied, 'The symptoms all together could only as far as I know take place by arsenical poisoning. I don't know anything else that would cause them—conjunctivitis and all.'

While other medical practitioners might accept such an opinion, it was the jurors who needed convincing. Most had little knowledge of medicine or physiology, let alone of arsenic and its deadly action on the human body. To assist the jury, the prosecutor questioned Marshall about arsenic in general. The doctor explained that it was not a constituent of the human body; it had to be introduced. If the person lived long enough, the arsenic would pass out of the body via the excretory mechanisms, mainly through vomiting and urination. Death from multi-organ failure sometimes occurred as suddenly as a few hours after ingestion or it might not happen until nine or ten days later, irrespective of the quantity. Healthy individuals tended to survive longer and Collins had seemed a healthy man.

Could he provide an opinion as to how much arsenic Collins had ingested and the frequency of the dosages?

'From the symptoms, I think it is probable that arsenic had been introduced more than once. I think it had been administered from time to time while I was attending. I could not say whether arsenic had been introduced before 28 June. I could not say whether the arsenic had been introduced in large or small doses.'

When asked how easily it could be administered, he explained that arsenic had no perceptible taste in small quantities. He knew because he had tasted it. He didn't add that arsenic in small doses was used as a medicinal tonic, that even the 'poison of poisons' had its beneficial uses. 'It is generally in a fine white powder. It is like flour but if you look closely it is in small crystals and it is sparkling.'

How easy was it to dissolve?

'If water is boiled on it, it is made more soluble than when it is dissolved in cold water.'

Coffey then asked the doctor about his encounters with Louisa herself. In his response, Marshall mentioned Louisa's inattentive, almost indifferent manner when listening to his instructions for her husband's wellbeing.

Heads twisted to look at her. Reinforcing the surgeon's remarks, she appeared inattentive and indifferent, showing little interest in the comments being made about her.

When Lusk began his cross-examination, he asked Marshall about the samples he had taken away for testing. Had Mrs Collins known he was collecting them?

'I spoke first to Collins about taking the vomit away. I don't know if Mrs Collins was present. I'm not sure if she knew of my taking away the vomit, but she did of the urine.'

Justice Foster was curious to know if she could have worked it out for herself. How much of the vomited matter had he collected?

'All that would pour out,' Marshall told him, 'so she would see that it was gone.'

Lusk enquired about the results of his tests. Marshall conceded that he was unsuccessful in discovering any traces of arsenic. 'That to a great extent removed my suspicion,' he added. 'I then attributed it to natural causes.'

So why did he collect another vomit sample on 6 July?

'I collected more of the vomit not from the symptoms but from general suspicion.'

That being the case, what had prompted his decision to go to the police and to later send the case to the coroner?

Marshall explained that Collins' rapid deterioration between Marshall's visits on the Friday and Saturday had alarmed him as it seemed inconsistent with the natural course of his disease.

Dr Martin was called to the stand. After Martin had corroborated Marshall's testimony, Lusk quizzed him about the quantity and frequency of the arsenic Collins had ingested. Martin couldn't provide the necessary clarification although he did report that, in general, arsenic was entirely eliminated from the human body within fourteen days, and mostly eliminated within a week or so, leaving traces only in the liver or spleen. If ingested as a liquid, it was usually expelled within forty-eight hours, so if arsenic was found in vomited matter, it indicated that it had been ingested within the previous two days.

Lusk asked about the normal timeframe for an arsenic death.

'If not expelled by vomiting or purging, the usual time for the fatal effect is two hours to three days.'

By the time Martin left the stand, the jurors and spectators were scratching their heads. Had one dose been ingested or more? Was it a large dose or a series of small doses or a mix of large and small doses? When had the dose or doses been administered? They were as confused after hearing the testimonies of these 'experts' as they had previously been ignorant about the subject of arsenic poisoning altogether. Perhaps the government analyst could enlighten them.

William Hamlet couldn't help them. It wasn't his job to speculate, only to communicate the scientific evidence. He described his discovery of arsenic in Collins' remains and also in the tumbler that was a third full of a milky liquid.

Lusk asked where exactly in Collins' remains he had found the arsenic.

'When I received the jar, I separated the liver and stomach from the rest. I washed them and added the washings to the contents of the stomach.'

It was an important clarification. Hamlet had just told the court that the large dose of arsenic found in Collins' stomach had not necessarily come from his stomach alone, which meant that the arsenic might not in fact have been recently administered.

Dr Milford, the autopsy doctor, was invited to offer his own opinions. He said that the post-mortem examination suggested that death had been prolonged and protracted, and that the cause was probably arsenic irritation. He thought it unlikely that a large dose had been recently ingested and more likely that the arsenic had been ingested in small, frequent doses with deadly effect.

When Milford left the stand, the hour was late and the witness list still long. Foster adjourned the trial and ordered that the jury be locked up for the night. Juries were not usually sequestered during criminal trials for the simple reason that most criminal trials began and ended the same day—in less than an hour, in some instances. Murder cases, though, were different.

• • •

Journalists hurried to their pressrooms to prepare the copy for the next day's edition. Spectators and court officials headed home for tea. As they sat down with their families, some couldn't help noticing the sugar bowl on the table and wondering, just for a moment, whether any of those shiny, crystal-like specks might be . . . no! . . . don't be silly . . . of course not.

Chapter 19

Out of the mouths of babes . . .

Psalm 8:2

Dr Hamilton Marshall was the other half of the investigative pair who had failed to find arsenic in Collins' vomited matter. He hurried through that part of his testimony then reported that he'd left the bottles on the top shelf in his dispensary until George Marshall had taken them away. 'Nothing could have happened to them without my knowledge,' he assured the court. 'I never touched them.'

As these samples were later found to contain arsenic, it was in the defence's interests to try to break the integrity of the chain of custody. Lusk asked what the bottles had looked like and whether they resembled any other bottles in the vicinity. Hamilton admitted that his pharmacy had contained many bottles of a similar appearance.

That being the case, since he and his cousin had been unable to find arsenic when they conducted their own tests, was it possible that his cousin had collected the wrong bottles to give to the government analyst?

The young surgeon said firmly, 'I saw the bottles containing the fluid where he put them. There were no bottles containing similar fluids.'

The constabulary soon replaced the medical fraternity in the witness box. Jeffes provided a lengthy description of his encounters with the Collinses, including Mrs Collins' actions when he picked up the tumbler later found to contain arsenic. The prosecution needed to convince the jurors that this link in the bottle's chain of custody was also intact. Jeffes assured the court that it was. 'I put a mark on the tumbler when I took it away. The glass was never disturbed till I gave it to the government analyst. It was about three parts full.'

Three parts full? Hadn't Hamlet just testified that the glass he had collected, the glass in which he had discovered a significant trace of arsenic, was only one-third full? While some noticed the discrepancy, Louisa's counsel failed to challenge either witness about the inconsistencies in their testimonies.

As the next group of witnesses was called—Louisa's friends and neighbours—the courtroom attendees were curious to see Louisa's reaction. What emotions would her face reveal if their words incriminated her? Perhaps the court would at last see a crack in her inscrutable visage, a fleeting expression of anxiousness or misery. But no, apart from an occasional glance at an acquaintance in the audience followed by a flutter of a smile, she seemed unconcerned about the picture they were painting, as if that world, that woman, bore no relation to herself.

Charles Sayers was among those called to testify. Under cross-examination, he repeated his inquest statement that he had not seen Louisa jump up and grab Jeffes' arm when the constable collected the tumbler. The prosecution was unhappy with Sayers' answer. Coffey returned to the subject under re-examination, asking what exactly he had seen.

'I saw Jeffes go up to the dressing table. His body was between me and Mrs Collins.'

So he couldn't swear that Mrs Collins *hadn't* grabbed Jeffes' arm?

'I could not swear that Mrs Collins did not put her hand on his,' he conceded, 'but I didn't see it.' When pushed for further clarification, he repeated stubbornly that while he couldn't swear that it hadn't happened, he had been in the room at the time and hadn't seen her behave in such a way.

Neighbour Catherine Mudge also told the court that she had seen Constable Jeffes talking to Louisa but hadn't seen him do anything—or Louisa herself for that matter.

The strength of the prosecution's case was being weakened by its own witnesses; the constable's report of Louisa's panicked response when he picked up what proved to be an arsenic-filled tumbler had been one of the most incriminating pieces of evidence in the Crown's case against her.

Coffey called Johannah Bartington as his next witness. She reported that she too had been present when Jeffes began collecting the items from the bedroom, although she hadn't been able to see everything he was doing. Coffey asked if she had noticed Mrs Collins' reaction.

'She seemed to get up, stand up, when he took some things. She seemed not to want him to take them.'

During his cross-examination, Lusk asked where Louisa had been standing. Johannah said that Louisa and Jeffes were standing almost side by side, a few feet apart. 'I didn't see any struggle,' she added pointedly. 'If she had tried to pull him off his feet, I'd have seen it. There was nothing like that.'

Coffey recognised that it was a recovery of sorts—thanks in part to Louisa's own counsel—but would it be enough to convince the jury?

• • •

In presenting its case, the Crown had scheduled its witnesses as if focusing on narrowing regions of influence. First, Sydney's medical profession, whose territory covered vast swathes of Sydney, then the narrower sphere of the Botany constabulary before contracting to the tiny world of Pople's Terrace. The bullseye was inside the Collins' house itself: Louisa's children.

Louisa's sons Fred and Arthur reported that Collins and their mother had lived together happily and had never quarrelled. Then their younger sister, May, was called to testify.

The fair-headed girl walked across the courtroom and climbed up the stairs to the witness box, which was positioned on the right side of the judge's bench. Like the other witnesses, she was told that she would need to swear an oath on the Bible, an oath declaring that she would tell the truth 'so help me, God'. Before she did so, the court needed to make sure that she understood the significance of this part of the court proceeding, the meaning of the oath she had to swear. By holding her hand on the Bible and calling on God as her witness, she was telling the court that she knew God was watching her. If she told the truth, God would be happy, but if she lied, God would punish her.

When her oath was sworn, Coffey stood up and asked her age.

'I am eleven years old,' May told him. (She wasn't really, not yet anyway; not for another two-and-a-half months.)

Coffey questioned her about her home life then asked about the night Mick died. May said she'd been dusting the kitchen shelves and that her mother had been in the same room.

'How do you recollect that particular night?'

'I don't know,' she said with confusion.

Coffey reminded her about her stepfather's death and she remembered that she had seen Collins' dead body on the table. 'That night, I missed off the shelf a little packet, a box,' she told the court. She added that she had previously seen it on the weekend before Mick died, on the Saturday.

What did it look like?

'It was a little round box with a lid.'

What was on the outside?

'There was nothing on the outside.'

Coffey reminded her that there was in fact something on the outside: the pictures . . .

'There were pictures of rats on it,' she agreed. 'The rats were red.'

He asked what the rats were doing. She said that they were on their backs.

'What did you do with the box after you found it?'

'I don't know what I did with it.'

When asked if she had perhaps opened it, she said that she had. It had contained a dark blue powder. Some had been taken out—about a spoonful.

What happened next?

'I put the lid on again.'

And then . . . your mother?

'I showed it to my mother.'

What did you say?

'I said, "Look what I found on the shelf." '

Then came the question the man seemed to think was really important. Did she know what the box was?

'It was Rough on Rats,' she stated.

The word 'arsenic' reverberated around the courtroom as if carried on the air itself.

Coffey asked how she knew that the box was Rough on Rats?

'I could read it.'

Coffey asked about her mother's response when she mentioned finding the box. What exactly had her mother said?

'I don't know whether she said anything to me about it.'

So what had she done with the box after showing it to her mother? Had she put it back?

'I don't know whether I put it back or not.'

The questions kept coming, one after another, a relentless and exhausting barrage. Coffey tried to get her to remember what she had done with the box. She said that she couldn't remember if she had put it back on the shelf or if she had done something else with it. She didn't think her mother had taken it. All she could remember was that she had never seen it afterwards.

He asked if she would know such a box if she saw it again. When she said 'yes', he enquired if she had seen such a box previously. She agreed that she had. He asked when.

'I saw it first on the very top shelf in the house. It was when we lived in the paddock about a year ago.'

The judge broke into the stream of questions, asking what was on the lid.

'Two rats,' she reported.

Coffey asked if she could remember when she found the box.

'It was before my own father took sick.'

• • •

Behind her inscrutable mask, Louisa was reeling. Horror stabbed at her like a hot poker, provoking feelings she would later put down on paper. She had just watched her only daughter saying things that could send her to the gallows. Before her own eyes, her little girl had stood in the witness box with a Bible in her right hand and had sworn to tell the truth, then she had said all those terrible things in such a straightforward manner that the words must surely have come from someone else's head and mouth.

Still, pride wouldn't let her reveal her anguish. She kept her face blank as if this profound betrayal caused her no pain.

• • •

Knowing the sensational nature of May's testimony, Coffey had kept the government analyst waiting in the wings. Now he called him to the stand. What could he tell the court about May's discovery?

'That box is Rough on Rats,' Hamlet confirmed. Questioned about the colour of the powder, he explained, 'It is a slate-grey colour because arsenic must be sold only when coloured with soot or indigo.' The populace was aware that colouring had been introduced in an attempt to prevent accidental poisonings. 'It contains between ninety-six and ninety-seven parts of white arsenic with three parts in a hundred of indigo.'

Could this be the source of the arsenic that killed Collins?

'What I discovered might be caused by that,' Hamlet acknowledged. 'It is sold all over the colonies in grocery shops. Restrictions have recently been placed upon its sale, but they have not yet properly come into force.'

A juror suggested that the odd colouring might deter someone from drinking a mixture containing Rough on Rats.

'A small quantity, large enough to be poisonous, put into a tumbler with milk would not discolour the milk,' Hamlet replied. 'It would not be perceptible.'

Louisa's counsel didn't ask the scientist if he had actually conducted such an experiment so he could make such a bold statement with certainty.

The prosecution recalled Dr Milford and asked for his medical opinion.

'That preparation, the Rough on Rats, would produce all the effects I saw in Collins' body,' he advised the court, 'the effects of arsenical poisoning.'

• • •

Lusk had known he was facing an uphill battle when he accepted Louisa's brief. Although she had compiled a list of people who could be called to testify in her defence, he couldn't subpoena those he couldn't find, particularly as he lacked the financial resources to search for them. One located witness was Walter Hayes, a fellmonger who had boarded at the Collins house for a couple of months earlier that year. Hayes' testimony might undermine the Crown's case to some extent. While the law declared that the Crown didn't have to provide a motive in order to secure a conviction, the public—the people from whom a jury was drawn—struggled with that principle. If they couldn't comprehend why someone would commit a crime, how could they decide that the person was guilty beyond a reasonable doubt, especially when the only evidence laid against the accused was circumstantial?

When asked about Louisa and Mick's relationship, Hayes told the court, 'They appeared to get on well together. I never saw any unpleasantness while I was there. Collins was a sober, respectable man and a pleasant man in the house.'

Lusk enquired about Collins' work situation. The court had already heard about his employment problems because the prosecution had read out Louisa's inquest statements. Hayes said that Collins was initially out of work but had obtained employment soon after he joined their household. He remembered Collins taking a trip to the Illawarra and coming back the same day saying that he couldn't find work. He hadn't heard anything about a lost or pawned watch, though.

Under cross-examination, Coffey asked about the other relationships within the family. How was May treated?

'She was not ill-treated while I was there.'

What about arguments in the household: between Collins and his wife, perhaps?

Hayes said that the couple hadn't argued, however Collins' relationship with his stepchildren was a different matter entirely. 'There was a row between Collins and Arthur while I was there, not between him and his wife. It had reference to a name Arthur had called Collins.'

It was a reminder that Arthur had shown no concern for Collins' wellbeing while he lay on his sickbed, only venturing into the bedroom at Louisa's behest on the day before his death. Clearly, there had been tension between the pair—triggered perhaps by Louisa's haste in marrying the man who had caused so much unhappiness between his own parents.

Another boarder, Augustus Nordgren, confirmed Hayes' remarks about the Collinses' relationship. Nordgren had lodged at the Collins house for three months over the summer period, departing in January that year. 'I always saw them live happy together. They seemed fond of one another. I did not hear any of the family ill-treated.'

Lusk changed his line of questioning when he called the body-washer, Ellen Price, to the stand. He asked her about Collins' attire at the time of his death. She testified that he was dressed in a shirt, trousers and socks. 'I took the trousers off,' she added. 'They were in a very soiled condition.'

Under cross-examination, Coffey asked about the contents of Collins' trouser pockets. Ellen said that she hadn't noticed anything. 'If there had been anything in the pockets, I would have felt it.'

When Lusk attempted to call additional witnesses, he discovered that they had left the courthouse, apparently by mistake. Legally, he couldn't call Louisa as a witness. New South Wales criminal law followed centuries of British tradition in refusing to allow accused criminals the right to offer sworn testimony in their own defence; not only would it be an invitation to commit perjury, it would reverse the burden of proof and would allow prosecutors to question defendants about past behaviour that was discreditable without being relevant. Louisa could, however, make an unsworn 'dock statement'—which could not be cross-examined—as most accused criminals chose to do.

This would allow the court to see her as more than just a wooden lump sitting in the dock. It would allow the jury to hear her voice, to feel the passion in her declaration that she was innocent of the charge against her, that she hadn't done such a thing, that she couldn't have done such a thing because she loved Mick. But she was not going to do so.

The courtroom regulars noticed the omission and wondered about it.

With no one else to question, it was time for Lusk to address the jury. However, it was six pm and he didn't want the jurors thinking about their rumbling stomachs while he was giving the speech that would help them decide Louisa's fate. He asked the judge if they could adjourn for tea. Foster agreed to a forty-minute break.

At six forty-five pm, Lusk began his closing address, homing in on the weakest link in the Crown's case: 'The Crown has failed to show any motive for Mrs Collins to commit the terrible crime with which she was charged.' He reminded the jurors of Louisa's anxiety to assist her husband throughout his illness, that among her many caring actions were her repeated trips to seek the doctor's assistance. Even the Crown's witnesses had shown that she had been kind and attentive to Collins and had been reduced to tears on a number of occasions. Their relationship had clearly been affectionate and her husband had shown no signs of suspicion regarding her treatment of him.

He admitted that there was no doubt that Collins had died from arsenical poisoning. 'But whilst there is no evidence of his having administered the poison himself; still, it was quite possible for him to have committed suicide.' He asked the jurors to recollect that Collins rarely volunteered any information about his health problems and that, despite the seriousness of his illness, he had continued to wear his trousers while in bed. Thus, it was possible for him to have hidden the arsenic in his trouser pocket as Louisa had suggested. Moreover, Collins had a motive for committing suicide as he was in and out of work and was struggling financially.

After speaking for over an hour, Lusk concluded, 'In view of the very grave responsibility cast upon you, I ask you to carefully consider these facts, and to give the accused the benefit of every reasonable doubt. If you find her not guilty, no irreparable injury would be done.'

Coffey attempted to undermine Lusk's defence by declaring that the medical evidence was not consistent with the suggestion of suicide. 'The doctors' evidence showed that the poison had been administered in small doses on different occasions, that the deceased was in great pain for days and continually vomiting. It would be absurd to suppose that he would, in committing suicide, submit himself to a week of torture.' He finished by stating, 'The evidence points in only one direction, and that is to the guilt of the accused.'

It was nine pm by the time Coffey finished, too late for the case to be wrapped up that night. Foster adjourned the case until nine-thirty the following morning when he would begin his own summation. Afterwards, the jury would have the rest of the day to consider their verdict. Louisa Collins should know her fate by nightfall.

Chapter 20

There is no such thing as an impartial jury because there are no impartial people.

Jon Stewart

When the *Evening News* pressman reached Darlinghurst Courthouse early on Wednesday morning, long before the usual hour of business, he was astonished at the size of the crowd huddling under its portico, particularly in view of the inclement weather. The rain that had threatened on Monday had commenced falling early on Tuesday and had continued throughout the day and night. Sydney had awoken to a gloomy morning, with cloudbursts at regular intervals. Not that cloudbursts would confine its sensation-loving citizens to the warmth of their blazing hearths. After the breakfast newspapers had reported that Louisa Collins' daughter had provided the most incriminating evidence against her, Sydney's men and women wanted to see for themselves the face of this accused murderer.

The doors opened at twenty past nine. The crowds pushed through. Three minutes later, every seat in the public gallery was taken. The courtroom itself was soon packed as well.

When Louisa appeared in the dock, the *Evening News* reporter noticed that she was dressed in the same hat and cloak and blue dress as on the previous two days. His female readers would be interested in those details. And what about her expression? Extraordinarily, that too was unchanged. She wore a look of unruffled coolness despite the fact that she would soon hear the verdict of the jury. Then the judge's voice drew the pressman's attention away from Louisa.

'Gentlemen of the jury,' Justice Foster began, 'the case which has occupied your attention during the past two days is one of very great importance, not only to the person who is charged here with the terrible crime of poisoning her own husband, but also to the public at large.' Foster commended the jury for having listened closely to the evidence, and also the Crown and defence for ably conducting their cases, although he had concerns about the defence's statement that no irreparable injury would be done if Mrs Collins were found not guilty. An irreparable injury would indeed be done if the jury made a mistake when reaching its verdict. 'In a case of this sort a mistake either on one side or the other cannot always be rectified. I once heard Sir Alfred Stephen say, in a case of murder, that he could not acquit the jury of a large share of responsibility, who had, on a previous charge of murder, improperly acquitted the prisoner.'

The scales of justice had just become a deadweight resting on the jurors' shoulders. Serving in a capital trial was a daunting responsibility. If they convicted the woman, they would forever have her death on their consciences. Yet if they failed to convict her and another person died, they would be forever burdened with the sense of their own complicity.

Foster reassured them that this burden of guilt would apply only if they reached an improper verdict. He explained the legal requirements in cases comprising circumstantial evidence alone: that the circumstances must not only be consistent with the prisoner's guilt, they must also be inconsistent with any other rational conclusion.

This was helpful advice for the jurors who had little experience of the judicial process.

Foster continued by saying that both the Crown and defence agreed that Collins had been killed by arsenical poisoning. 'This is a question of paramount importance,' he told the jury, 'because otherwise the prisoner must be acquitted.' If they were satisfied that Collins had been poisoned with arsenic, they would have to decide whether the evidence proved beyond a reasonable doubt that Louisa was responsible. He said that the Crown had shown that Louisa had 'means', reminding them of the Rough on Rats evidence provided by Louisa's daughter. She also had 'opportunity', both because she had lived with and cared for Collins during his illness and because she had stated on several occasions that she alone had given him his medicine. 'This strikes two ways. It shows that the prisoner had a better opportunity of doing this than any other person but, on the other hand, that she had not endeavoured to conceal it in any way.'

As the judge continued his summation, the *Evening News* reporter glanced at Louisa to see how she was reacting. While she continued to display an air of unruffled coolness, her eyes were alert as she watched the judge tip the scales one way then the other.

Regarding the defence's case, Foster remarked on Louisa's two inquest statements, the first before there were suspicions that she had poisoned her husband, the second afterwards. 'If she knew, when the inquest was held, that her husband had had a strange packet of powder in his possession, why did she not say so at the inquest? It was only after she was charged that she mentioned seeing him with such a paper. No trace of the powder has ever been found, and her statement is not corroborated by any other evidence.' As for her claim that this explained Collins' trouser-wearing, the jurors had to ask themselves if he was wearing them to keep warm or if, as the prisoner alleged, it was to conceal a packet of poison. As for the suicide argument, Foster said that Collins was unlikely to have repeatedly dosed himself because of his weak state and the additional suffering it would have caused him.

Then there was the question of the arsenic-filled tumbler. 'It is to this matter that you should give the most careful attention,' he told the jurors. He reminded them that Louisa had told the police that she herself had supplied Collins with the milk in the tumbler and that Jeffes had testified that she had tried to stop him taking it away. 'Why should she try to stop him unless she knew there was something in it?' Foster challenged the jury. 'But then again, if she did know there was anything in it, why did she not remove it? It is an extraordinary fatuity that, in many cases, poisoners do not do away with the traces of their guilt, which could easily have been done away with, and some stupid thing left undone is often the thing which brings the crime home. I cannot say it was so in this case, but such is the case in many criminal cases.'

Of course, there were other points in the prisoner's defence that they should equally consider, including her anxiety to have the doctor's assistance. 'This is a most important point for you to consider. This is contended on one side to be a sign of her innocence, but the Crown contended that she did this to screen herself in case of discovery. If the prisoner was committing a secret crime, why did she call in medical men, the men most likely to discover her? The fact that she did so must be considered in her favour.' They should also consider the fact that she sent for a vomiting powder to help her husband. If she was trying to poison him, it was hardly likely that she would give him a powder that would rid his body of that very poison.

Finally, three-and-a-half hours later, he concluded: 'The responsibility rests on you, and I do not think I can help you very much. If, after you have given the matter your most careful consideration, you are unable to remove any doubt that may exist in your minds, then it is your duty to give the accused the full benefit of that doubt and find her "not guilty" even if you think the evidence is greater against her than in her favour. If, on the other hand, you come to the conclusion that she administered the poison, you will bring in a verdict of guilty.'

• • •

The spectators filed out of the courtroom at one pm to allow the functionaries a respite for lunch. They huddled outside in the rain for half an hour before being allowed back in. By that time, Justice Foster had retired to his room. He would be alerted as soon as the jury had reached a verdict.

The clock struck two then two-thirty, three . . . three-thirty. Still there was no word. With weary determination, the spectators remained in their seats, knowing that the court wouldn't wait for them to reappear if they took a 'necessary' break at an inopportune moment.

At ten minutes past four, the judge's associate and the Crown prosecutor entered the courtroom. The spectators' chatter ceased as if a tap had been turned off. Eager eyes focused on the two men. Had the jury reached a verdict?

Two minutes later, the judge entered the courtroom and took his seat on the bench. Louisa was returned to the dock. The reporters saw her watching the jurors as they took their places, all the while wearing her usual look of complacency.

'Gentlemen, have you reached a verdict?' asked the judge's associate.

The silence was so intense it was as if the air itself sizzled with expectation.

'No, Your Honour,' replied the foreman.

The bubble had been burst. The spectators slumped in their seats. Strangely, the only person who seemed unmoved by the foreman's response was Louisa herself.

Justice Foster asked how they were positioned.

'There is no likelihood of the jury reaching a verdict,' the foreman advised. 'We paid careful attention to the whole of the evidence, and one or two of us even took full notes throughout the trial, which we read over and fully considered after we retired last night, but we found it impossible to agree.'

'I am very sorry that you could not arrive at a verdict,' said the judge. 'I would willingly release you now if I could, but it is not in my power to do so. By law I am compelled to lock you up for twelve hours before I can discharge you.'

The foreman pressed for the jury's discharge, but the judge said that he couldn't change the law. The foreman pleaded, 'If we were locked up for a week we wouldn't be able to come to any agreement.'

'Even if, as you have stated, there was no chance of agreeing, I would not be at liberty to release you until one o'clock in the morning. As many of you live out of town, it would not be convenient for you to be discharged at such a late hour. I will attend the court as early as possible in the morning—say nine o'clock—at which time I will discharge you.'

• • •

The crowds were smaller on the fourth day of the trial. The foreman's unequivocal declaration that the jury hadn't a hope of reaching a unanimous verdict had quenched much of the excitement of the previous day. Even so, many Sydneysiders were determined to see the finale for themselves. Perhaps some of the jurors might have experienced a Damascus-like conversion of opinion overnight.

Again the jury filed in; again Louisa took her seat in the dock. The *Echo* reporter remarked: 'Her appearance certainly did not leave the impression that she had passed an anxious night, and was not such as would have been presented by many undergoing such a trying ordeal.'

Again the judge took his seat; again the question was posed: 'Gentlemen, have you agreed upon a verdict?'

'No, Your Honour. It is impossible to agree,' said the foreman emphatically. 'The opinions of the jury seem immovable. We have been considering the case for over twenty hours and there is no possibility of us reaching a unanimous decision.'

The *Daily Telegraph* reporter watched Louisa as the foreman explained the jury's predicament. His keen eyes noticed a momentary lifting of her mask of indifference as an air of relief settled over her, accompanied by a faint smile of satisfaction.

Justice Foster asked the foreman about the division of opinion and was told that it was nearly equal. The judge then thanked and officially discharged the jurors. Before they departed, he added, 'I think the case is one upon which conscientious gentlemen might hold different opinions.'

Chapter 21

Trial by jury has been termed the palladium of British liberty.

Evening News

With Louisa's case again sub judice, the press refrained from commenting on her guilt or innocence, although the *Evening News* couldn't resist publishing an editorial on the subject of trial by jury. The editor expressed concern about the fallibility of juries, saying that their verdicts were sometimes so incomprehensible that shocked judges had been known to recommend that names be struck off the jury lists. Many in the community thought that jurors left their commonsense outside the jury box, that their semi-superstitious sense of responsibility deprived them as a group from exercising the sound judgement they might have used as individuals. Stories had even been told of disagreeing jurors tossing a coin to decide whether the verdict should be 'guilty' or 'not guilty', as if the fate of the person standing in the dock was of no more importance than a choice between beef or mutton for dinner.

What really concerned the editor, though, was the significance of a hung verdict. He recognised that a defendant might sometimes end up with a friend or two on the jury, people whose personal feelings prevented the jury from reaching a unanimous verdict. Clearly, though, that was not the situation in Louisa Collins' case. Twelve jurors had heard exactly the same evidence, yet half—or thereabouts—had reached one conclusion and the other half the opposite conclusion. What's more, they had formed their conclusions based on their own judgements because the judge's summing up had been so impartial that it was hard to know how he would have voted if he himself had been sitting in the jury box.

This also raised the question as to whether a jury of twelve ordinary men was capable of reaching a unanimous verdict unless the judge provided a clear direction as to which way—in his opinion—they should cast their vote. That being the case, it was not only an unsatisfactory outcome, it was damaging to the prestige of trial by jury as a means of arbitration.

• • •

Meanwhile, frustration creased the brows of the Crown law officers. Where had they gone wrong? They had proven that Collins was killed by arsenic poisoning, that Louisa by her own admission was the only person giving Collins nourishment, and that arsenic had been found in a tumbler she had given him, one she'd tried to stop the constable from taking away. So what 'reasonable doubt' had led half the jurors to want to acquit her?

Others were pondering the issue as well. Obviously, the Crown's inability to establish a motive was a critical factor. When only circumstantial evidence was available, an apparent motive helped glue it all together. Instead, the Crown's case had communicated the opposite. The fact that Louisa had married Collins so soon after her first husband's death suggested that their relationship was based on passion rather than convenience, which was supported by the Crown's own witnesses, who had testified that the couple lived on good terms.

Moreover, Collins was a temperate man who was usually at home in the evening, so in her hasty remarriage Louisa hadn't embraced a drunken bully she might later have wished to eliminate from her life. True, Collins was only an intermittent worker, but the Crown had been unable to demonstrate that Louisa would financially benefit from his demise. Worse, it had shown that Collins' death had shut off Louisa's primary source of income, the money she and her children needed to survive. The Crown had also shown that her behaviour reflected concern for Collins' wellbeing rather than callousness and that there was no air of subterfuge in any of her actions.

Additionally, the Crown's witnesses had brought to light some odd behaviour from Collins himself—like his comments to the police that he was 'all right' and would be 'up in a day or two' even when he was on his deathbed. Did this suggest that he didn't want people nosing around too much? Perhaps it wasn't surprising that even the judge himself had recognised that there were grounds for reasonable doubt. So how would the law officers deal with these difficult issues when they brought the case to trial for a second time—if they decided to do so?

The Crown's next step was obvious when Louisa was brought before the Central Criminal Court on 15 August to be arraigned again on the same charge. They would delay retrying the case until the court's next sitting, which commenced on 29 October. The law officers hadn't yet arraigned her on the Andrews' charge, so this would allow the Crown another two-and-a-half months to decide how to proceed with both cases.

As Louisa was returned to Darlinghurst Gaol to await the Crown's pleasure, the law officers asked Coffey for his recommendations. Coffey mentioned the Crown's failure to establish a motive but said that, in his opinion, the evidence had been strong enough to prove her guilt. Still, he suggested that the authorities attempt to trace the purchase of the Rough on Rats and also find out more about the Collinses' relationship in the months before Collins' death, perhaps by questioning May Andrews. Additionally, the Crown should question everyone who was at the house on the Saturday evening before Collins' death to clarify when the liquid in the arsenic-filled tumbler was last changed and by whom.

• • •

Senior Constable Sherwood was charged with reinterviewing the witnesses. In mid-September, he forwarded a number of witness statements to his superiors, along with a summary of his newly discovered information. He had established that the arsenic-filled tumbler taken from the Collinses' bedroom had first been used on the evening before Collins' death and that Ellen Pettit had collected and thoroughly cleaned the tumbler before handing it over. He also reported that Louisa had obtained some paper, ink and a pen after the police left that same night and had put them on the table in the front room—although no one knew why.

May had answered questions about her home life, saying, 'Since my father died, my mother and Collins used to beat me and my little brothers with a walking stick, and tell me I was like my bloody father.'

Sherwood offered no opinion about May's remark. It was an ugly revelation. Yet perhaps they were acting merely on the Christian principle of 'spare the rod, spoil the child'. Whatever their motives, it was clear that Louisa's feelings about her first husband were bitter and long-lasting.

• • •

Those with a keen interest in Louisa's case continued to keep an eye out for reports about her; however, the press maintained its silence. Before long, the Botany Poisoning Case was eclipsed by startling reports arriving from Britain.

'Horrible murders in London,' announced the *Sydney Morning Herald* on 10 September 1888. Some women of the 'unfortunate class' had been murdered in the Whitechapel area—horribly mutilated in fact. Who was the culprit? It was an anatomist who wanted organs for medical exhibition in America, declared the London coroner late in September, without stating why he was attributing responsibility to one of those upstart Americans.

A day later, the Whitechapel Murderer was at it again, leaving two more mutilated bodies in his wake. By 22 October, the press was reporting that the police had practically abandoned all hope of catching the perpetrator unless he revealed his secret during an unguarded moment or was caught in a future act. Then there was another murder. Soon afterwards, a letter was published in the press, supposedly sent to the London police by the murderer himself. 'I am down on whores,' howled Jack the Ripper, 'and I shan't quit ripping them till I do get buckled.'

It was a reminder that killers often keep killing until someone or something stops them in their tracks.

Chapter 22

> I desired liberty; for liberty I gasped; for liberty I uttered a prayer; it seemed scattered on the wind.
>
> Charlotte Bronte, *Jane Eyre*

Sitting in the dock had been frightening, but at least the eyes boring into her had testified to the reality of her existence. Behind the gaol walls, it was as if she were invisible. Although she hadn't been convicted of any crime, she was being treated as if the verdict was already in, as if the clanging gates of Darlinghurst Gaol had screamed 'guilty' more loudly and authoritatively than any jury.

Her letters to the law officers and the police were being ignored. Worse, she had discovered that her letter to her defence counsel had been redirected by the gaol's governor to the sheriff. It was only forwarded to Lusk after he complained that he hadn't received it. Lusk was horrified when he learnt of this breach in legally mandated confidentiality, more so when he discovered it was a customary practice. He warned the sheriff that, if the practice continued, he would be forced to raise the matter in the proper quarters.

Her request to the Crown Solicitor for the inquest depositions relating to Andrews' death was also ignored, as was Lusk's reminder.

It was only after Lusk sent another threatening letter to the Crown Solicitor that the office deigned to respond.

Clearly, Lusk was her only conduit to the legal authorities. What chance would she have had of properly defending herself if she'd had no one on the outside to argue for her rights? Indeed, how many people had gone to the gallows because of the Crown's reluctance to grant them their legal rights—or indeed the Crown's breaches of those same rights? It was obvious why the sheriff was the automatic recipient of private letters from prisoners to their barristers: the Crown wanted him to assess the contents and communicate anything necessary to the relevant authorities. Did this include the Crown law officers who were trying her case, indeed trying all of the prisoners' cases? Where was the 'justice' in that?

• • •

The days were slow and tedious, spent working silently in the laundry or sewing room. The food never varied: hominy and bread for breakfast, meat and potatoes for the midday meal, and hominy again for tea. Late each afternoon, she was returned to the female dormitory, a tall, rectangular, stone building known as D wing. It had three tiers of cells with an open area in the centre, which was sometimes used by charitable ladies who read to them once a week.

Although still awaiting trial, she was incarcerated in the same building as the convicted women. She enjoyed some privileges in terms of diet, dress and visitors; however, similarly to the convicted women, she was locked in her cell every evening at five, where she remained until six the following morning. Her bed was a hammock: a strip of canvas attached to iron rings on the wall, which was rolled up during daylight hours. She could read until the light faded, but the nights were long—too long. There was little else to fill the mind but unwelcome thoughts and dreams.

She began another letter to the sheriff, begging for an answer to a question that had troubled her. While she belonged to the Church of England, her husband was a Roman Catholic. Despite these differences, she had attempted to do the right thing for him before and after his death.

> When he took ill, I wanted to send for the priest. In fact, I begged of him to let me send for the priest. He said, 'No, my love. I will neither see priest nor parson. I only want you. I don't wish to see anybody.' I could not in any way persuade him to see the priest while he was alive. So after his death I sent for the priest at Randwick as there are none living in Botany. The priest came in his buggy to my place. He had scarcely alighted when the two Botany police that was stationary on my house all the morning . . .

She interrupted her account to complain that she'd thought the policemen were there as her friends but had later discovered they were acting on information from the doctors. As she continued writing, she tried to hide the depth of her bitterness.

> When the priest was about to come to my door, the police detained him for a considerable time, talking to him. I wondered at the delay then sent someone to invite the priest in. He came in and read prayers over the dead body of my husband that was lying on the bed and spoke a few kind words to me and then he left.

She added that she was writing this letter because she wanted to know what the police had said at such length to the priest. Could someone tell her?

The days passed without any response. In a second letter to the sheriff, she asked to see the Sisters of Mercy who visited Catholics in the gaol. 'I am sure they would only be too glad to take pitty on me and see the priest in Randwick. I am sure it would throw some light on the subject of the death of my late husband Collins, which is schrouded in mystery at the present time.' She admitted that Governor Read had refused her request to see the sisters. 'In fact, he most grossly insults me and speaks to me as though I was one void of feeling. I am only waiting trial, as you know,' she added plaintively.

Finally, she begged the sheriff to permit a prisoner's woman to attend her. 'For I have some awful disclosures to make before my trial comes of which will make things look very different to what they do at the present time.'

• • •

While Lusk dealt with Louisa's legal issues, Senior Constable Sherwood was the recipient of communications directed to those living in the Botany district. He too was ignoring her letters. She started another, repeating her previously unheeded request for the photograph of herself and Collins, the one published in the illustrated newspapers. She provided directions to the photograph's location, making it clear that she didn't expect him to make a special trip to the gaol; she just wanted him to bring it to the court when her case came to trial again. Why did she want it? 'It was not money I wanted from Collins, it was himself,' she wrote. 'If Death had come and offered me a Million of Money for Mr Collins, I would not have taken it in place of him.'

She couldn't help avowing her innocence: 'I am no Murderess or Drunkard or Liar!' In the long hours of enforced silence and inactivity, it was hard not to dwell on the dreadful things people were saying about her, both in the courtroom and out of it. She continued by telling Sherwood that she was honest and upright in all her dealings and that, after her trials, she would pay all of her bills, including the cost of feeding her and of the cab fares to the various courts before her incarceration. 'I shall only be too happy too give the Government a cheque for the full amount no matter what becomes of me if I should get hung or imprisonment for life. I shall not let the Government be at the loss of one halfpenny by me.' She didn't want him to think ill of her for saying such a thing, though. 'You need not think for one moment that this letter is a Bribe or a Sweetener for it is nothing of the kind; it is the truth. I let you, Mr Sherwood, and everyone else see who I am.' To make such payments, she would need money, of course, and she admitted that she had some stashed away. 'I am independent, thank God.'

She also penned another letter to one of her creditors, a Botany gentleman, saying, 'I hope you do not think of me as most people do, as one of the deepest dye, black. As soon as my trials is over, I will call and pay you what I owe you. Hoping that your wife and dear children are quite well, I remain, yours truly, Louisa Collins.'

• • •

A reply from Sherwood and the photograph at last. But no visit from Arthur as she had also requested. According to Sherwood, Arthur was too busy to leave his work. She responded tartly, 'Sir, I do not blame Arthur for not coming to see me because he would not be let come by you and Jeffes and my son Herby Andrews and Mrs Bartington.' She suggested that her correspondence had been withheld from Arthur and reminded Sherwood that he was responsible for investigating all crimes. 'That is what you are paid too do and not stop Arthur from coming too see his Mother in prison.'

She also took issue with Sherwood's claim that he had acted according to the law when taking her into custody. 'Sir, you know in your heart and soul that you never read no Warrant to me when you came to my house at candle light and told me too go in the Tram too Sydney too tell me something about the inquest. I went without the slightest resistance, thinking, of course, that all was right.' And she challenged him to treat her decently. 'We are all born but not Buried. Mr Sherwood if you don't want to go headlong too your doom with four others, the best thing I would advise you too do is too be civil with me for I have done you no harm nor anyone else.'

• • •

As the date of the next criminal session drew near, offers of support from sensation-loving barristers reminded her of her obligation to Hugh Lusk. In a note to the *Sydney Morning Herald*, she asked that the attached letter be published, one that explained her decision to reject these other offers:

> Sir, it is out of no ill-feeling or disrespect or injury too any other Barrister for I wish them all well but it is out of pure respect and the deepest gratitude for all he has done for me and my welfare he richly deserves all the respect I can show him and I am only too happy too call him the Champion Barraster of New South Wales and I wish all the other Papers to copy this letter.

The gaoler appended a note saying that Louisa wanted the letter to be sent to the press after her case was finished. Instead, it was sent to the colonial authorities where it was filed and forgotten.

Chapter 23

Eat arsenic? Yes . . .
Consenting, he did speak up;
'Tis better you should eat it, pet,
Than put it in my teacup.

Ambrose Bierce, *The Devil's Dictionary*

A different wig graced the bench in the Darlinghurst courtroom on Monday, 5 November. Justice William Windeyer was presiding over Louisa's second trial, again on charges of killing Michael Peter Collins. Those watching Windeyer as he made himself comfortable saw a handsome face marked by strong features and a brusque, forbidding manner. Some were aware that under this formidable exterior lay a liberal heart. He was an advocate of social reform, particularly of women's rights. Indeed, as a one-time parliamentarian, he had been responsible for the passage of the Married Women's Property Act of 1879, which granted married women the legal right to their own income and inheritance. Nevertheless, some of his harsh rulings in the criminal courts had created widespread controversy. He believed that criminal justice demanded retribution and his sympathy lay with the victims, particularly female victims. As the judge presiding over a sensational gang-rape trial two years previously, he had sentenced nine of the perpetrators to the gallows. Such rulings were responsible for his nickname, 'the hanging judge'.

A different wig also sat in the Crown's prosecutorial chair. Henry Cohen usually gravitated towards cases involving commercial interests and the civil law, so he seemed a surprising choice for the Crown's lead prosecutor in a murder trial. Sitting beside him, though, was the previous prosecutor, William Coffey. The Crown hoped they would make a formidable team.

• • •

As the clerk called out the jurors' names, one was familiar to Louisa: Alexander Geddes. His surname was well known in the Botany district. Many locals were employed by members of the Geddes family in one of their wool-washing or fellmongering establishments. Mick had worked for Thomas Geddes in the months before his death. Charlie had been employed by Alexander Geddes himself until shortly before his own death. Would anyone challenge Geddes' presence in the jury box? Would he reveal his own distant connection? No . . .

The new prosecutor began his opening address. Louisa listened intently. Perhaps he'd found new evidence against her. But as he traced her case's history up to the time of her arrest, he added nothing new. She'd already heard it recited twice before. Her eyes glazed over and she retreated into the same protectively indifferent state as before.

'Dr George Archibald Marshall?' the prosecution called. Rumours regarding Marshall's demise had been wrong, much to the prosecution's relief. A dead man's words were never as powerful as those of the living.

For the third time, Marshall stepped into the witness box. Nothing new was elicited from his examination; however, Lusk was more prepared for his cross-examination. He asked the surgeon about his experience with arsenic poisoning cases and wondered if he had considered the possibility that Collins might have been an arsenic-eater.

An arsenic-eater? Now that was a new suggestion. Was it possible?

Lusk knew that it was indeed a possibility. The claims of arsenic-eating as a health benefit had first surfaced in a Viennese medical journal in 1851, with reports that peasants living in the mountainous Styria region regularly consumed doses of arsenic that were well above the lethal level. The peasants began by taking small amounts several times a week then they slowly increased the dose until they were eating four to eight grains at a time, even twenty-three grains in one instance. Men found it increased their energy and endurance, making it easier to work in their tough, mountainous environment. Hangovers were a thing of the past, as were the usual coughs and colds. Longevity increased—not just in life but also in death; the exhumed bodies of long-dead arsenic-eaters often bore recognisable features when others buried around the same time had been reduced to skeletons. Virility increased. And since female arsenic-eaters were transformed from wraiths into voluptuous, libidinous, rose-cheeked beauties, illegitimate children abounded.

After the report was published, the rumours of arsenic's potency spread around the globe. Men began taking arsenic pills while women added arsenic preparations to their beauty regimes—and the 'Styrian defence' became a new tool in murder trials. 'She died not because I murdered her,' the husband would proclaim, 'but because she was an arsenicophagist.' Or: 'I have arsenic in my possession because I was trying to make myself more alluring for my husband, not because I intended to murder him.' Was the young, virile Collins an arsenic-eater?

'I had no reason to suppose that the man was an arsenic-eater by choice,' Marshall informed the court.

With no other evidence than Louisa's mention of a missing packet of powder, Lusk let the 'Styrian defence' drop, hoping that it might have introduced an element of reasonable doubt.

Then a juror asked a question.

• • •

It is almost a truism that barristers should only ask questions to which they already know the answer; many a well-prepared case has been undermined by an unexpected and unwelcome response. A single barrister, though, wasn't the only person steering the course of Louisa's trial. While the defence, prosecution and judge each held their own reins, another twelve individuals could tug at them at any moment. It was like steering a horse through a minefield.

'Do you know what occupation the deceased followed?' the juror asked Marshall.

'Collins was employed before his illness in carting green skins for a wool-washing establishment,' the surgeon replied. He had heard enough testimonies and read enough newspaper reports in the previous four months to be aware of Collins' occupation, even if he hadn't been privy to that information when he actually treated the man.

'Don't you know that, in this country, all squatters and fellmongers treat skins with arsenic?' the juror asked.

'That is very important,' said the startled judge. Looking back at Marshall, he asked, 'Do you know that as a fact? It ought to be in evidence.'

'I do not,' Marshall replied.

Prosecutor Cohen tried to grab back the reins, asking the doctor if arsenic could have been introduced into Collins' body in such a way.

'If Collins had suffered from blood-poisoning by following his occupation, I would not expect to find so much arsenic in the body as was found.'

The juror piped up again, asking about hand wounds.

'Of course, Collins might have cut his finger and, working with arsenic, have placed his finger in his mouth and in this way have introduced the drug into his system,' Marshall admitted. 'It would depend very much on the quantity and strength of the arsenic used.'

The prosecutor asked if this was likely in view of what he had seen.

'Collins' symptoms were inconsistent with those that should be presented by arsenical poisoning from working with a solution of arsenic.'

The juror interjected, 'I knew a case in which a man had suffered through working with arsenic.'

'Such a statement should be made on oath,' said the judge firmly, 'in order that true facts might be elicited in cross-examination. There is no evidence to show that the deceased had cut his hands or fingers and thus got arsenic into his system.'

The spectators' heads were swivelling backwards and forwards as questions flew around the courtroom: from the prosecutor to the witness, from the judge to the witness, from the judge to the juror, from the juror to . . . everyone. What an extraordinary development. How had this faceless adjudicator transformed himself into defence counsel-cum-witness?

Called to the stand, Dr Martin was asked his own opinion about the possibility of arsenic absorption through Collins' skin. He said that he thought it impossible that such a large amount of arsenic could have been found in Collins' liver if it had been absorbed by any other means than ingestion. 'If that quantity had been absorbed through the skin, it would have caused a good deal of irritation on the skin's surface. I saw nothing of the kind. The skin was clear except for the wound on the bone.'

'Taking it for granted that Collins had not been at work from the twenty-eighth of June and had handled no skins after that date, and supposing the poison had passed through the skin and that he had vomited as stated, would you expect to find arsenic in the body after death?' Cohen asked.

'I would expect to find only a slight trace of arsenic.'

Lusk was delighted to pursue this new trail of evidence and questioned Dr Milford about the possibilities. Milford said, 'I know of cases in which the external application of arsenic has caused sore hands. I myself suffered from sore fingernails for three years through using arsenic in dealing with bodies. This has also happened in the case of numbers of medical students dealing with dissection.'

Asked if Collins' body had shown signs that arsenic might have been absorbed through the skin, Milford said that he had seen no such signs on Collins' hands or around the necrosis on his leg but that there might have been traces that he hadn't noticed.

Was skin-absorbed arsenic likely to cause vomiting?

'I have never known a person to vomit after absorbing it through the hands,' Milford responded, then admitted that he knew of cases in which clothes washed in arsenic had poisoned the wearers and that some cases of externally absorbed arsenic had led to deaths.

As Lusk sat down, the juror remarked, 'In removing the wool from skins, the tanner might occasionally rub his hand across his mouth and thus in a short time swallow a fatal dose.'

The prosecutor asked Milford if he could comment on this point. Milford replied, 'Had the poison been taken in the manner suggested and six days had elapsed since the last skin had been handled, I would not expect to find arsenic in the man's vomit. The poison would be eliminated and would not accumulate.'

• • •

That afternoon and the following morning witnesses continued to tread the hallowed path to the witness box. The pressmen continued to scribble notes, all the while recognising that their published reports would likely omit most of these testimonies; their subscribers had little interest in reading the same information for a third time.

During these interminable days, Louisa maintained the same composed demeanour. Occasionally, on making eye contact with someone she knew, she would twitch her lips in a slight smile, but otherwise she seemed as indifferent as previously.

Senior Constable Sherwood reminded the court that Louisa had made no verbal response after being officially charged with murder. Nobody could miss his insinuation: that if the woman had not poisoned her husband, surely she would have loudly protested her innocence. Under cross-examination, he conceded that she had spoken openly to the policemen about her husband's illness and had seemed genuinely surprised that the surgeon had refused to sign a death certificate. He also admitted that, despite exhaustive searches of her house—even with the children's assistance—he had found nothing that suggested she might have poisoned her husband.

When neighbour Charles Sayers testified, the juror piped up again, asking him about Collins' poisoned hands. Sayers said, 'I do not remember Collins having poisoned hands. He had sore hands caused probably by handling wool and skins.'

Justice Windeyer had had enough. He looked towards the jury box and said, 'If any juror knows anything about such a fact, or about the case, it is your duty to be sworn and examined in the usual way.'

'I know nothing about the case, sir,' responded the juror. 'I don't know the woman, or ever spoke to her in my life.'

'Your question implied that you knew something about the case.'

'I only know that men do suffer from poisoned hands after handling skins, and I think it possible that Collins had been affected in this way.'

'Then you simply drew the inference that it was possible in this case,' accepted the judge and directed the question back to the witness.

Sayers agreed that while workers' hands could become soft and swollen from the wool friction, Collins did not suffer in that way. His skin was firm.

When James Law was called to testify, Lusk under cross-examination asked about the Collinses' relationship—apparently happy—and Botany's opinion of Louisa.

'Until the death of her first husband, she was very much respected in the neighbourhood,' Law replied.

What about afterwards?

'Her remarriage very close upon the death of her first husband was talked about,' he said primly.

Aware of Law's equivocation, the prosecution prompted him for a direct answer.

'Since the death of her first husband, her reputation was not so good.'

• • •

The first suggestion that all might not have been rosy in the Collins household came a few witnesses later. Rosetta Mapstone reported hearing a man and woman wrangling and someone vomiting when she visited Catherine Mudge one Saturday night in mid-June. Mrs Mudge's sister, Mary Ellen Cavanagh, also testified to hearing Collins vomiting at night on several occasions around that period. They were certain that it was mid-June and not later in the month as they were helping Mrs Mudge with her ailing baby who died on 22 June.

To the more percipient in the courtroom, these testimonies were a source of confusion rather than clarity. If the vomiter was indeed Collins, why hadn't he mentioned his earlier health issues on the numerous occasions he was questioned about his illness by the doctors and police officers?

When young Fred Andrews was called to testify, he assured the court that there had been no rows between his mother and Collins.

His brother Arthur agreed that the couple lived on good terms, although he admitted that her drinking was a problem. 'Mother was sober a few months before Mick died. I saw her drinking about a month before Collins died. He often said he would have it stopped.'

The prosecutor asked how often she drank.

'She could be under the influence once or twice a week, sometimes not that.'

Lusk asked about her degree of intoxication. Arthur said that he had never seen her drunk. Nor had he heard any arguments, except about her drinking, and he'd never seen Collins use physical violence against her.

Then May Andrews was called to testify. Clothes rustled and chairs scraped as spectators shifted to catch a glimpse of the young girl. Few were unaware of her previous revelations. Did she have more startling information to communicate?

May repeated her tales about seeing Rough on Rats in the house, more confident in her testimony on this second occasion. The prosecutor asked what her mother had said when she mentioned the discovery.

Those who had attended the previous trial knew that the girl had been adamant that she couldn't recollect what her mother had said or what had happened to the box, except that her mother hadn't taken it. Now, three months later, she had an answer. 'She asked me where I found it. I said, "Under the big basin on the shelf," and I showed her the place.' The prosecutor asked what had happened next. May said, 'She went away then and I think she took the box with her.'

The *Evening News* reporter happened to glance around the courtroom at that moment and noticed that some of the jurors were crying, horrified that the girl was being asked to condemn her own mother. He looked at Louisa and was startled to see that her mask of inscrutability had vanished, washed away by her tears. Was her misery caused by her sense of betrayal or because she saw a vision of her daughter's future horror when she realised what she had done? Because May wasn't just repeating the incriminating information from the previous trial. There was more.

'Once, when Collins was ill, Mother said if I went to get a pint of beer, she would give me two pence. She said we were going to live in Waterloo, that the money was no use to her whilst Mick was alive, that she was going to get some money from Mick when he died.'

Money from Mick? Had his life been insured? No previous witness had suggested such a thing.

The prosecutor asked when her mother had made the comment.

'I think the doctor had been there before she said this.'

Asked if she had fetched the requested beer, May said that she hadn't as her brother told her not to. The prosecutor enquired if beer was her mother's normal drink. May replied, 'Sometimes I saw Mother drink beer and brandy. I sometimes fetched it for her sixpence worth at a time. I went about once a day for that.'

What was Collins' reaction to her drinking?

'I heard Collins speak to my mother when he came home about her drinking. Sometimes he would speak cross. This happened once or twice a week.'

When Lusk took over the questioning, he enquired about the jug May had mentioned, the one that held Mick's milk.

'I remember having a jug of milk in the kitchen that night. It came off the milkman. It was the jug the milk was usually kept in. My little brother was taking some of the jug of milk to put in his tea. He took a little drink and mother said it was for Mick and she did not let him have it and he put the jug back on the side table.'

What about the condensed milk?

'She boiled some condensed milk for Mick and put it in another jug. This was on the Saturday afternoon before the milk came from the milkman. What came from the milkman she put on another table for our tea.' Then May realised that she had made a mistake in her previous statement. 'What she would not let my brother have was the boiled condensed milk,' she corrected. 'That was what she said was for Mick.'

Hamlet was recalled to the witness box and questioned about condensed milk in general. He explained that it comprised milk and sugar—thirty-three per cent sugar—as well as maize and starch, the starch being added to make up bulk. He reported that the constituents of condensed milk tallied with what he had found in the arsenic-filled tumbler.

The prosecution was delighted. Not only had May hammered another nail into her mother's coffin, she had been helped by none other than Louisa's defence counsel himself.

Chapter 24

Of all kinds of murders that by poison is the most dreadful, as it takes a man unguarded, and gives him no opportunity to defend himself.

Counsel for the Crown, *R v. Mary Blandy*, 1752

As country New South Wales baked under a scorching sun and drought gripped the western regions, the courtroom attendees were grateful for the cooler Sydney temperatures and the breeze that stirred the courtroom air. With only the defence and prosecution's closing addresses and the judge's summation to be heard, the fate of the poker-faced woman sitting in the dock should be known by day's end. Would her barrister succeed in keeping her from the noose's deadly embrace?

'We have now been engaged for three days in considering what on the face of it appears to be a very difficult case,' said Hugh Lusk as he commenced his closing address at ten am on Wednesday, 7 November. 'But when we divest it of a large amount of suspicion, it is found to be not such a difficult case.' He asked the jurors to listen carefully as he examined the *facts* of the case and distinguished them from matters of *opinion* that were not, properly speaking, part of the case itself. He said the facts revealed that Mrs Collins had shown great anxiety for her husband's wellbeing and would not benefit in any way by her husband's death. Furthermore, the medical texts revealed that arsenic often failed to take effect for days, so if Collins had absorbed the poison before he saw the doctor, there was nothing to connect his wife with his death.

He accepted that the arsenic found in the tumbler played a large part in the Crown's evidence, but queried if the jurors should place so much weight on this evidence because of the discrepancies between the various testimonies. 'The liquid in the glass had diminished in quantity between the time it was found by the constable and when handed over for analysis. Is it not fair to assume that it might have been tampered with in other ways?'

Evidently since the previous trial Lusk had realised that the discrepancy between the quantities mentioned by Hamlet and Jeffes was an important point he could use to undermine the prosecution's case.

As for the box of Rough on Rats: was it reasonable to suppose that Mrs Collins would simply hide it under a basin on a kitchen shelf rather than carefully conceal the existence of such a well-known poison, if she had indeed used it to commit such an awful crime? The same could be said for the liquid in the tumbler. If she had put it there, why hadn't she later thrown the contents away?

There were other ways Collins could have been poisoned. He might have purposefully committed suicide or even accidentally poisoned himself (an allusion to arsenic-eating). He might have absorbed poison into his body by handling arsenic-treated skins while working at the wool-wash. 'In conclusion,' Lusk said, 'there is no evidence whatever upon which you would be justified in convicting Mrs Collins of the crime with which she has been charged.'

Naturally the prosecutor disagreed—at length.

• • •

Louisa's expression was alert as she waited for the judge to begin his summation. She had listened to two days of testimony, some of it extraordinary and unexpected. What approach would the judge take when he summed up her case?

Others were wondering the same thing. Would Windeyer's directions to the jury reflect evenly weighted scales of justice or would he place a greater weight on one side or the other? With a reputation as 'the hanging judge', his likely leaning wasn't hard to surmise.

'Of all forms of murder that by poisoning is one that most shocks us, by reason of the treachery, the falsehood, and danger that necessarily surrounded it,' the judge began. 'But you are required to be careful in investigating it so as not to be hastily carried away in arriving at a conclusion which ought only to be arrived at after due and deliberate inquiry.'

It was an impartial beginning.

Windeyer explained that circumstantial evidence alone was often the only evidence available in poisoning cases because those who were cunning enough, cruel enough and calculating enough to bring about a person's death by poisoning did so in such a manner that others could not see the fatal dose being mixed and administered. Therefore, it was necessary to view all of Mrs Collins' actions with the utmost caution. 'You will have to consider whether her acts of kindness and consideration might have been part of the scheme to bring about Collins' death,' he counselled.

Regarding the evidence itself, he said that the jurors could accept that Collins died from arsenical poisoning because the testimonies from the government analyst and doctors proved it to be so. It was the jurors' role to determine how the arsenic had been absorbed into his body. Had Collins committed suicide? Windeyer asked if it were feasible to believe that a man so young and so healthy would destroy himself, particularly when there was no evidence to show that he had lost control of his reason. Moreover, most who attempted suicide did so as speedily as possible. In fact, he had never heard of a man destroying himself by inches. It was his opinion that the theory of suicide could not be supported. Nevertheless, if the jurors had any doubts, they must give Mrs Collins the benefit of those doubts.

Could Collins have absorbed arsenic while carrying out his work? 'That proposition arose in consequence of a question put by one of the jurymen and not by the counsel for the prisoner,' he reminded the court, while conceding that, in a case of such importance, they should explore all possibilities. He said that the evidence showed that Collins had not suffered in this way as no arsenic had been used in his workplace and as he had been engaged only in carting untreated green skins in the weeks before his death. The medical evidence also showed that it was impossible for such a large quantity of arsenic to have found its way into Collins' stomach by absorption through the skin. 'However, if you feel that death was brought about in this way,' he advised the jury, 'there would, of course, be an end of the case.'

If they could not adopt the theories of suicide or absorption, they were brought face to face with the likelihood that Collins was poisoned by another person. The Crown's case was that Collins' wife had the opportunity and the means for doing so. Windeyer repeated the evidence supporting the Crown's case, then concluded, 'If, after having considered the facts, any doubt remained in your minds as to the guilt of the prisoner, it is your duty to give her the benefit of that doubt. But if, on the other hand, no doubt exists in your minds, it is your duty to find the prisoner guilty.'

• • •

The jury's retirement allowed the spectators a welcome break from the increasingly hot and stuffy courtroom. Many an eye had drifted closed as the judge repeated the evidence presented. Still, they couldn't remain outside in the fresh air for long in case the jury reached a speedy verdict. Listening to a murder case unfold was exciting, but there was nothing better than hearing the verdict for themselves.

By suppertime, however, some of the spectators had decided that their empty stomachs triumphed over their need to hear the verdict firsthand. Others hung on until nine-thirty pm, when the foreman announced that the jurors hadn't yet reached a verdict. After the judge ordered the jurors' sequestration, the spectators spilled out of the building, making plans to be present when the trial resumed at ten am the following day.

• • •

Men, women and children swarmed into the courtroom on Thursday, 8 November, buzzing with excitement. The foreman hadn't said that the jurors were unable to reach a verdict, just that they hadn't yet done so. There would be a resolution this time—wouldn't there?—one way or the other.

The spectators sought out Louisa, desperate to see how she was reacting. Astonishingly, she wore the same air of indifference as on the previous days of her trial.

At 10.08, the jury filed into the witness box. As the atmosphere tensed, the judge's associate asked, 'Gentlemen of the jury, are you agreed upon your verdict?'

Not a murmur; not a rustle.

The foreman replied, 'No, we are not agreed.'

A moan of disappointment swept through the courtroom.

'Swear him in the usual way,' said the judge resignedly. He then asked if there was any chance they would reach an agreement.

After the abortive first trial, no one was surprised at the foreman's reply. 'There is not the slightest probability of our agreeing, Your Honour.'

'Then, gentlemen, you are discharged.'

Turning to the prosecutor, Windeyer asked, 'What course do you propose to take in regard to the accused?'

'I apply, Your Honour, that she should be remanded to her former custody until I consult with the attorney-general.'

• • •

The smile that had begun to tweak Louisa's lips when she heard the foreman's announcement turned radiant after she had spoken with her counsel. Two hung juries. The law officers wouldn't bring her to trial on the same charge for a third time, surely. Such a situation would be unprecedented.

Chapter 25

> We have a criminal jury system . . . [whose] efficiency is only marred by the difficulty of finding twelve men every day who don't know anything and can't read.
>
> Mark Twain, Fourth of July speech, 1886

'As the judge who tried the case,' Justice Windeyer wrote to Attorney-General George Simpson soon afterwards, 'I think it right to inform you that, in my opinion, there has been a miscarriage of justice.'

Windeyer was annoyed at the hung verdict. He reported to Simpson that a plainer case of poisoning was hardly possible to conceive, and that there were circumstances connected with the trial that made the verdict most unsatisfactory. He wanted to alert the attorney-general officially—to begin with, at least. 'If you care to inquire into it, I will communicate it to you *personally*,' he added.

No doubt the attorney-general agreed to meet this important judicial figure; however, the reason for the requested meeting and the result of any such meeting was kept out of the official records. Did Windeyer want to discuss the impact of the juror's intrusion, or to recommend changes in court procedure or in the Crown's handling of Louisa's case so as to minimise the possibility of a future hung jury?

Meanwhile, prosecutor Henry Cohen was preparing his own letter to the attorney-general, in which he revealed that the breakdown of votes in Louisa's second trial was reportedly ten for an acquittal, one for a conviction, and one undecided. Louisa had almost walked out of the Darlinghurst courtroom a free woman—on the charge of killing her second husband, at least.

Cohen also offered his opinion about the Crown's future course of action. He remarked that the facts certainly pointed to Louisa having administered the poison that killed her husband; yet there was evidence that raised doubts about her guilt: namely, her persistence in seeking the doctor's assistance, her failure to dispose of the contents of the arsenic-filled tumbler, and her insistence that she alone had given Collins his nourishment. 'As I am asked whether she should be tried again for the offence of murdering the deceased Michael Peter Collins, I beg to state that, in my opinion, she should not be put upon her trial again to answer this charge, two juries having now disagreed upon the question of her guilt in this case.'

• • •

The public wasn't privy to the breakdown of the jurors' votes although it wasn't hard to comprehend the lack on unanimity in this second jury's deliberations. While motive remained a problem, another weapon had been added to the 'reasonable doubt' armoury. The juror's questions had been dynamite.

No doubt the 'not guilty' voters included the juror who had expressed scorn at the establishment for its ignorance about arsenic's use in the wool industry. Indeed, anyone associated with the industry knew of its uses and benefits—and the horrors of working with it. The juror might have explained to his brothers-in-sequestration that sheep needed to be 'dressed' at regular intervals; that is, they were immersed for a minute or two in a vat of liquid in the hope of eradicating ticks, lice and other skin-irritating parasites. While the liquid sometimes comprised carbolic acid or mercury salts or lime-and-sulphur or even tobacco, most shepherds and flock-masters praised arsenic as the most effective ingredient, not only because of its deadliness as a pest eradicator, but because enough arsenic might be absorbed through the sheep's skin to improve its fleece and increase its value. The benefits of arsenic-eating had penetrated even into the pastoral industry.

Some farmers purchased a brand-name product while others made up their own solution. Until the laws restricting its sale took effect, arsenic was easy to purchase by the hundredweight over the counter of many a grocery or huckster's store. It wasn't rare for a sheep to die an agonising death because a manufacturer or pastoralist was careless in his calculations or because the animal was exposed to the poison for too long.

The sheep-dippers dreaded the exercise. They knew that their struggles with recalcitrant sheep would expose their own skin to the dip's arsenic-laced contents. Some complained of a burning feeling in their bowels as if they were being consumed by fire—a sign of skin absorption. Most wore a protective waterproof apron or washed themselves thoroughly after completing their day's work. Nobody appreciated a raw, bleeding scrotum or one covered with blisters and boils.

Thus, no one with a sound knowledge of such practices would automatically assume that a man working in the industry who died of arsenic poisoning had been wilfully murdered. At the very least, the fact that a fleece-worker had been killed by the poison used to protect fleeces should offer some grounds for reasonable doubt, particularly if the other evidence was not altogether convincing.

No doubt, this brought to mind other stories of arsenic's deadly intrusion into the lives of the unwitting public. Arsenic not only filled the sheep-dip vats on pastoralists' properties and the basements of rat-infested tenements, it had a tendency to find itself on the dinner table because of its resemblance to foodstuffs like flour, sugar and baking powder. Other sources of dinner-table ingestion included crops sprayed with arsenic-laced pesticides and meat from animals that had ingested these pesticides. It could be found in wells in areas where arsenic was used as a rat poison and in the groundwater in districts where it was used in manufacturing. It could also be found in green paper, green yarn, green artificial flowers, green paint and green wallpaper. Those who worked with these products were the ones most likely to suffer symptoms of arsenic poisoning. Others might show the tiniest of traces in their systems—if tests were ever undertaken.

• • •

Even before receiving Cohen's letter, the attorney-general had been unsure if the Crown should try Louisa for a third time on the Collins charge. In mid-November, he advised the press of his indecision, yet also of his determination to pursue her for her first husband's murder. When he read Cohen's letter soon afterwards, he recognised that the barrister was not the best choice to lead the Andrews trial, let alone a third attempt at trying the Collins case if they decided to bring it to trial again.

The inquest depositions, recently collected witness statements and other pieces of investigative paperwork were passed to Charles Heydon, who had been authorised to prosecute the Andrews case. As Heydon and his team sifted through all the documents, they realised that the Andrews case was in many ways stronger than the Collins case. The Crown's inability to offer a solid motive was one of the main reasons for the prosecution's failure to convict Louisa in the first two trials. In the Andrews case, however, there were motives aplenty.

Some of this information would be critical as trial evidence. Most, though, wouldn't be needed for the purposes of a conviction so it wouldn't be brought out at trial. Still, it helped paint a picture of the troubled world of Pople's Terrace in the summer of 1886–87, in the period leading up to and after Charles Andrews' painful death.

Chapter 26

> Happy families are all alike; every unhappy family is unhappy in its own way.
>
> Leo Tolstoy, *Anna Karenina*

Senior Constable Sherwood knew that he was bringing unwelcome news when he arrived on the doorstep of 10 Pople's Terrace on Anniversary Day, 26 January 1887. Being informed that two of your boys had been getting up to mischief and were now in the lock-up wasn't the sort of information that parents enjoyed hearing, particularly when they were suffering financially.

Andrews had just lost his job. It wasn't his fault. He was reputed to be one of the hardest-working men in the district, even though at fifty-three he was, in the eyes of most, elderly. Since settling in Botany, he had worked for wool merchant Alexander Geddes; however, Geddes' nineteen-year-old business had shut its doors at the beginning of the month, forcing Andrews and his fellow workers into living off their savings. While jobs might be hard to find in these economically trying times, boarders weren't. George Osborne, James Wilkie and Augustus Nordgren were lodging in the back room of the Andrews house and their payments were helping to cover the family bills.

After Sherwood had explained to Louisa why he was visiting, he learnt that he wasn't just doubling the family's problems, but trebling them. She told him that Andrews was sick in bed, having been ill for the past few days. She didn't offer to take him to see her husband, so he was surprised to encounter the man later that afternoon in the Sir Joseph Banks Gardens. He asked Andrews about his health. Andrews complained of retching and vomiting but said that he was more concerned about his boys' plight. They discussed the situation, with Andrews praising the policeman for his efforts on the boys' behalf. Unbeknown to Sherwood, it would be the last time he saw the ailing man.

The following day, Sherwood spotted Louisa at the Redfern police court where the boys were facing a magistrate who'd decided they needed to be taught a salutary lesson. When Sherwood had a moment to speak to her, he asked how Andrews was feeling.

'Very bad,' she said. 'He's very ill and I think he is dying.'

• • •

John Rail, the secretary of the Mutual Life Assurance Company, heard a similar prognosis from Louisa the following Monday when she called at his company's city office. She told him her husband was ill and was not expected to recover. Could he provide details about her husband's life insurance policy?

'Is there a will?' Rail asked. 'If he has not prepared one, there will be a difficulty in getting the insurance money.'

Louisa said that her husband didn't have a will so she would need assistance in preparing one. Perhaps he could direct her to the right person. 'My husband will be leaving everything to me,' she assured him.

Rail felt sorry for her. 'If you get me a form,' he offered, 'I will write out the will for you.' He explained where the form could be obtained.

Louisa returned a short time later with the requisite form. He asked what she wanted the will to say. She said that it needed to make everything over to her: all her husband's money and insurance and other possessions. He filled in the details then told her how to get it witnessed, adding that, in the event of her husband's death, she should take it to Mr Dowling's office for probate.

Louisa wasted no time getting the necessary signatures. Neighbour Mary Law received a visit from her later that afternoon requesting that her husband witness the signing of the will. When Mary replied that James was out but would be available later, Louisa said she was in a hurry and would need to find someone else to help her.

Margaret Collis was standing near her back gate when Louisa called out to her, 'Is Mr Collis or any of the other men in?'

'No,' Margaret replied, 'but my brothers will be at dinnertime.'

'That won't do. I've been to Sydney and got the will drawn up and I want the witnesses to see him sign his name. I want it soon as Charlie is dying.'

'He is not that bad, is he?' asked her concerned neighbour.

'Yes, he's very bad. He'll never get out of his bed again. It will save me trouble to get the will signed before he dies.'

Mrs Stephen was standing nearby. She said that her husband would come over and sign the will. With William Farrar as the second signatory, the will was signed a short time later.

When Louisa called at the Botany police station that afternoon, Sherwood asked about Andrews and again received the answer that he was extremely ill. 'He might die any moment,' she added.

'If he's too bad for you to come to the court in the morning, you needn't mind,' said the concerned officer. 'You can send any person to take the boys home. They will be discharged by the magistrates.'

Even so, it was Louisa who fronted up the following day to collect her boys. To Sherwood's query about her husband's health, she said, 'He's very bad and will probably be dead when I get home.'

Sherwood thought that Louisa seemed surprisingly untroubled by her husband's condition, which was in marked contrast to her concern for the wellbeing of one of her sons. Yet she showed as little interest in the other miscreant as she had shown for her sick husband.

'You needn't have come,' Sherwood told her. 'I said I would send the boys.'

She shrugged it off.

'I'll get the case called as soon as possible so you can return home,' he assured her.

• • •

Having heard that Louisa was desperate to have her husband's will signed, James Law was surprised at her dismissive attitude when he dropped by on the Tuesday to enquire about Andrews' health.

'There's not much wrong with him,' she said unsympathetically, and headed into the back room, leaving Law to talk to Andrews alone.

Andrews was lying on a stretcher in the front room, clearly exhausted and anxious. Still, his voice remained strong when he complained of persistent vomiting and retching and of pains in his neck and shoulder. Either he was one of those usually healthy men who lost all stoicism at the onset of ill-health or his ailment was more serious than his wife was willing to admit.

When Dr Martin visited at four pm that same Tuesday, he thought that Andrews' condition was serious indeed, although not necessarily fatal. The news soon spread. Neighbours and friends dropped by to pass on their best wishes.

Charles Sayers visited around seven-thirty the following morning. Louisa was shifting Andrews' pillows to make him more comfortable. When Sayers asked how he was feeling, Andrews complained of constant vomiting, a burning sensation in his throat, and of pains in his bowels. 'If I don't get relief,' he said, his face etched with fear, 'I think I will die.'

The grocer had worked with Andrews prior to opening his store and knew he had a hardy constitution. The contrast was disturbing—even more so because the fellow was in such low spirits. Sayers tried to cheer him up, saying with kindness more than tact, 'You are worth half-a-dozen dead men.'

Another one-time co-worker, Henry Kneller, called in late the same morning. He too found Andrews in the front room with Louisa in attendance. Andrews politely asked after his wife and family, and they talked together for a while. About one pm Andrews gave two or three pronounced gasps. 'He is dying,' Kneller said gravely, looking at Louisa. Tears began to run down her cheeks. He left soon afterwards, saying that he would come back later in the afternoon. He was leaving them to say their private goodbyes.

• • •

Mary Law was the first to hear that Andrews was dead. Shortly after three pm, nine-year-old May Andrews came to her house saying that her father had just died and that her mother wanted Mary to come over. Mary accompanied the child back to the house and saw Andrews' body lying on the stretcher. No attempt had been made to straighten him out, let alone to tend him in any other way. She found Louisa dressing, showing no signs of distress. Was she going out? So soon?

'I am going to Sydney by the next tram to let the insurance people know and to go to the Savings Bank,' Louisa said. Then she asked her daughter to purchase some tram tickets while she finished getting ready.

John Rail confirmed the precipitateness of Louisa's visit. He was at work at the Mutual Life Assurance Company that afternoon when she returned to the office.

'My husband has just died,' she informed him.

He offered his condolences and asked when the man had died.

'About half an hour ago.'

• • •

Ellen Price, the midwife and body-washer, entered the picture much later than normal. Around eight o'clock that night, she received a message saying that Mrs Andrews required her services. She caught the next tram and found Louisa on board. She asked why Louisa wanted her.

'Mr Andrews is dead,' Louisa said.

'What did he die of?'

'He was only sick about a week and was suffering from diarrhoea.'

'It is very sad,' Ellen said. She was surprised when Louisa didn't answer.

Reaching the Andrews house, Ellen found the body on the stretcher near the window, straightened and suitably positioned. When she touched the body, she discovered it was stiff and cold. Obviously, he had been dead for hours.

'It is a pity you did not send for me sooner,' she admonished Louisa, knowing that rigor mortis would make it difficult to tend to the body.

Henry Kneller was standing nearby. He said, 'Poor fellow. I straightened him. She went away in the tram when he died.'

'I had business I had to attend to,' Louisa said. Yet Ellen noticed that, even with her husband's body in the same room, she seemed untroubled by his death. Instead, she scolded her boys, saying, 'Why did you let the fire go out? You knew your mother would want a cup of tea.'

'When are you going to send word to Herby?' asked her second eldest son, Reuben, knowing that his brother in Newcastle would want to be informed.

Reuben's return home that day had been unexpected. He too had lost his job when Alexander Geddes' business closed, although he had managed to find work at Rookwood. Journeying home after a week's employment, he had encountered his weeping mother in the same tram. She told him of his father's death.

'I will be in no hurry to let Herby know,' Louisa told him. 'I don't want him and won't have him.'

• • •

Neighbours trooped to the house the following day to farewell Andrews. After Margaret Collis had expressed her condolences, she mentioned seeing Louisa catch the tram the previous afternoon and wondered where she had been going. Louisa said that she had gone to see the insurance doctor before Charlie was washed and laid out because the insurance doctor hadn't attended him. She had been fearful there might be trouble over his death for that reason and was concerned because of the will.

Friday was the day of the funeral. Her observant neighbours noticed that Louisa was suitably dressed and veiled when she rode off in the funeral coach—with her old boarder, Mick Collins, accompanying her. Afterwards, instead of adhering to the mourning tradition of wearing black clothes and accessories for a year, her only concession was to wear a black hat.

Two days later, Margaret Collis and Mary Law saw the pair walking arm in arm. Mary sniffed, 'That looks nice, the poor man hardly cold yet.'

The following morning, Ellen Price saw them near her own home waiting for a Sydney tram. She noticed that Louisa had discarded her mourning attire altogether and wondered where they were heading.

William Scott was able to answer that question. An employer of the Haymarket branch of the Government Savings Bank, he attended Louisa that day. When he asked how he could help her, she reported that her husband had just died and that she needed to have his money released straight away. She had already been to the office of solicitor James Dowling with a note of introduction from the secretary of her husband's insurance company and had signed the necessary paperwork. Dowling had told her to take the paperwork to the bank to close Andrews' account.

Scott explained that such money was not released for a month after a death was reported so the paperwork could be thoroughly examined.

Louisa begged him to help her, saying that she greatly needed the money. Her financial predicament was easy enough to describe: deceased husband who had been unemployed for a few weeks; children to feed; medical bills.

Scott took pity on her and said he would make an exception to the usual rule. He told her to come back the following day to collect her money—the sum of £10 5s 4d. It was equivalent to a month of her husband's wages.

That night, Collins moved back into Louisa's cottage.

Naturally, the neighbours gossiped about it, wondering if the couple had already tied the knot. A week later, Mary Law saw the pair waiting for the tram, dressed in normal attire. Later that day, she spotted them returning home. 'Well, have you done it?' she asked. 'Am I to wish you joy?'

'Oh, it's all over long ago,' Collins said. Then he laughed and Louisa joined in.

Obviously, the neighbours were not aware that the joyous day wouldn't transpire for another two months. In fact, the date of their nuptials fell two days after probate was completed and Louisa received the insurance payout of £178.

The neighbours did notice that Collins chose not to seek work after moving in with Louisa and that, a couple of months later, the pair went on a spending spree. The once-impoverished Collins began strutting around in a new suit and sporting a watch and chain. He also took a trip to Melbourne to visit his family. Louisa treated herself to new clothes and furniture. No doubt, the photograph of the well-dressed couple that had been published in the illustrated newspapers, the photograph that Louisa had begged Senior Constable Sherwood to send her, was taken around the same time.

Eventually, according to neighbours, Collins was forced to find work, although his efforts were sporadic. When the employment situation in Botany worsened, the family moved to Waterloo, where their baby John was born on 28 November.[5] Louisa dealt with the social niceties by declaring on his birth certificate that she and Mick had been married on 13 February 1887, around the time of the Pople's Terrace dance.

In February 1888, the family returned to Botany—to cottage number one in Pople's Terrace, not far from their previous residence. There the baby died two months later. It was then, according to Louisa's own family, that she began to drink heavily and that tension began to develop in the Collins household.

Chapter 27

> Louisa Collins, unless the unanimous verdict of the press and the public has done her a grievous wrong, proceeded to do to death her first husband by small doses of arsenic with a serenity, with a profound calmness, comparable only to that of some snake deliberately killing and swallowing a rabbit or a squirrel.
>
> *Brisbane Courier*

Justice Sir Joseph Innes looked with interest at Louisa, whose face bore its usual expression of stolid indifference. He was presiding over her third trial, although the charge in this instance related to the killing of her first husband, Charles Andrews. Opening his notebook, he wrote 'Regina v. Louisa Collins' and the date, 19 November 1888. He added, 'She is a good looking woman of about 38 or 40, dark hair, about five foot six inches, rather slight, big eyes looking somewhat hollow now.' He also mentioned the previous unsuccessful attempts to convict her.

Innes himself had a murky heritage. He was a grandson of Australia's most famous female convict, the English horse-stealer and colonial businesswoman, Mary Reibey. Openly ambitious, he had used politics as a springboard to a seat on the bench, much to the disgust of the *Bulletin*'s editor, who pointed out that he had never achieved the legal eminence to warrant such an honour. A man of deep emotion and empathy, Innes was once so distressed at pronouncing a death sentence that he told the prisoner's counsel to find something—anything—that could be used to argue for mercy. Would he need to do so in Louisa's case as well?

The new prosecutor, Charles Heydon, stood up and began his opening address, indicating to the court that he was taking a broader view of the case than suggested by the indictment. 'I am entitled,' he declared as if challenging the judge to stop him, 'to produce evidence showing that another person, to whom the prisoner had access, died from the effects of arsenical poisoning.' He cited several cases as precedents.

Justice Innes was wary about this approach, declaring that he would reserve his ruling until the actual evidence was tendered.

There was little sign of Heydon's proposed strategy when his first witnesses testified. They repeated much of the information elicited at the Andrews inquest four months previously. Dr Martin reported that the death certificate he had signed listed 'acute gastroenteritis' as the cause of death but he now had a different opinion. He had thought it an odd case at the time because his medicine usually checked the vomiting caused by gastroenteritis. Moreover, constipation was more common than diarrhoea in cases of gastroenteritis, while the vomiting/purging combination was more common when an irritant poison like arsenic had been ingested. Since arsenic had been found in Andrews' remains, he now believed that arsenic poisoning caused the gastroenteritis that led to Andrews' death.

The government analyst provided another brief but precise description of his tests and discoveries; however, Judge Innes was troubled by the possibility of inaccuracy when dealing with such tiny proportions. 'Small as this amount appears to be to us, are you sure that you have made no mistake about tracing it?'

'None whatever, Your Honour,' Hamlet reassured him. 'I could detect a five-thousandth part of a grain.'

When the prosecutor asked if more arsenic might have been present at the time of Andrews' burial—if the coffin's deteriorated condition, for example, could have had some impact—Hamlet replied that the water that drained from the coffin might have dissolved the arsenic in Andrews' body and carried it away.

Upon cross-examination, Lusk queried if the opposite might have occurred. Could the arsenic have entered Andrews' body after death rather than before?

Hamlet admitted that this was feasible. 'The possibility is present of arsenic being in the soil or in the coffin plate or metal fittings or dyed substances used in the coffin.'

This was not the answer the prosecution wanted the jury to hear. It offered the type of reasonable doubt that could torpedo the Crown's third attempt at convicting the woman. When Heydon asked if post-death absorption was likely, Hamlet said that he had analysed soil samples from three different areas in the coffin's vicinity without finding any traces of arsenic. He thought it more likely that the arsenic had been introduced into Andrews' body during his lifetime.

Lusk raised another possibility: that the arsenic might have been ingested as an impurity in the bismuth prescribed by the doctor.

'Bismuth is sometimes impure,' Hamlet conceded, before adding that Inspector Hyem had collected some bismuth from the chemist shop responsible for preparing Andrews' medicine, and that he himself had tested it without discovering any traces of arsenic. 'The bismuth sold in Sydney is generally pure,' he added.

Was Lusk going to point out that 'generally' was not a strong enough confirmation when a woman's life was at stake? Would he ask if the bismuth sample tested in August 1888 was extracted from the same bottle used in January 1887? Given the popularity of bismuth in medical preparations, the answer should have been obvious. Yet he failed to ask this critical question.

Lusk returned to the question of the water-filled coffin when the post-mortem doctor testified, asking Knaggs if he thought it likely that the water had washed away some of the arsenic.

Knaggs said that the water had barely reached the centre of the body. 'I don't think it reached the stomach. The water was not washing through the body and any arsenic in the body would not in my opinion have been washed away by the water.'

• • •

As the sun sank towards the horizon, the first of Louisa's children was called to the witness box. Previously, only the testimony of Louisa's daughter had been incriminating; however, this trial dealt with the death of the children's father. Could the older boys have information to support the prosecution's case?

Arthur talked about the quarrel that had led to Collins' ejection from the house, adding that the friction between his parents hadn't ended there. One evening, shortly before his father's illness, his parents had been in the front room arguing. Then his father said something he would never forget. 'He said, "You and Collins wish me dead," ' Arthur told the jury, adding, 'He said this at a time prior to his death.'

'Well, I presume it was,' was the judge's dry interjection.

'My father seemed angry when he made use of the expression,' Arthur continued. 'He was talking pretty loud and sharp to Mother. Mother said something in a low tone of voice, but I can't remember what.'

The prosecution asked about Collins' return to the house after Arthur's father's death. As Arthur mentioned the dance in the neighbouring cottage, heads pivoted towards Louisa—not to see her reaction to her son's comments, but because she had laughed. It was odd behaviour from a very odd woman.

Their attention was drawn back to the witness box when Lusk questioned Arthur about his parents' relationship. Arthur said that he had often heard his father say angry and nasty words to his mother. His father's alcohol intake? Arthur admitted that his father drank a lot of beer; however, he was never drunk.

Everyone in the courtroom knew that alcohol was usually an issue when wives killed their husbands. Seemingly, Andrews was not an inebriate who failed to pull his punches when his wife displeased him—not that wife-beating justified husband-killing. Still, it might have offered the type of mitigating factor that a judge like Innes could use to recommend mercy.

Then the prosecutor called May Andrews.

As Lusk listened to the child telling the jury how she had seen Rough on Rats in her home shortly before her father died and also before Collins died, he realised they had reached the moment that Heydon had alluded to, the moment when the Crown would attempt to try Louisa for the deaths of both husbands rather than Andrews alone. He asked the judge, 'Can the Crown produce evidence of this nature to show that a person who had died subsequently had exhibited similar symptoms and that the prisoner had had access to the person?'

The point was argued at length by both sides with various authorities being quoted. Heydon indicated that it was important from a probative perspective. Lusk expressed his concern that it was too prejudicial. Innes said that the jurors would be intelligent enough to know that it wasn't their responsibility to determine whether Louisa had poisoned Collins; rather, the question was whether the evidence about Collins' death was relevant in the Andrews trial because of the similarities between the cases. He felt that the arguments on both sides had merit and that he would be failing in his duty if he rejected the evidence. The prosecutor could continue.

And with that important ruling, Heydon asked the girl to repeat all the devastating details she had provided at the previous two trials. Then he called or recalled other witnesses to do the same. Soon, all the evidence covering 'means' and 'opportunity' for both cases and 'motive' for the Andrews case had been introduced.

Most of the evidence had been brought to light in previous trials, although Louisa's neighbour Margaret Collis had some new information to share. She told the court that she had been sitting with Louisa late on the Saturday night before Collins' death when Louisa made a revealing comment. 'She said she never liked Andrews,' Margaret told the court. 'She said, "My mother forced me to marry him because he had money and was comfortable, but I never liked him. I hated him and all belonging to him."' Louisa also said that she didn't like Andrews' children either, that the only child she did like was Mick's baby, the infant who had died.

Lusk asked how they had come to have such a conversation.

'She was saying how much better she liked Collins,' Mrs Collis explained. 'The conversation came up about her disliking all of Andrews' brothers and the children. She said she liked Collins, though.'

• • •

When Lusk commenced his defence, the *Evening News* correspondent was startled to recognise his only witness. It wasn't because the man had testified at a previous trial; rather, he had been one of the jurors. And here he was testifying in Louisa's defence.

Lusk asked wool merchant Alexander Geddes if arsenic was used in processing the skins. Geddes said that some of the squatters put arsenic over the skins to preserve them from weevils. He added that some of the men experienced sore hands, but that the effects had never been serious.

Soon afterwards, the jurors were locked up for the night with Geddes' evidence echoing in their minds. Perhaps Andrews had indeed suffered a severe case of gastroenteritis, with the minuscule traces of arsenic in his remains resulting from contact with arsenic while working at the wool yard.

Chapter 28

How oft the sight of means to do ill deeds make deeds ill done!

William Shakespeare, *The Life and Death of King John*

The morning's *Herald* was filled with news from abroad, the agony caused by the silent telegraph cable being an almost-forgotten memory. Among the colonial news was a discussion about an equally important link with the outside world: the individual who represented the Queen's supreme authority, the Governor of New South Wales.

Those with a particular interest in Louisa's case were watching out for developments that might have an impact. The identity of the governor—more accurately, the man's personality and political views—was among them. The current governor, Lord Robert Carrington, had been appointed three years earlier in an experiment of sorts. He was the first of the 'non-professional' governors to be given such a posting—the 'untried and juvenile noblemen,' a bitter ex-governor would snipe—yet he had fulfilled his political and social duties so admirably that similar appointments had already been made. Some would prove less satisfactory. Accordingly, Sir Henry Parkes was asking the New South Wales Legislative Assembly to vote this day on the subject of governor appointments, namely to implore the

English authorities to allow the colonial governments the right to veto their choices.

The community knew that the current governor had a few more years to serve so the impact on New South Wales wouldn't be felt for some years. Nevertheless, the article was a reminder of the role Lord Carrington might play in Louisa's life—and prospective death—if the court's verdict did not go her way.

Elsewhere, the *Herald* provided a detailed report about her case, adding that Lusk would begin his closing address when court resumed at ten am.

• • •

'I submit that the evidence given by the prosecution was wholly inadequate to prove that Charles Andrews was poisoned at all,' declared Lusk as he began summarising the case. He reminded the jury that Andrews' doctor hadn't suspected poison at the time of his death and had only remembered the case fifteen months later when another incident led him to question his diagnosis. 'It makes all the difference in the world through what medium a person looks at bygone events,' he warned sagely.

He moved on to the subject of the chemical evidence, saying that the minute traces of arsenic could have entered Andrews' body after death and that there was no evidence to prove that arsenic had been present prior to death. That being the case, there could be no presumption that Andrews had, in fact, been the victim of a deliberate poisoning.

As for the evidence suggesting that Louisa Collins had poisoned Andrews, that too was weak. True, she had evinced a strong liking for another man while her husband was living, but her social and moral character was not on trial. The Crown had argued that she killed her first husband to obtain his money, but the evidence showed that she was not the only person to benefit. 'I do not wish to say anything disrespectful of the dead, but there was one other person who profited more by Andrews' death than the accused did, and there has been nothing whatever to show that Collins himself had not easy means for administering the arsenic, if arsenic had been administered at all.'

He finished by urging the jury to dismiss all that had been said regarding Collins' death. 'You must deal with the present case upon its own merits and give the accused the benefit of any doubt which might arise in your minds.'

Justice Innes had made only brief notes during Lusk's one-hundred-minute address; nevertheless, he silently applauded the man's endeavours by jotting in his notebook, 'A capital speech.' Then he signalled that he was ready to hear the Crown's closing address.

Heydon drew the jury's attention to the history of Andrews' illness and to the similarities between his death and that of Collins. He asserted that the Crown had shown that Louisa was the only person who could have administered the arsenic that killed her first husband, and that she had two strong motives for doing so: to obtain Andrews' money and to marry Collins. 'The suggestion made by the counsel for the accused—that the deceased might have been poisoned by Collins—will not admit of belief at all,' he added scornfully. 'I contend that there is only one conclusion at which you could arrive, which is that the accused is guilty of the crime with which she has been charged.'

'A conclusive and pitiless reply,' Justice Innes jotted in his notes.

• • •

The courtroom regulars knew that the judge's direction to the jury not only heavily influenced the decision-making process, it was, for that reason, a clue to the likely verdict. In Louisa's first trial, Justice Foster had been impartial and the jury had split almost evenly. In her second trial, Justice Windeyer had made clear his conviction that she was guilty, yet ten of the jurors had voted for an acquittal. If Justice Innes also directed the jury towards a guilty verdict, what chance did she have of dodging this third bullet?

Everyone listened closely as Innes began his summation. He told the jury that they needed to decide if arsenic was the cause of Andrews' death or if the traces might have come from his coffin or the surrounding soil or even his work. If they were of the opinion that arsenic had killed Andrews, they had to decide if it had been deliberately administered and, if so, whether his wife was responsible. He drew the jurors' attention to the fact that the Crown's case offered opportunity—Louisa was the only person looking after Andrews—and also motive: passion and money. He added dryly that, while she had shown a great want of decency in her haste to possess both of them, the jury would also have to consider the possibility that Collins himself had committed the crime.

Then there was the question of means. He said, 'Even supposing that the box of Rough on Rats was introduced into the house for the purpose of destroying rats, still the jury would have to consider whether, having it at hand at the time she became seized with her passion for Collins, she was not tempted to use it.'

Finally, he told the jurors that they mustn't allow themselves to be influenced by any opinions they might have formed regarding Collins' death as the evidence was admitted only to show that two persons who were attended by the same person had died from arsenical poisoning. With a few additional words about guilt, innocence and reasonable doubt, he ordered the jury to retire and consider their verdict.

At two forty-five pm, the jury filed from the courtroom. At five o'clock, a clerk hurried from the jury room bearing a message for the judge.

Chapter 29

> No court presumes to tell a jury that they are to try a capital case with the same indifference and unconcern as . . . a case where the results of their decision would be less important.
>
> Lysander Spooner, *The Illegality of the Trial of John W. Webster*

It had happened again! Another hung jury. Another unsatisfactory non-verdict.

A few weeks hence, radical parliamentarian David Buchanan would write to the *Sydney Morning Herald* railing against the law requiring unanimous jury verdicts, and citing Louisa's trials as evidence of the problems it caused. He argued that, under this law, the opinions of eleven honest, upright men (or perhaps ten or nine) could be set aside by that of one man. He admitted that the resisting juror might also be honest and upright, yet wasn't the judgement of eleven men more likely to be accurate than that of one? Alternatively, the resister might have reached his opinion from private considerations—there were black sheep in all societies—and by his single voice negate the combined votes of the eleven. 'As human nature exists, and ever will exist, it is little short of lunacy to demand unanimity from any body of men empowered to decide any given thing under the sun,' he asserted.

He added with wry perspicacity, 'What chance would there be for legislation if the parliament was required to be unanimous in all it did?'

While Buchanan failed to provide any reasons as to why 'honest, upright' jurors—or black sheep, for that matter—might deliberately hold out against a conviction, the public knew of one reason at least: the death penalty. 'The opponents of the death penalty are now so many, and so determined, that it is very seldom that a jury does not include one or more of them,' observed the *Australian Star*, 'and when such men are included, the jury in capital cases degenerates into a debating society formed to argue the point as to whether capital punishment should be abolished. The question of guilt or innocence becomes of secondary consequence.'

Was anyone aware that one of the jurors was in fact an opponent of capital punishment, a man named Henry Prior Palser who had helped found the Society for the Abolition of Capital Punishment two decades previously? No doubt he was one of the jurors who thought there was not enough evidence to justify an execution.

The increasing aversion to capital punishment was a problem faced by many societies that retained death as the ultimate sanction. When the community that supplied jurors was not unanimous in its support for the law's legislated punishment of death, it created not only a legal quandary, but a personal one. The power to order a judicial execution was put into the hands of ordinary individuals, men who had not asked for such a responsibility nor necessarily believed in the principle of 'an eye for an eye', lawful though it might be. Even those in favour of capital punishment soon realised that there was a gulf between stating *in principle* that one was willing to follow the law's sentencing regulations and the reality of looking into the eyes of a person standing only a few feet away and ordering their execution. It was not just a question of society's laws, but of individual conscience.

Another parliamentarian declared that there would be more convictions if it were not for the death penalty, that jurors were more likely to err on the side of mercy for fear that the punishment might be too great. A letter-writer disagreed, saying that such a comment reflected poorly on the integrity of the juries in Louisa's trials. 'Doesn't the honourable member know that these juries were sworn to give a true verdict and, if so, did he not insinuate that they infringed that dreadful oath?'

But what did a 'true verdict' truly mean? In fact, what did 'beyond reasonable doubt'—the grounds for a 'true verdict'—actually mean?

While both capital and non-capital cases should—in the eyes of the law—require the same degree of certainty, the term 'beyond reasonable doubt' was never defined in such a way that jurors had a simple set of rules to follow. It was ephemeral, elusive, an invisible fence positioned somewhere along the spectrum between certain guilt and undoubted innocence. In each trial, it was the jurors' role to make a calculated guess as to where that fence might sit, a particularly difficult guess when only circumstantial evidence was available. Such a guess could be made with relative equanimity when the accused's family and friends stood on one side of the fence and a gaolhouse door on the other. However, when the gaolhouse door was replaced by the gallows, that guess was a life or death decision. Inevitably, the jurors found themselves under another sort of pressure, with the result that one eye remained focused on the evidence, on trying to determine where that 'reasonable doubt' fence should be placed, while the other was drawn inexorably towards the grim spectacle of the gallows. Human nature being what it was, the 'beyond reasonable doubt' fence was inevitably positioned differently in a capital trial, so much so that a unanimous guilty verdict was harder to achieve. It was one of the many reasons why the cry against capital punishment would ultimately be heard.

Certainly, the problems with hung juries didn't end with their non-verdict. What about the right to a future fair trial? If the mere act of standing in the dock was prejudicial, what statement was being made to the jury when the accused was returned to the dock? Indeed, what statement was being made when Louisa was returned over and over again on what were almost the same charges? No person walking into the jury box could have been unaware of her story or of the authorities' persistent attempts to convict her. No potential juror could have failed to hear the authorities' silent scream: 'Listen here! Do you think we would have brought her to trial for the second . . . or third . . . or even fourth time if we were not absolutely certain of her guilt?'

There were further problems associated with bringing her to trial so many times. Each time the witnesses testified, their memories were reinforced through repetition. Yet it wasn't repetition alone that acted as a reinforcement. Their moment of fame wasn't limited to the witness box. The press printed their testimonies almost verbatim—not just a single newspaper, but many of them. What witness wouldn't buy the newspapers to see what was written? What witness would limit his or her reading to a single instance? Indeed, some witnesses might even read the reports to friends and relations, or act out the original encounter so as to claim the limelight for an instant longer. As they read the reports, they wouldn't restrict themselves to their own testimonies. They would read those of the other witnesses as well, accounts of statements they might otherwise have never heard. Each witness statement was like a piece of a jigsaw puzzle so, by reading the other statements, the witnesses could see where their own piece lay and what picture it helped to paint. The net effect wasn't just the reinforcement of their own testimonies; rather, it perfected each link in the circumstantial chain. Each time Louisa was put to trial, the chain of evidence presented to the court was neater and stronger and harder to break and the chances of a conviction increased. Would the authorities attempt to do so enough times to obtain their desired result?

So it appeared. Soon after the third hung verdict was announced, the newspapers reported that Louisa was to be tried a fourth time. Which husband? A third attempt would be made to convict her of the Collins murder. But if this prosecution also failed, the Crown would probably abandon the idea of putting her to trial for a fifth time.

Many were surprised that the Crown hadn't already abandoned its pursuit. There were substantial financial costs associated with each of Louisa's lengthy murder trials—unlike the majority of criminal trials that were completed within a day. Furthermore, there were rumbles in the community about the Crown's repeated attempts to convict her. Many thought the authorities had already crossed the line.

Meanwhile, the Crown seemed to be doing everything in its power to ensure a conviction in Louisa's fourth trial. In fact, parliamentarian Thomas Walker would later claim that the Crown organised to have the scheduled trial judge replaced with one of its choosing. 'Mr Justice Stephen has not power, eloquence, and force enough to convince a jury of this country,' Walker said by way of explanation, 'so arrangements were made to get a particular judge who, because of his force of language, his clearness of diction, and other qualities of a judge, would be able to get a jury to convict her.' The scheduled judge, Matthew Stephen, was indeed replaced at the last minute, seemingly at the urging of the Crown according to a letter written by the prosecutor himself. And Stephen's replacement was one whose position did indeed attest to his pre-eminence in judicial circles.

Was this the only reason for the last-minute change? Another parliamentarian would reveal that Stephen had expressed concern about the impropriety of repeatedly bringing Louisa's children to court to secure their mother's conviction, particularly when they were forced to loiter among its population of undesirables. So was the Crown's reason for ousting Justice Stephen partly founded on a fear that he might intercede in its decision to call the children as witnesses? The Crown knew that without May's testimony it had no 'means' in addition to the problematic lack of motive. Without May's testimony it had no case.

Chapter 30

The cursed crimes of the secret poisoner
We must confess are the worst of all,
You bless the hand that smooths your pillow
But by that hand you surely fall.
You put your trust in those about you,
When you lie sick upon your bed,
While you are blessing they are wishing
The very next moment would find you dead.

Chambers' Edinburgh Journal

And so it began again, the extraordinary case that refused to go away. Trial four; hearing six. Another packed courtroom. This time the biggest wig of the legal bigwigs was presiding: Chief Justice Sir Frederick Darley.

Darley was so distinguished in appearance, so dignified in his air of command, that he looked as if he were born to wear the robes of office. His was indeed a forthright voice of authority making pragmatic decisions that would serve society well for a quarter of a century. Yet history would also condemn his judicial pronouncements as sometimes lacking legal brilliance. Would his rulings reflect wisdom or imprudence when he presided over Louisa's fourth trial?

Charles Heydon was again the lead prosecutor when the trial began on Wednesday, 5 December; it had been delayed for two days to allow Darley to preside. Naturally, as Heydon began his opening address, he didn't mention the Crown's previously unsuccessful attempts to convict Louisa, the three abortive prosecutions that hovered like ghosts behind the jury box.

Although paler than the last time, Louisa still appeared calm and collected according to the *Evening News* journalist—a praise of sorts, if she were a man. 'Callous,' spat other reporters, seeing her dauntlessness as 'unfeminine' and a sign of the cold-blooded nature of the killer they believed her to be.

The Crown began its case by calling Dr George Marshall. The only time the courtroom regulars pricked up their ears was when Lusk asked why he had failed to find arsenic during his own testing procedures.

'I did not strictly follow the rules for making the Reinsch test,' Marshall admitted. 'I did not allow sufficient time to elapse to allow arsenic to deposit on the copper.' He added that, some weeks later, when he had looked again at the test tube and copper foil, he had noticed unmistakable traces of arsenic.

The members of the prosecution recognised that Louisa's counsel had just made their case easier for them.

Constable Jeffes was the next to testify, followed by the government analyst, then by Louisa's children. Heydon was determined to drive home the most damning evidence at the start of the proceedings. Both Fred and May told the court that, on separate occasions, they had each poured condensed milk from a jug into their cups of tea but that their mother had stopped them from drinking the brew, saying that the condensed milk was only for Collins.

Louisa remained cool and self-possessed while her children hammered more nails into her coffin. Her pride wouldn't let her show the court how betrayed she felt.

• • •

Heydon was pleased. The critical testimonies of the doctor, constable and government analyst had built a robust cage of circumstantial evidence. Louisa's three children had succeeded in pushing her inside by offering opportunity, means and a motive of sorts. But could he lock the cage door? The prosecution hadn't succeeded in the previous trials partly because of doubts about how the arsenic had found its way into the men's bodies. Heydon hoped that his larger array of expert witnesses would succeed in quashing those inconvenient doubts.

However, the prosecutor felt the key to the cage slip from his fingers when Dr Milford, who had conducted Collins' post-mortem examination, returned to the witness box. Milford reported that he had noticed a considerable discharge from the wound on Collins' leg and a disagreeable smell. If an open wound was dressed with arsenic paste, he explained, it would be absorbed more quickly than undamaged skin, which might account for the large quantity of arsenic found in Collins' body. He mentioned cases in which such a situation had occurred.

A juror asked if anything about Collins' leg sore suggested that arsenic paste had been applied to it. Milford replied that it did not appear to have been healed or treated but that Collins probably knew that arsenic paste would prevent a bad smell from arising so he might have treated himself in such a way.

'Pardon me?' said Mr Heydon. '*I* did not know that. Why must *he* have known it?'

'Oh, pardon me,' was Milford's polite response. 'I have given evidence in this case two or three times and have heard all that has been said about curing skins with arsenic. The deceased must have known that arsenic is used for curing skins.'

Heydon had a witness lined up to counter any skin-absorption claims. Sydney University's Dr Alexander McCormick told the jury unequivocally, 'If arsenical paste had been applied to the wound on Collins' leg, he would have died from poisoning before five grains of arsenic could have accumulated in his system. If the paste was strong, it would destroy the tissues; if weak, it would cause irritation at the place where it was applied. Considering the quantity of arsenic found in Collins' body, I think it is impossible for it to have been absorbed by the wound on his leg.'

• • •

Dr Martin's evidence was a crucial part of Heydon's strategy. He asked the doctor detailed questions about Charles Andrews' death in February 1887 and the conclusions he had reached then and now. He then questioned him about the death of the Collins infant, eliciting from Martin that the child was five months old when it died in April 1888 and was not premature.

Lusk called out, 'I object to the character of the evidence being adduced as it tends to show a motive for getting rid of Andrews. I cannot see how it can possibly affect the present case.'

No one had the slightest doubt that he was objecting because he could see most clearly how the evidence would affect the present case. Heydon was attempting to repeat the strategy used in the Andrews trial, that of introducing evidence about the other husband's death so as to suggest a pattern of murderous behaviour on Louisa's part.

The judge turned to Heydon. 'Unless you intend to show a motive for Collins' death, the testimony could be regarded as not pertinent.'

'If light could be thrown on the relationship existing between the prisoner and Collins, light would be thrown upon the case,' said Heydon.

'Is there not in the evidence a suggestion that the motive was for the murder of Andrews and not of Collins?' Darley asked.

'The question is a difficult one to answer,' Heydon said, sliding around the unwanted challenge. 'Nevertheless, the course of the evidence in chief might tend to throw some light on the family history with regard to Collins.'

Darley decided to allow Heydon to continue his line of questioning. Lusk accepted his ruling without asking that the point be reserved for later consideration, a request that a more skilled barrister—or a healthier one—would have made. Similarly to the previous day, he asked for an adjournment when the clock reached five-thirty pm. He had been feeling ill on the first day of the trial and was still unwell on this even more critical second day.

• • •

The prosecution finished with its witnesses the following day. Just before the midday break, a court official handed a telegram to a juror. The juror read it and called out 'It is all right' in an attempt to communicate a message to a spectator. The judge didn't appear to notice, but Louisa did. She was paying closer attention to the proceedings than most people realised.

In the afternoon session, Lusk called only two witnesses in Louisa's defence: a boarder who testified that Collins and Louisa had lived on good terms, and one of Collins' workmates who provided information about the day he fell ill. At four thirty-three pm, Lusk informed the chief justice that the defence had no further witnesses.

It was a simple statement that spoke volumes to everyone in the courtroom. The end was nigh. After two inquests and three previous trials, the current trial had witnessed few startling revelations; yet, what might have seemed banal through repetition was still dramatic when set against the backdrop of the gallows. Moreover, whatever the verdict, Louisa Collins would not be seen in the dock again. Even if this jury was unable to reach a verdict, the Crown wouldn't risk bringing her to trial for a fifth time. Four failures would not simply be a misfortune; it would be politically mortifying.

As the jurors moulded their faces into suitably solemn expressions, Lusk began his fourth closing address. No motive; an arsenic-filled tumbler that seemingly had been tampered with; reasonable doubt. The courtroom regulars had heard it all before. As for the Andrews evidence, Lusk said that the jury should discard it. 'In Collins' case, we are dealing with something substantial, inasmuch as the man died from arsenical poisoning; but in the case of Andrews we are simply dealing with vague suspicions. If Andrews was not proved to have died of poison, then all the evidence which has been submitted is completely thrown away.' On the other hand, even if the jury was satisfied that Andrews had died from arsenical poisoning, it proved little as there was a reasonable possibility that some other person had committed the deed.

After speaking for two hours, he offered his concluding remark: 'I submit that the case admits of doubt from beginning to end and that it is your duty to give the accused the benefit of the doubt and acquit her.'

With the courtroom dimming as night fell, Darley indicated that he would not begin his summing up until the morning. There was still time, though, to hear the prosecution's closing address.

Heydon's was a carefully crafted address, not only in its presentation of the facts but in its deliberate manipulation. He appealed not just to the jurymen's intellect but, more importantly, to their egos. He began by declaring that Mrs Collins' guilt had been conclusively proven, that the prosecution had clearly shown that Collins had been poisoned by a series of arsenic doses and that Collins' wife was the only person who could have administered those doses. He added, 'I contend that no sensible man could for an instant bring himself to believe that the most direct and most positive evidence of wilful poisoning had not been adduced—and abundantly adduced.' Attempting to stave off any reluctance to convict, he told the jurors that they mustn't let themselves be paralysed by their feelings and responsibility. And he admonished them sternly, 'If you return a verdict of not guilty, you will proclaim yourselves unfit for the grave duty that has been cast upon you.'

At seven-fifty pm, when the judge adjourned the trial for the evening, the jurors retired with the prosecutor's words ringing in their ears. If you pride yourself on being sensible, the Crown was telling them, you will accept the evidence of wilful poisoning. If you consider yourself worthy of the grave responsibility of sitting on a jury, you will put aside your emotions and convict the woman of murder.

Heydon had eliminated four jurors before accepting the twelve he was addressing, perhaps in an attempt to make sure that this jury didn't contain any men with an aversion to capital punishment. These jurors had been deliberately chosen to embody the ideal of 'twelve good men and true', so the prosecutor's demand went directly to the heart of *who* they were. Yet there was a subtle challenge underlying his words, one that went to the heart of *what* they were. 'Only the lily-livered would be afraid to uphold the law,' the Crown was saying.

It took a certain type of man to resist such a challenge to his masculinity and Heydon was hoping that none was sitting on his jury.

Chapter 31

A jury consists of twelve persons chosen to decide who has the better lawyer.

Robert Frost, quoted in *Fire and Ice: The Art and Thought of Robert Frost*

Early on Saturday 8 December, warders escorted Louisa from her cell to the stone steps leading to the tunnel entrance. At the bottom of the steps stood a large iron door. She waited while the key squealed in its lock then she passed through the doorway and began walking along the narrow, low-ceilinged tunnel built of immense sandstone blocks. It was impossible not to feel dread as the courthouse entrance loomed closer and closer.

According to the press reports, she would never walk along the tunnel towards the courthouse again. But would she be making the return journey? If she were lucky—if the jury decided she was not guilty or was unable to reach a verdict—the courthouse doors would open to release her to freedom. But if the jury decided she was guilty . . .

• • •

'The prisoner at the bar, Louisa Collins, stands indicted for having murdered her husband, Michael Peter Collins,' began Chief Justice

Darley when the whispering had died away. He continued in the usual way, advising the sombre jurors of the seriousness of the case and of their own formidable responsibility.

After briefly outlining the family's history and discussing the particulars of the case, he drew the jury's attention to the evidence concerning Charles Andrews' death. He said that the court was not trying Louisa for that death; rather, that the evidence had been admitted to show that it was improbable that an accident had taken place. If Collins alone had died from arsenical poisoning, there would have been the possibility that his death was the result of an accident or suicide. But when two men died of the same symptoms within a seventeen-month period, and when traces of arsenic were found in one body and conclusive evidence of arsenical poisoning in the other, there was a strong presumption that it was no accident—especially when it was found that the same woman had attended both men. It suggested that the deaths were the result of an individual's design and it was up to the jury to decide if Louisa was that individual.

Darley then ran through the evidence regarding Collins' death and read out Louisa's statement, pointing out the discrepancies between her statement and those of other witnesses. He drew the jury's attention to her actions during and after Collins' death and to the evidence of arsenic's presence not just in the body but in the tumbler. 'The suggestions made by counsel for the defence—that the police or someone else had tampered with the milk in the tumbler between the time that it was taken from the house and handed over to the government analyst—can scarcely be entertained,' he added, 'as there is no ground whatever for supposing that anyone had been guilty of the diabolical act suggested.'

He reminded the jury of Louisa's anxiety about her husband's health and her repeated calls for medical assistance. He also admitted that there was no apparent motive for her taking Collins' life, although it was unnecessary for the jury to have a distinct motive laid before them as it was often impossible to understand the mind of another person. Nonetheless, aware of the difficulty faced by a jury when assessing a motiveless crime supported only by circumstantial evidence, he added, 'It might be that the prisoner, after having poisoned Andrews without being discovered, took the same means of dealing with Collins after she had got tired of him.'

Soon after the court clock chimed the midday hour, he told the jury that it was now time to retire to their room to consider their verdict. 'If, as a result of your judgement, you are left with any reasonable doubt in your minds, you are bound to give the prisoner the benefit of that doubt and acquit her. But the doubt must be a reasonable one, and not a doubt conjured up out of the imagination. If, on the other hand, after careful consideration of the evidence, you can come to no other conclusion but that this unfortunate man met his death by poison administered by his wife, then you have to discharge but one solemn duty and pronounce that verdict which the law of the country requires you to return.'

• • •

An excited babble filled the courtroom as the spectators weighed the odds. Would this jury succeed in reaching a verdict? An hour later, when the jury hadn't returned, Darley realised that this trial was not going to produce a speedy result. He ordered that the court be adjourned for a meal break so that he and the functionaries could at least wait with full stomachs.

As the courtroom started filling again at two pm, word spread that the jury was returning. Only two hours? Those who had intended to remain in the fresh air for a while longer hurried back inside.

The jurors took their seats. Louisa rose and faced them with the same air of detachment controlling her features. Again, a deathly hush settled over the room.

The clerk asked, 'Gentlemen of the jury, have you agreed upon a verdict?'

'We have, sir.'

After three hung juries, the words were almost a shock.

'How say you, gentlemen of the jury?' continued the clerk. 'Is the prisoner, Louisa Collins, guilty of the charge whereof she stands arraigned or not guilty?'

The silence in the courtroom was absolute.

'We find the prisoner guilty.'

• • •

The *Evening News* reporter was watching Louisa closely. He noticed that she blanched as the foreman announced the verdict. Trembling, she glanced around the courtroom, then she clutched the small desk in front of the dock. Her back straightened, her head lifted, and she looked the clerk of arraigns in the eye as he began to address her.

'Louisa Collins, you have pleaded not guilty to the murder. The jury have found you guilty of murder. Have you anything to say why the sentence of the court should not be passed upon you, according to law?'

Louisa turned to the judge and said calmly, 'Nothing whatever, Your Honour.'

With due solemnity, Chief Justice Darley picked up the scrap of black cloth known as the 'black cap' and placed it on his head. 'Louisa Collins,' he began, 'after a most careful trial, after being defended with much skill and ability, you have been found guilty of the murder of your husband, Michael Peter Collins. No one who has heard this case throughout can have any doubt that this verdict is a true and honest verdict. In fact, no other verdict could be arrived at by a body of intelligent men such as those who have so carefully attended to this case throughout. The murder you have committed is one of peculiar atrocity. You were day by day giving poison to the man whom above all others you were bound to cherish and attend. You watched his slow torture and painful death and this apparently without a moment's remorse. You were indifferent to his pain and gained his confidence by your simulated affection. There is too much reason to fear that your first husband Andrews also met his death at your hands; that him, too, you watched to the end—saw his torture day after day.

'I hold out no hope of mercy to you on earth. It would be wicked of me to do so. But I implore of you to seek forgiveness where it will assuredly be found. Seek the assistance of the clergyman to whose faith you belong. He will point out to you the way to gain such forgiveness. Your days are surely numbered, and it now remains for me only to pass the last dread sentence of the law upon you.'

The *Evening News* reporter had continued to watch Louisa. Not a muscle of her face quivered as she listened to the judge's condemnation. In fact, she appeared as calm as it was possible for any person to be. Certainly, she was calmer than the judge himself, who was deeply affected by his task; calmer than the jury, several of whom had burst into tears; calmer even than the spectators—few dry eyes could be seen in the courtroom.

The judge concluded, 'The sentence of the court is that you be taken to the place from whence you came, and on a day hereafter to be named by the governor in council, that you be taken to the place of execution, and there be hanged by the neck until you are dead. May the Lord have mercy on your soul.'

Part 3
WRATHFULNESS

[It] reminds me of the story of the only survivor of a shipwreck who was cast upon a beach. He struggled to his feet and made his way across the sand to the woods. In them, he found a cleared space and in the middle of it was a gallows, upon which he is alleged to have said, with a sigh of relief, 'Thank God, I have fallen among Christians.'

Kenneth McCaw MLA

Chapter 32

> The conviction of Louisa Collins . . . is the termination of the most remarkable series of trials on the capital charge which any prisoner ever had to undergo in this colony.
>
> *Daily Telegraph*

Louisa kept her head high as she moved to the dock staircase, refusing to catch anyone's gaze. They had dissected her enough, exposing the sordid details of her family life, her drinking, her adultery. She didn't want to see them delighting in her misery.

Descending the dock steps, she began walking through the familiar tunnel to Darlinghurst Gaol, her final journey through its claustrophobic confines. She had plodded its course so many times it was difficult to keep a tally, yet each time a glimmer of hope had lit the passageway. Now it had been doused by that single word: 'Guilty!' Yet on whose authority was the speaker, via the pronouncement of this word, able to dictate who lived and died?

• • •

The subject of capital punishment was being discussed more frequently as Victorian society tried to throw off the shackles of a 'barbarous' past and grapple with the issues of crime and punishment from a more civilised perspective. Could the death penalty really be deemed a modern form of punishment, an *enlightened* punishment?

Of course, executing the wicked had been a custom since ancient times, with rulers attempting to outdo each other in the horrors they inflicted on their citizens. Crucifixion, stoning, hanging, drowning, beating, beheading, boiling, burning and burying alive. What deeds merited these hideous punishments? Naturally they included crimes like murder, rape and theft. Yet, in some societies, they also included such heinous acts as making a night-time disturbance or singing an insulting song. 'Crime' is defined by what a monarch or dictator or legislature decides is criminal rather than by any intrinsic evilness in the deed itself.

The deadliness of Louisa's guilty verdict stemmed from the rights assumed by long-dead monarchs. In early modern times, sovereign power had rested on the sword. As the folkloric tale of Robin Hood reveals, the sword wielded the right of seizure—of money, goods, services and human freedom—for the purpose of empowering and enriching the sovereign as well as those in his hierarchy who maintained his power base. The defining privilege of sovereign power was the right to shed human blood. Kings and queens saw themselves as God's agents on earth and believed they had been granted the divine right to decide who should live or die.

Over time, absolutist monarchical power was replaced by the bureaucratic state, which took upon itself the right to exclusively represent the nation's affairs. The focus began to shift towards enriching rather than exploiting the people, through financial, social and even medical means. Still, implicit in its maintenance of authority was the ability to use violence as a means of asserting that authority, both against members who transgressed its rules and against outsiders who breached its boundaries.

Hanging was its deadliest punishment—in Australia, at least. Introduced into England by invading Germanic tribes during the fifth century, the noose had long been a symbol—second only to the cross—of supreme authority over life and death. In 1788, the First Fleet brought the lethal practice to the Australian continent, executing a convict for thieving food only a month after Sydney Cove's serenity was disturbed by settlers building accommodation for their 'civilised' society. November 1789 saw the first female execution, that of Ann Davis for stealing clothes; she was so drunk she had to be carried to the gallows. Its heyday came four decades later, after conservative military autocrat Ralph Darling assumed the New South Wales governorship. In 1830, fifty felons were hanged from a population of forty thousand, compared with only forty-six from the thirteen million inhabitants of England and Wales. English attitudes were turning against capital punishment and these would gradually flow through to its colonial outposts.

Forgery, cattle stealing and various thieving offences were struck from the New South Wales Bloody Code in 1833 and other offences in 1838. The colony leapfrogged England by abolishing public executions in 1853, joined by Victoria and Tasmania in 1855. When England broached the same subject in 1866, influential figures argued that, since Australia had already done so, England should follow suit—and it did, in 1868. Meanwhile, England had leapfrogged New South Wales by reducing the number of capital crimes to five, although, in practice, the only crimes that continued to be punished by death were murder and, on rare occasions, treason. New South Wales, however, remained obdurate. Eleven capital crimes were still on its books when Louisa stood in the Darlinghurst Courthouse on Thursday, 8 December 1888, awaiting the jury's verdict. Murder was one of them.

Thus, with his pronouncement of the word 'guilty', the jury's foreman had set the gallows clock ticking. No one knew when it would be silent again. Certainly, it wouldn't tick for long—less than a month, most likely.

• • •

Louisa knew there was still hope. Her death sentence had to be ratified by the Executive Council—or the 'Execution Council' as it had once been nicknamed—whose members might choose to stop the gallows clock prematurely. Seven other criminals had been sentenced to death in New South Wales courts during the centennial year, yet only twice had the gallows clock continued ticking until the bolt was drawn.

There was a further source of hope. No woman had been executed in New South Wales for twenty-eight years—and it wasn't because women had been criminally guiltless throughout that period. Rather, a merciful Executive Council had commuted all of their death sentences.

When would the council meet? Soon, she was told.

It couldn't come soon enough. She'd had months to consider the possibility of a conviction, months to craft a suit of armour to protect herself from the shock and to prevent others from witnessing her horror. But the armour of the imagination is never strong enough to withstand the brute force of reality. Once the chief justice had pronounced his judgment, once he had articulated those deadly words, a picture inevitably crystallised: a noose hanging from a sturdy beam.

'They will never hang a woman!' she told herself. Or would they?

• • •

Most prisoners under sentence of death were incarcerated in the gaol's 'condemned cells' in the northernmost part of the gaol, a couple of dozen steps from the first-floor gallery that served as the scaffold. The authorities claimed that condemned prisoners would suffer less emotional torment if their final journey was short, ignoring the proximity-induced torment they endured for the weeks beforehand. No doubt, the authorities' primary intention was to maintain the dignity of the occasion, to ensure that the pressmen attending the ceremony would return to their newspaper pulpits and preach another lesson about the triumph of justice and the law. The last thing the authorities wanted was for the public to hear an account of guards dragging a hulk of a man for dozens of yards to the gallows or a woman whose screams cracked windowpanes a block away. It would generate sympathy for the sufferer rather than awe at the law's majesty.

But Louisa wasn't being taken to the condemned cells; she was returning to the female wing. The condemned cells were in the male wing, and nobody wanted a woman residing near the men. It might inflame the more brutal and cunning of those rogues, with disastrous consequences for everyone concerned.

The warders took her along the well-known route back to D wing, but not to her usual cell. As she stepped through the doorway into a three-bedded cell, she saw that two of the beds had been removed and a chair placed in one corner. She was told that a female warder would sit with her, not just throughout the day but during the night as well. The warder would even remain in the room when she received visitors.

Why?

'Protection' was the reason: protection not only against the actions of others, but against those she might inflict upon herself. She had broken society's laws—so society must not be denied its right to kill her.

Chapter 33

Louisa Collins' method of procuring a divorce by means of arsenic is open to serious objection.

Sydney Morning Herald

After four nail-biting trials and months of reportage, the press couldn't let Louisa's conviction pass without some editorialising. The *Daily Telegraph* applauded the verdict and also the Crown for its astute decision to introduce the evidence regarding Louisa's first husband's death. The *Sydney Morning Herald* found the evidence convincing and the verdict unsurprising and had no qualms about imposing a death sentence. 'Hiding the fiendish purpose behind the sanctity of wedlock and dealing out slow and torturing agonies to one who believes the hand that is giving him poison is trying to preserve his life belongs to a species of crime for which death punishment hardly seems retribution enough.'

'Murder by poisoning!' It was always said in tones of outrage, as if the secrecy and duplicity of this largely 'domestic' crime, this predominantly 'female' crime, made it more iniquitous than any other. Indeed, the *Herald* roared that crimes of poisoning struck at the very heart of society. 'If a man's life is not safe in the hands of one who has sworn to love and cherish him, where shall there be safety?'

Parliamentarian Thomas Walker agreed that domestic poisonings should shock the instincts of even the most brutal man in the community, failing to recognise that brutal men should indeed be the most shocked—and fearful. Brutality wielded its mightiest fist in the domestic sphere, so a brute faced the greatest risk of having a poisonous cocktail served with his supper.

As it happened, the outrage voiced by press and politicians had its origin in ancient common law. Until a mere half-century previously, husband-killing had been deemed a more heinous crime than murder. In the medieval world, society had envisaged itself as a framework with each person having an appointed place. If a wife killed a husband or a servant killed his or her master, it was considered an act of betrayal that threatened the fabric of society itself. The Treason Act of 1351 codified this murderous betrayal of a superior as 'petit treason'. Even though legislative changes had subsumed 'petit treason' under the broad 'murder' umbrella, social attitudes were little changed. The public still saw husband-killing as a form of treachery and duplicity to rival Judas' kiss.

However, those railing against women and their choice of poison as a weapon failed to recognise that the 'gentle sex' had fewer options than men. Physical violence was rarely on the list. Any attempt to beat, strangle or stab an unwanted partner would likely incur physical violence, which was generally what the woman was trying to escape in the first place. A killer-for-hire? That required money and a broader social network than the domestic sphere inhabited by most women. In truth, poison was cheap, accessible and non-confrontational, making it the only weapon in an urban woman's arsenal.

Nonetheless, the notion that poisoning was the most evil of crimes readily meshed with the view that women were the most evil of creatures. Biblical Eve, corruptible and corrupting, had long served as a metaphor for womanhood, so much so that many of the medieval church leaders had held the female gender in utter contempt. St Clement of Alexandria had opined that 'the consciousness of their own nature must evoke feelings of shame', while the Catholic Church's witch-hunting manual, *Malleus Maleficarum*, stated, 'All wickedness is but little to the wickedness of a woman.'

Throughout history, the nexus between women and sex and death had horrified yet titillated. The siren of Greek mythology—half-woman, half-bird —who lured sailors to their deaths; the femme fatale of romantic poetry who sucked out man's life-force. Witch, siren, sorceress, temptress. The Eve mythology proved persistent and deadly.

Women were expected to be more like Mary, pure and unsullied. Their place was in the home, submitting to a husband's authority, breeding children and nurturing their family. But, even in the Victorian era, society still believed that Eve lurked within her modest robes, capable, like the black widow spider, of devouring her mate. And this particular black widow had eaten not just a single partner; seemingly, she had eaten two.

Colonial society fixed its gaze on Louisa with a malevolence rarely directed at male killers. She became the epitome of the corrupting Eve, the venal Jezebel, the witch whose evil could only be vanquished when she was burned at the stake. The press and public nicknamed her 'Lucrezia Borgia' because 'there was no character more sublimely terrible, and more fiendish, than that of Lucrezia Borgia. Though her relatives were villains, they could not compare with her in her atrocities.'[6]

Even Louisa's coolness during her court cases was seen as proof of her wickedness. 'There is no reason to doubt,' wrote the *Daily Telegraph*'s editor when offering a second reason for her conviction, 'that the unfeeling indifference and complete callousness exhibited in the court by the prisoner throughout the four trials fitted her for the act of which the verdict convicted her.'

Meanwhile, the Crown's strategy of linking the two deaths had slipped free from its courtroom confines. The press and public now accepted, in the main, that Louisa was guilty of two murders, even though she had only been convicted of one. In a democratic society, the voices of the people were heard by their political representatives and influenced their decision-making. Thus, the public's belief that Louisa was guilty of multiple murders and should be treated accordingly could have a profound impact on the men who would raise their hands in judgement as to whether she should live or die.

• • •

On 13 December, the members of the most powerful body in New South Wales prepared to meet at Government House. The Executive Council was the official arm of government, granting legal authority to the decisions made by the people's representatives. Among the matters under its purview were the capital cases: the judgments imposing the punishment of death. The law allowed the council a final say as to whether Louisa should go to the gallows or have her sentence commuted to life imprisonment.

As the council members headed to Government House, Sydney's punters speculated as to how these men would vote. The Governor of New South Wales, Lord Charles Robert Carrington, would be the host. The young moustachioed aristocrat with liberal leanings and a kind, generous nature was immensely popular with the people and their representatives. He understood the conventions limiting his role as the Queen's representative, yet he had also shown himself willing to grab the wheel of his supreme authority when he felt that the ship of state was steaming towards a dangerous abyss.

The New South Wales premier would also sit at the august table. Seventy-three-year-old Sir Henry Parkes was serving the fourth of five terms as premier. In these merry-go-round years of the early

New South Wales parliament, when governments frequently rose and fell, he had risen above all others. 'The wily knight,' the *Bulletin* called him.

Parkes had found his political voice four decades previously. Then a young British-born radical, he had held loosely Chartist dreams of a broader franchise and representative government at a time when Britain still retained the autocratic hope of dumping its criminal refuse on New South Wales soil. His success in helping to thwart these imperial ambitions had fired his blood with the fever of political ambition. Soon afterwards, he had established the radical *Empire* newspaper, using it as his bullhorn to rally for change—for progressive reform, though, rather than revolution. When his dream of representative government was fulfilled, he had manoeuvred himself onto the political podium.

Capital punishment had long been one of his concerns. In the aftermath of an 1852 execution, he penned an *Empire* editorial declaring that it was time to consider the ethicality and efficacy of death sentences. As he saw it, the arguments in favour of capital punishment were threefold, being drawn from scripture, abstract justice and expediency. He dismissed the expediency argument as invalid because history's example had already proven that death punishments were inexpedient as crime correctives. And the blindness of abstract justice was akin to the sin of retaliation, which was forbidden under the Christian code. All that was left were the biblical passages, yet their advocacy of the death penalty had been questioned—indeed impugned—by men of judgement. That being the case, he declared that it was both offensive and revolting to use such passages as the authority to take a life, particularly as a life wrongly taken could never be restored.

While philosophically a staunch abolitionist, Parkes' political success had been founded on his pragmatism, so it was difficult to know what stance he would take regarding Louisa's case. Two years previously, while a member of the Opposition, he had privately approached Governor Carrington to plead against the death penalty for the 'larrikins'[7] convicted of a brutal gang rape at Mount Rennie in the Moore Park area of Sydney. Among other reasons, Parkes argued that so many men should not hang for a single crime. Of course, their victim, sixteen-year-old Mary Jane Hicks, might argue that she was not the victim of a *single* crime—that, rather, nine discrete criminal acts of a similar nature had been perpetrated consecutively. Whether rapists should be hanged at all, however, was a different question. Indeed, it was a particularly troublesome one considering that England, the source of much of the colony's judicial wisdom, had tossed rape's capital statute into the legal fire some decades previously, as had other Australian colonies. That being the case, Parkes' willingness to speak out against the death penalty in the Mount Rennie case could not be considered a litmus test for his likely response to Louisa's case.

Against this plea for mercy must be set Parkes' Machiavellian manoeuvring in the case of the Duke of Edinburgh's would-be assassin two decades previously. Parkes had concealed evidence proving that the plot was hatched not by a Fenian anarchist, but by a mind addled with alcohol and insanity. Without this mitigating evidence—and despite Prince Alfred's own pleas—Henry O'Farrell had been refused mercy and dispatched to the gallows.

So, would opportunism or expediency drive the premier when he cast his vote?

Parkes' men—the members of his cabinet—would join him at the Executive Council table. Parkes usually focused on power and leadership rather than political scruples when he chose his cabinet but—according to widely accepted rumours—even baser reasoning underpinned this choice of ministers. Struggling as ever to keep himself above the quicksands of insolvency, Parkes had reportedly offered the cabinet's prestigious and financially remunerative positions to men he owed money. He had won his huge majority on a 'free trade' platform with the slogan 'good government and commercial freedom', and one of his cabinet choices was the Freetrade Association president. Yet ministerial portfolios were also offered to three men who had recently advocated commercial duties to protect local industries from cheaper international or intercolonial prices. The critical Ministry of Justice portfolio, for example, was now in the hands of businessman William Clarke, a politician derided by the *Australian Town and Country Journal* as 'the most personally disliked man in the Assembly'.

These men would not 'toe the party line', all the same, as party politics was still a distant dream. However, that dream was closer to fruition with Parkes' government because the premier's resounding victory had reshuffled political allegiances into party-like divisions, the first stage in the demise of the unstable faction-driven system that had dominated parliament for three decades. Factional alliances were based on loosely held principles pasted together with self-interest. With a support base about as resilient as a house of cards, some governments lasted only a matter of months—or weeks. And the issue that triggered their downfall could be as unexpected as it was catastrophic.

The question of appropriate criminal punishments had already proven deadly for a Parkes government. His first premiership had ended after the governor's controversial decision to allow the early release of a bushranger—although Parkes' downfall owed more to his own petulance at the government's censure of his actions than any weakening of his support base. The fact that rash decisions could swell into a tidal wave capable of washing away a government would not be forgotten by these men—Parkes in particular—as they discussed Louisa's case.

• • •

Lord Carrington convened the meeting and advised that the first matter on their agenda was the case of the capitally convicted prisoner, Louisa Collins. He tabled the report written by Chief Justice Darley and invited his companions to consider the matter.

The report was read to the members. Parkes thought it detailed and thorough, so much so that he would later declare: 'It was the fullest and most careful report from a judge I have ever seen in my whole life.' Even so, the council needed the most detailed information possible. Accordingly, Darley himself was called into the room.

In this type of situation, Lord Carrington recognised his place and took a back seat. The leader of the government was also leader of the council, so Parkes took charge. He questioned the chief justice on the quality of Louisa's defence.

'I think she had a very able defence,' was the response.

'Can you suggest any recommendation to enable the Executive Council to take a merciful view of the case?'

'I can give none,' Darley replied deliberately.

After Darley had departed, the council began its discussion. The council's minutes are brief, providing no guide as to how long the exchange lasted or how readily the members reached agreement. When Parkes later referred to the meeting, instead of saying, 'The council decision was unanimous,' he spoke cautiously—'I think I am justified in stating that the Executive Council was unanimous' and 'I think I am stating what I may be fairly pardoned for stating when I say that that was the decision arrived at'—as if, perhaps, such unanimity had not been easy to come by. Capital punishment was a contentious subject that divided the populace so it is likely that passions were aroused before a firm hand guided them towards a unified position.

If some council members wanted to reprieve Louisa despite the judge's refusal to offer any grounds for doing so, Parkes made his own position clear. He probably expressed himself in words similar to those he would later use in parliament: 'We did not hear the trial. We did not see the witnesses. We never had the responsibility attaching to the legal investigation and this solemn decision of a court of law. How can we, then, presume to set aside the solemn decision of a jury of Louisa Collins' countrymen?'

The council members knew that the Westminster system of government stressed the importance of the separation of powers between the executive and the judiciary in order to protect liberty and promote good governance. Yet, at the same time, the law permitted the executive to venture across the tightrope separating the two powers by requiring the council members to either ratify or veto the courts' sanction of death. It recognised that despots could build thrones in judicial as well as political kingdoms. It also recognised that mitigating circumstances sometimes existed that the courts could not take into consideration.

So what should they do? The council members all knew Parkes' personal views on capital punishment. Everyone did. Nevertheless, as he no doubt reminded his cabinet, the issue here was not the question of capital punishment itself; rather, it was the rights and obligations of the council in upholding and implementing the colony's laws.

But to execute a woman? That question must have been asked by at least one of the men. Even among those who advocated capital punishment, the execution of a woman was often a moral and emotional stumbling block.

Again, Parkes no doubt reminded them that the law was blind to gender, perhaps also in the words he would later use in parliament: 'Are we to bend down to the circumstances of the sex of the criminal? It is abhorrent to every feeling of humanity to see a woman hanged. It is abhorrent to mine. If it were in my power by any means possible to save the country from such a spectacle, I would spare no pains to save it, but while the law remains in force must I save us from this spectacle at the sacrifice—the hanging—of justice itself?'

Certainly, this philosophical argument could be challenged on the practical grounds that no woman had been executed in New South Wales for nearly three decades—and it wasn't because the fair sex had refrained from killing during that period. It was inevitable that someone would remind the council of the 'Maitland murderesses'.

Mary Ann Burton and her stepdaughter, Sarah Keep, had been accused of murdering Sarah's husband in November 1883 by means of strychnine poisoning. The case against the women was circumstantial because the women themselves said that Keep had committed suicide. A hung jury ended the first trial, however the second resulted in a death sentence. A month later, the Executive Council reprieved the women to life imprisonment. The council's reasons for doing so were not published; however, the *Maitland Mercury*'s editor thought its decision was probably influenced by four factors: that the women might still have been innocent even though the circumstantial evidence suggested otherwise; that the first jury had been almost evenly divided yet the second jury, hearing little extra evidence, had reached a unanimous verdict; that the public strenuously objected to the hanging of women; and that, as murders by women were rare, the deterrent effect of capital punishment was unnecessary, so a reprieve to life punishment would satisfy the community that justice had been served and society protected against similar outrages.

Shouldn't the Maitland case serve as a precedent? Weren't the actions of the Maitland murderesses even worse than those of Louisa Collins? Not only had the women committed murder, they had conspired to commit murder—a serious criminal offence in its own right. So when they had been reprieved, the people had thought that a critical precedent had been set, that women would never again be executed. Yet here was the council, a mere three years later, arguing the merits of executing another woman.

Neither Parkes nor his men explained why they ignored this precedent. Perhaps a journalist captured the essence of their reasoning: 'The clemency exhibited in the Maitland cases might have rendered Louisa Collins more reckless than she otherwise would have been, and that so far from having any fear of the scaffold before her eyes, she might have considered that, if the worst came to the worst, the law would never take her life.'

Of the council's debate and decision-making process, all that has survived is the brief notation in the minutes: 'After careful consideration, the Council are unable to see any ground for mitigation of the capital sentence and therefore advise that the sentence of Death passed upon Louisa Collins be carried into effect.' They also set a date for her execution: Tuesday, 8 January 1889.

Louisa would be sent to the gallows in twenty-six days unless somebody could come up with a convincing reason to reprieve her.

Chapter 34

> We kill an adder or a scorpion because its life imperils us. Must we spare Lucrezia Borgia or Madame de Brinvilliers?
>
> *Queenslander*

The Executive Council approved her execution? It wasn't what Louisa had been expecting. Women were not executed, not according to the Darlinghurst warders. They said that no woman had ever died on the gallows at Darlinghurst. Since Darlinghurst had been Sydney's only gaol since 1840, this meant that no women had died on a Sydney scaffold for half a century, if not longer. Surely they wouldn't execute a woman now.

There was more news. The Executive Council had set a date: one month to the day since her conviction.

What could she do? Appealing to the judge wouldn't help. She had stood in the dock trying not to tremble as he berated her with his excoriating judgment, as he dismissed her case, her life, with his unforgiving conclusion, 'I hold out no hope of mercy to you on earth.' So how could she convince the authorities to reconsider their plan to kill her?

• • •

As the news spread, the public's reaction was intense. Prior to the council meeting, most were satisfied with the verdict, being convinced that Louisa was guilty of one if not both murders. The less satisfied were not necessarily doubtful of her guilt; rather, their concerns focused on the legality and morality of her conviction. However, with the council's decision to ratify her death sentence, the public mood changed.

'In this our centennial year, drawing to its close, let it not be stained with blood,' begged An Anxious Mother in a letter to a Sydney newspaper, 'particularly the blood of a woman and mother.'

An Anxious Husband snapped back: 'Persons who object to being hanged in our centennial year have only to abstain from murdering their fellow citizens during that particular twelve months' period—not much to ask of them.'

It had begun again: the squabbling about capital punishment. The subject had long split the community, arousing passion and anger on both sides. Correspondents spat at each other through the letter pages of the newspapers, determined to have their own views heard on the subject of Louisa's hanging and on capital punishment in general.

'If the law is death,' wrote D.Y., reducing the argument to its simplest legal foundation, 'surely the law should be allowed to take its course.'

But laws change, countered Citizen. He reminded his readers that those who advocated death as a punishment for murder belonged to the same cult who had once advocated death as a punishment for petty theft. Moreover, when these people argued that Louisa should be hanged because 'it's the law', they were attempting to place responsibility on the legislators of yesterday for a deed carried out today. 'This won't do,' Citizen declared firmly. 'No past parliament can force us to hang Louisa Collins.'

Justice attempted to push the law's foundation back another step, arguing that it was biblical in origin and therefore divine and immutable. 'He that killeth any man shall surely be put to death,' he quoth. Fire-and-brimstone believer Zachary Pearce Pocock unleashed another biblical lightning bolt: 'Who so sheddeth man's blood, by man shall his blood be shed.'

G.E. Penly countered that these views might accord with the Old Testament Law of Moses but that, like the codicil to a will, Christ's teachings had nullified such bloodthirsty commands. 'Let him that is without sin cast the first stone.' And he asked if the judges or cabinet members were so pure and holy that they should arrogate to themselves the powers of a deity and take a life that God had given?

His query produced snorts of disgust from those who knew the truth about their recently widowed premier. Parkes had long enjoyed the pleasures of a young mistress and was the father of her three bastard children.

The *Bulletin*'s editor weighed in, exposing the absurdity of the life-for-a-life biblical injunction. Since Nosey Bob, the executioner, was to shed the blood of Louisa Collins who had shed the blood of Michael Peter Collins, who then was going to shed the blood of Nosey Bob? And who would shed the blood of Nosey Bob's executioner? 'Where are we to stop?' he demanded, because if the hangman represented the community then the lives of the entire community should be forfeited.

He also observed that all the scriptural reasons raked up by the hangman's apologists were not so very long ago given for the burning and drowning of witches, an act that in current times was universally regarded as a piece of superstitious savagery. He added, 'In much less than two centuries more, our own official stranglings will be justly looked upon in a similar light.'

• • •

Since capital punishment was still 'the law', abolitionists tried to motivate the public to think about what the law was aiming to achieve—justice for the victim, obviously, and punishment of the criminal—and whether it was succeeding. To some, retribution was, of course, the purest form of justice and the most effective deterrent.

Still, was death the ultimate punishment? The *Bulletin*'s editor, J.F. Archibald, recalled that when King George III granted pardons to two dozen female prisoners on the condition they accept transportation to New South Wales, six turned down the offer, preferring death to antipodean exile. Archibald felt that death, if it struck quickly, was not an appalling terror, that a lifetime of penal servitude with long stretches of solitary confinement would be a greater punishment. Moreover, with a lifetime behind bars, another aim of criminal punishment might be achieved: reformation. Needless to say, executed criminals could not be reformed.

As for 'protecting society' from the criminal herself, could Louisa be considered a serious threat? 'She is not an evil exhalation which can arise in the night and defy prison walls and prison roofs,' the *Bulletin* pointed out. To repeat her evil, she would require a lover, arsenic, milk and, of course, freedom, which could be prevented by the simple expedient of a sturdy prison door.

As for 'deterring would-be criminals', the hanging advocates believed that the only effective deterrent was to hang all criminals so that others would be too afraid to commit crimes. They claimed that reprieves gave hope to the wicked and spurred further crime. However, one letter-writer reminded the public that crime had *not* increased in England since the huge reduction in the number of crimes punishable by death—far from it. And the *Bulletin* added that capital punishment's proven ineffectiveness as a community-wide deterrent was one of the reasons why a number of countries and American states had already legislated to abolish the barbaric practice.

Of course, setting aside the statistical evidence, one could simply mention the name of John Price, the English hangman who was himself hanged for murder. If a hangman—of all people—wasn't deterred, could society truly expect anyone else to be?

No one talked about the financial benefits of executing criminals. It seemed too pragmatic, somehow, too brutal, particularly when one could use advocacy arguments that spoke of the supremacy and infallibility of divine will.

But what about the moral effects of capital punishment on society as a whole? Letter-writer Philanthros declared that it was an act of savagery disgraceful to the present age. Humanity argued that this relic from the dark ages had a hardening and brutalising effect upon society, and that a brutal society committed more crimes, not less. 'Abolish it' was the plea from many others as they flooded the press with reasons why such a punishment breached all standards of human decency.

The 'death' advocates, such as parliamentarian David Buchanan, declared that the notion that hanging inflicted a stain on society was the weakest and most perverted of all the weak and perverted notions being propagated by the 'spurious, imbecile philanthropists pouring out their mawkish, miserable cant and diseased, rotten sympathy with crime and criminals'. It would take stronger arguments than these to convince the gallows' apologists that the double-dyed murderess should be granted the indulgence of a reprieve.

• • •

As letter-writers sat at their desks furiously penning their opinions, a rumour began to spread. On the day Louisa was informed that the Executive Council had ratified her death sentence, she had 'pled the belly'. According to that night's *Evening News*, the premier had been notified. His response? If she were indeed pregnant, she would have to be withheld from execution.

Yet, how could she suddenly claim to be pregnant? Her husband had died five months previously and had been seriously ill for some weeks beforehand. Wouldn't the gaol warders know if the woman was more than six months pregnant? Of course, it wasn't unknown for female prisoners to fall pregnant during their incarceration. No prison was run solely by women.

A week later, the *Evening News* reported that the gaol physician, Dr O'Connor, had examined Louisa and had communicated the results of his examination to the authorities. No one would say what he had discovered. The authorities were keeping surprisingly quiet about the subject.

Chapter 35

The fell spirit of the Borgias is stalking through . . . society.

Michael Harris quoted in W.F. Bynum, *Medical Journals and Medical Knowledge*

Apart from the fascinating tidbit about Louisa's possible pregnancy, the journalists for the *Evening News* were struggling to find the type of information about Louisa that would motivate their readers to buy more newspapers. 'Louisa Collins is one of the most uninteresting cases of condemned people that have ever been dealt with in Darlinghurst,' one reporter lamented.

The pressmen continued delving. The editor sent reporters to the gaol itself, to Botany, even to the Merriwa and Scone districts where she had spent her youth, so they could ferret out every morsel.

What a minx the young Louisa had proven to be. Locals said she'd been the pet of the village, an especially appealing little girl. Blessed with good looks and winning ways, she'd become a country coquette by the time she reached her teens, soon earning for herself the reputation of being a heartless flirt. Despite her many suitors and youthful sweethearts, she hadn't married any of them. Rather, she'd chosen Charles Andrews, a good-hearted fellow who was respected and esteemed by all who knew him. Reportedly, she had taken to drink within a couple of years of her marriage, which had caused tension in the household and had perhaps contributed to their decision to relocate to Sydney.

The Botany locals had their own stories about Louisa and the goings-on at Frog Hollow—or 'Arsenic Flat' as they had facetiously renamed the area. They gossiped about Louisa's poor reputation, her drinking, her flirtations with the boarders—wishful thinking on the part of some, no doubt—and finally her 'great intimacy' with Collins. Some even mentioned seeing the couple kissing in tram cars or cavorting in the Botany bush.

Local draper Mr Bullock told a reporter that, shortly before Charles Andrews' illness, Louisa had asked him what steps she would need to take to obtain her husband's insurance money if he fell ill. Bullock said that he was suspicious when Andrews died soon afterwards, but had preferred not to make his suspicions known to the police. He had also thought it curious when Louisa ordered dress material of a light colour after Andrews' death instead of the usual black mourning attire. When asked why, she had replied in a careless manner, 'I can mourn in my heart without carrying my grief in my clothes.' Bullock said that she had always seemed a bit eccentric. For instance, she refused to have her dresses fitted on her by the modiste but had never explained why.

The pressman thought this behaviour extraordinary. Why would Louisa relinquish what most women considered one of the joys of life?

The tales continued. Louisa, reportedly, didn't tell her eldest son Herbert about his own father's death. Apparently, he'd heard the news when he encountered an old friend and had travelled to Botany for confirmation where he discovered that Louisa had already found a replacement. She answered his indignant inquiry in her usual cool manner and, when questioned about his father's money, told him that she had spent it all. Her astonished son said that he could have used his share to open a small business at Botany and help support the family.

The gossips alleged that she afterwards disowned him—although logic would suggest that the family discord had occurred sometime before and would explain why Louisa hadn't told him of his father's death in the first place.

Neighbours said that the Collins baby was a sickly infant and that Louisa showed him little affection and disliked others looking at him. She would excuse herself by saying, 'It's only a very little thing.' After the infant died, Ellen Price was called to wash and dress him. She told the pressman that she was disturbed by the infant's swollen lips and tongue but saw nothing to justify alerting the police—no doubt a wise decision as the doctor had reported that he'd noticed nothing odd about the infant's appearance.

And what about Collins himself? The pressmen's questions received the type of knowing looks that spoke volumes. For a man with such indolent habits, a woman with a purse of gold was the ideal catch.

• • •

It was hard to sift fact from fantasy so the editor of the *Evening News* decided to publish it all, no matter how absurd. There were allegations that Louisa was a relative of the bushranger Ben Hall. Some even claimed that Hall had flown into a violent rage when he heard about Louisa's marriage and had threatened to shoot Andrews at the first opportunity. (The *Evening News* was quick to point out that Hall had been killed some months before Louisa's wedding while others confirmed that there was no connection between the two families.)

One gossip said that a Chinaman had died of opium poisoning in the same room as Andrews, as if the room itself contained an evil miasma. And a boarder, a hale and hearty ex-cavalry officer, had begun to waste away while residing at the Andrews house. He'd been 'cured' when he moved away but had fallen ill again after his return; eventually, he had packed his bags and sailed for England.

There were claims that Louisa had visited the house of a week-old infant, a most unusual occurrence in itself, and had suggested that the babe be given some condensed milk, which she insisted on preparing and administering herself. The baby had reportedly fallen ill after her departure and died soon afterwards.

Inevitably, 'the ghost of Pople's Terrace' terrified some members of the locality with its bloodcurdling moans and violent retching. The reporter observed dryly, 'As the house is still untenanted, it is not unfair to surmise that the ghost conjuror has been overawed by the solemn stillness of some lovely night and that recollections of a "good night" drink have muddled a superstitious brain.'

After the Botany locals had finished gossiping, they were asked if anyone had anything good to say about Louisa. Well, they replied, she always paid her way.

While offhand and dismissive, it was in its own way a curious accolade, suggesting a deep-seated honesty and integrity that was at odds with the picture of the drunken Jezebel drawn by the press. It was also a reminder of Louisa's fortitude, which she was still managing to maintain, according to the gaol reports, despite a looming horror that would cause most people to collapse in despair.

Chapter 36

Something is rotten in the state of Denmark.

William Shakespeare, *Hamlet*

Abolitionist Frederick Lee had long wanted to cast the Bloody Code into the hellfires of history. So passionate were his feelings about this disgrace to humanity that he had helped found the Society for the Abolition of Capital Punishment in the aftermath of Henry O'Farrell's iniquitous execution in 1869. Even prior to the society's foundation, he had offered practical assistance to the condemned—like O'Farrell himself and, in more recent times, the Mount Rennie rapists. He believed that no one should be put to death for any crime, that the law's purpose was to seek justice, not punishment, and that punishment itself was intended for the reformation rather than the destruction of the criminal.

Especially troubling was the irrevocableness of capital punishment. Lee liked to use Shakespeare's poetry to make his point: 'But once put out thy light, I know not where is that Promethean heat that can thy light relume.' Lee and his fellow abolitionists were particularly alarmed when the convicting evidence was weak—for example, when it was founded on circumstantial evidence alone or the testimony of a single witness.

In recent times, Lee had given himself a title: the Standing Counsel for Condemned Prisoners. He monitored the capital cases moving through the court system to see if any might benefit from his philanthropic services, in particular those that lent themselves to suspicions of official malfeasance. Naturally, the reports of a woman standing in the dock on a murder charge—or two—had caught his attention.

Women had continued to be indicted on capital charges in the half-century since the Bloody Code had dropped theft from its statutes; however, in recent times, indictments and convictions had been few. In the current decade, only four other women had received capital convictions: the two Maitland murderesses (1885), along with Mary Laye (1882) and Harriet Williams (1886), the latter two for child-killing—both reprieved. Prior to the Maitland case, there had been no husband-killing convictions for a quarter-century.

And then Louisa Collins was indicted for killing *two* husbands, making hers a unique case in Australia's criminal history. Its singularity also meant it was the type of case in which the government, or perhaps an influential member of the government, might act improperly in an attempt to gain a conviction.

Could Lee find evidence of unfair behaviour—or perhaps worse—in the Crown's actions? Most certainly. The problems were manifest and manifold. It began with the Crown's decision to put Louisa to trial four times. Many people thought this decision reflected a 'spirit of unreasoning vengeance'. The conservative press wasn't concerned and, surprisingly, the *Bulletin*'s editor wasn't either. Archibald claimed that the custom of trying a case three times was not only ancient but, in the main, benevolent to the accused. If three juries failed to convict, the public opinion held that the accused merited their freedom.

Except that the authorities had tried *four* times to convict Louisa. 'I believe there is no record in England of a criminal under such circumstances being placed on trial more than twice,' Lee wrote in a letter to the *Evening News*. 'Where is the limit to be? If four times, why not eight times?'

Notably, neither before Louisa's fourth trial, when the public first expressed concern about the Crown's seemingly relentless pursuit of her, nor in its aftermath had the Crown provided examples of triple-trial precedents in an effort to allay community concern. This indicated that no one in the Crown's law office or in its circle of contacts knew of any such examples—or ones recent enough to seem relevant. So, even though the number of attempts to try her might not reflect malfeasance on the Crown's part, it certainly reflected an unprecedented level of zealous determination in its endeavours to convict her.

And what about the fact that three previous juries had been unable to reach a verdict? Any attempt to dismiss the fact that *three* juries had experienced these doubts by arguing that only *two* were making a judgement on the Collins case lost its traction when it was recollected that the prosecution admitted evidence relating to both husbands' deaths in the third trial. Three hung juries. Yet, despite that profound evidence of uncertainty, Louisa was going to the gallows because a fourth jury had managed to reach unanimity. When added to the fact that the convicting evidence was only circumstantial, wasn't the Crown's decision to refuse a commutation both unfair and unwise?

This raised another question: what procedural or evidentiary difference in the fourth trial was responsible for the different verdict? The answer was obvious: the admission of the evidence relating to Andrews' death. But should this evidence have been introduced? Not in Lee's opinion. As he explained in his letters and correspondence, Collins' death was undoubtedly caused by arsenical poisoning—scientific analysis had provided unequivocal proof—so it was reasonable for the Crown to introduce the Collins evidence into the Andrews trial to help argue that Andrews had also been killed by deliberate arsenical poisoning. Although doing so was prejudicial, this was outweighed by the probative value of the evidence. By contrast, Andrews' death certificate listed 'gastroenteritis' as his cause of death and the chemical evidence suggesting otherwise was flimsy. No scientist, medical practitioner or other expert would ever be able to *prove* that he had died from arsenical poisoning; it could only be a matter of *opinion*. And how often had the public read of medical or scientific experts standing in the witness box swearing to an opinion that was diametrically opposed to the opinion of a previous medical or scientific expert?

What would have happened if the Andrews evidence had not been admitted? The chief justice himself said in his summation that the jurors might find it hard to dismiss suicide or accidental death as possibilities when the Collins evidence was examined on its own, but that the likelihood of it being an accidental death was considerably reduced when the Andrews evidence was admitted. Clearly, both the Crown and judiciary had been asking the jurors to conclude that the possibility that Louisa poisoned Andrews made it more likely that she also poisoned Collins. However, this lost sight of the fact that Louisa might have had a motive for poisoning one man and not the other.

Thus, in his opinion, the Crown's actions were prejudicial and probably illegal. The only way to prove it, though, would be to bring her case before the Supreme Court so the full bench could make its own ruling.

• • •

Unbeknown to Frederick Lee, the *Bulletin*'s editor was putting his own concerns on paper. He argued, similarly, that the Crown's theory assumed that there was a double murder or none. Was that reasonable? The final jury had been asked to form their verdict in the Collins case based partly on an opinion regarding the Andrews case. Yet the Andrews jury had been unable to agree that Louisa had killed her first husband; moreover, it couldn't be taken for granted that the current jurors would have found her guilty if they had heard the Andrews case alone. True, it was difficult to keep the two cases distinct, particularly as there was a subtle but legitimate cogency in the Crown's line of argument—the 'similar facts' foundation. Nonetheless, to an ordinary jury, it suggested that the probability that Louisa Collins poisoned Andrews made it very probable that she also poisoned Collins. 'This is dangerously close to what reasoners know as the vicious cycle,' warned the *Bulletin*, referring to the fallacy in reasoning in which the premise is used to prove the conclusion and the conclusion the premise.

And what about the speediness of the final verdict? Three juries had previously sat through the night without reaching unanimity, with the only difference in the fourth trial being the inclusion of the Andrews evidence. That being the case, the fourth jury's speedy unanimity didn't make the verdict itself more credible. Rather, it confirmed the influence of that same 'vicious cycle' reasoning.

Which raised the subject of the adequacy of Louisa's legal representation. Her cases were complicated and circumstantial. The prosecution's arguments were intricate, particularly because of the vicious-cycle reasoning. Even the most skilled advocate would have had his resources and experience taxed. Yet the Crown had appointed only a junior barrister. It should be the Crown's duty to provide the best legal talent at its disposal when a person's life was at stake. This was especially important in Louisa's case because each of the witnesses—including her own children—had graduated from hesitancy to letter-perfection by the time they stood in the witness box for a third . . . fourth . . . fifth . . . sixth time and spoke the critical words that had sentenced her to her death.

• • •

In the meantime, Frederick Lee was continuing to gather information to add to his mercy pleas. Among the issues that worried him was the discrepancy between the amount of liquid claimed to be in the arsenic-laced tumbler—the strongest piece of mute evidence against Louisa, in his opinion. Extraordinary as it may sound, this all-important tumbler had remained in an open cigar box, unsealed and unsecured, for two days. Worse, in that time something had happened to it. Yet no one had made any attempt to account for the diminished liquid. In fact, the authorities treated the problem as if it were of no importance whatsoever. Wasn't this, at least, grounds for mercy because new information might later come to light explaining the discrepancy?

And what about the fact that May Andrews had admitted, while in the presence of a gaol warder during a visit to her mother, that she had never previously seen the tumbler pointed out to her in the courtroom, the tumbler that the government analyst said contained arsenic. Could May, an intelligent child embroiled in a difficult situation, have provided the answers she thought the threatening authority figures wanted to hear? Clever children were the first to recognise the benefits of a self-serving lie.

Another area of concern was the police's inability to trace the poison directly to Louisa which, surely, was a critical weakness in the Crown's chain of circumstantial evidence. While May had said that she saw Rough on Rats in the house, her statement was not supported by anyone else who lived in the house or visited the house or searched it in the aftermath of Collins' death. Nor had the police been able to find anyone who had sold Rough on Rats to Louisa or purchased it for her or lent it to her. In all cases of poisoning based on circumstantial evidence alone, the ability to trace the poison to the alleged perpetrator was considered crucial. It was even more important in Louisa's case as there were others living in and visiting the house who could have administered the poison.

Yes, Louisa could have poisoned Collins. But why would a poisoner tell the police—unasked and on multiple occasions—that she alone had given Collins his food, beverages and medicines? Moreover, if she was responsible for administering the poison, why hadn't she disposed of the contents of the arsenic-filled tumbler? This brought them back to that pivotal yet troubling piece of mute evidence.

Finally, in terms of motive, the Crown had struggled to provide an explanation as to why Louisa would want to kill Collins, which undermined its 'double murder' scenario. On the other hand, regarding Andrews' death, it must be remembered that Collins had as much to gain as Louisa if her husband was eliminated.

• • •

The question of Collins' possible culpability in Andrews' death was one that also intrigued Archibald, the *Bulletin*'s editor, so much so that he crafted a story that might account for Collins' actions. 'His mind was low in type, and he had no conscience,' began Archibald, 'and his illicit love had become an infatuation.' With little inclination to work but unable to live on credit at his new lodging house, Collins faced a dilemma—until he devised a solution. All that separated him from his lover and financial freedom was her husband. He had spotted a box of Rough on Rats during his illicit visits to the house, which led to an idea. But should he involve Louisa? Even though she was delightfully immoral, it didn't mean that she would join him in carrying out his plan. If she spurned the idea, she would no doubt spurn him as well. If she fell in with his scheme, what certainty did he have that she would not turn on him if their crime was discovered? So, secretly, on his visits to the house, he began leaving smidgens of arsenic in the beer Andrews would consume in the evening. Before long, he had gained everything he desired.

Fifteen months later, his beloved son was dead, his finances were pitiful because of intermittent work and gambling, and he was in despair. Horror at what he had done—what he had become—overwhelmed him. In this state of despair, he decided that he needed to suffer as his victim had suffered. That was when he consumed the first dose of arsenic. He thought it would kill him, but it didn't. He took more and more again, keeping an arsenic packet in his trouser pocket to allow ready access. His concerned wife kept calling the doctor, but he didn't tell anyone what he was doing. Finally, he put a large dose into his bedside cup and succeeded in killing himself.

'We do not seriously say that the foregoing story is the true story of Collins' death,' Archibald concluded. 'The theory that Collins murdered Andrews and afterwards committed suicide may not be, prima facie, as strong as the elaborate and well-woven theory on which the Crown has obtained a conviction; but, still, it is one of the many hitherto unconsidered explanations of this mysterious crime.' He argued that the Crown had perfected its case as it went along, and that little incidents which would be meaningless outside the Crown's case or would pass as the words and actions of a half-tipsy woman had become laden with significance when viewed through the prism of their theory. Many of these incidents would become unimportant again if his new theory was argued, while others would present themselves as powerful sources of confirmation.

Significantly, for example, his theory offered a motive for Collins' death whereas the Crown had been unable to provide a motive that adequately explained Louisa's decision to kill him. 'All this we do say while believing Mrs Collins to be guilty,' Archibald added with brutal honesty, 'but we have lived to be disillusioned of many ideas just as strong as that which we entertain concerning the guilt of Mrs Louisa Collins.'

In his own deliberations about the verdict, Archibald had reached the conclusion that the question of Louisa's guilt or innocence was not the primary issue, but whether the jury had reached its verdict in a manner that invested it with legal certainty. Yet how could the verdict have legal certainty if the jurors were victims of fallacious arguments and if the defence hadn't the skills to adequately counter them? Moreover, while there should be legal certainty to justify a guilty verdict in any trial, there must be the highest moral certainty to justify an execution. And how could the highest moral certainty exist when twenty-four men—or thirty-six, if the Andrews jurors were included—had deliberated long and hard without being able to reach that necessary legal certainty?

Surely, the absence of legal and moral certainty should serve as an impassable gulf between Louisa and the gallows. 'Men should never voluntarily put it out of their power to unsay a thing said, to undo a thing done,' he warned. He reminded his readers of the recent reports about two English prisoners found innocent after ten years of hard labour and the impossibility of freeing them if they had already been hanged. The men were tried before a British jury under British law. Would a Sydney jury have done any better?

• • •

As the gallows clock kept ticking, letters continued to be written in cottages and terraces, farmhouses and mansions, not only in New South Wales but all across the country, as if the final 'death' or 'mercy' decision would rest on the number of different arguments proposed.

Community tension increased. And when the community wasn't happy, one group of men soon learnt about it: those who occupied the most influential house in Sydney.

Chapter 37

The punishment of death was not intended by the Author of life to be entrusted to the fallible discretion of ordinary human governments.

Henry Parkes

Ninian Melville had been reading the reports about Louisa Collins' case and was among those troubled by her situation. The one-time undertaker with his long black coat, bulbous pipe and colourful stories had been reincarnated as the member for Northumberland. In that role, he had decided to bring his concerns about Louisa's case before the Legislative Assembly. Fortunately, parliament was in session although little was getting done.

Relations between Sir Henry Parkes' government and George Dibbs' opposition were tense and acrimonious. The financial estimates needed to be completed before parliament closed for Christmas yet the tussle had become 'a veritable tug-of-war'—vented the *Sydney Morning Herald*—'with the whole Parkes' clientele walking off with the government end of the rope while a batch of gesticulating iconoclasts struggle manfully at the other end, figuratively howling, "Stop thief!"' During election rallies two years previously, Parkes had promised to extricate the colony from the government's financial slough if his men were voted into office. Once he held the reins of government, though, he realised that the much-maligned deficit was his own government's biggest windfall. Others, who saw through the trickery and deceit, begged the leaders to stop behaving like greedy, petulant children and to start putting the colony's welfare first.

Melville, a Dibbs supporter, knew that he couldn't randomly introduce the subject of Louisa's execution. What topic under discussion would be appropriate? He decided to raise the matter on 19 December under the guise of discussing the financial estimates of the justice department.

'I trust that the remarks I am about to make will not be misunderstood and that what I am about to say will be received in the spirit in which it is uttered,' he began.

A look of confusion crossed the faces of some of his companions. It seemed an odd beginning for such a dry subject as the justice department's bills; however, the 'bird of evil omen'—as he had been nicknamed—had the floor and no one interrupted him.

'I intend to refer to the case of the woman Louisa Collins.'

Some were reminded that 'noisy Ninny'—he of the 'nimble lip'—had once been the butt of Henry Kendall's scathing wit in *The Song of Ninian Melville*. Was the 'windbag' about to commence another 'howling swell' in the voice described by a political commentator as being as loud as a trumpet and as discordant as bagpipes?

'I admit at once that the decision of the Executive could be justified and defended, but I think the circumstances of the case justify me in asking that the decision should be reconsidered.' He mentioned some of his concerns about Louisa's case, including the Crown's relentless attempts to bring her to trial, and he challenged the Minister for Justice to provide a parallel case.

The chairman was used to members attempting to steer parliament's time in their own direction. 'I will point out to the honourable member that your remarks are scarcely relevant to the question before the committee.'

Aware that his action would be open to challenge, Melville had prepared a response. 'With a view to putting myself in order,' he replied, 'I intend, as a matter of form, to move a reduction in the salary of the Minister for Justice.'

Parkes thought this an outrageous ploy. 'The Minister for Justice had really nothing to do with the case!' he protested.

'Perhaps the Minister for Justice was not directly responsible for the course taken by the Crown in this prosecution,' Melville admitted, 'but the honourable gentleman is the only minister in the House who represents the Department of Justice. There is no attorney-general present.'

'The attorney-general has nothing to do with it!' Parkes exploded.

'The attorney-general has everything to do with it,' Melville declared firmly, 'for he filed the bill which caused this woman to be placed on her trial.' He told the House that he was not going to argue that the woman was innocent, that although there were doubts about the evidence he would accept the inevitable and say that she was guilty. He also recognised that, in confirming her sentence, the Executive Council had not acted improperly. With the judge's report and the jury's verdict before them, and with no fresh facts or appeals offered for their consideration, they had little alternative but to let the law take its course.

Still, it had been years since New South Wales had been disgraced by the execution of a woman, so why was it happening now? He wouldn't stop to argue the question of capital punishment generally—which he didn't believe in—except to say that he didn't see what good would be achieved by executing the woman when she could be adequately punished by substituting life imprisonment for death. He believed that if an appeal was made to the government by a representative of the people, one that covered the concerns he had already mentioned, that appeal would be grounds enough to reconsider the case.

'To put the discussion in order,' he concluded, 'I move that the item "Minister for Justice £1500" be reduced to £500.'

Parkes picked up the gauntlet. He chastised Melville for embarking on such a course of action, saying that it would have no good effect on Louisa's fate or, more importantly, on the policy of capital punishment. He declared that if it were ever justifiable to take away a person's life, it would appear to be so in Louisa's case. She had been tried by one of the most capable judges in the colony, a man who had personally told him and the council that the woman had been ably defended and that there were no grounds for mercy. 'If the conviction is complete,' Parkes continued, seemingly unaware that his use of the word 'if' revealed a doubt as to whether her conviction was truly 'complete' or not, 'it is one of the most cruel, inexcusable, terrible murders ever perpetrated in the world's history.'

Of course, the members could think of a few worse murders in world history; nevertheless, they wouldn't interrupt their leader's flight of hyperbole.

Parkes admitted that he didn't believe in the deterrent effect of capital punishment; however, the legislature remained obdurate in its refusal to give up its hold on human life. That being the case, neither the members of the executive nor those of parliament had any other option than to uphold the law—a law that saw no difference between man and woman. And why should it see any difference when the lessons of history—of French streets running with blood during the time of the Revolution, for example—showed that women who forgot their sex were responsible for the worst of humanity's crimes? (The *Echo*'s political correspondent noted that the premier revelled here in painting a picture of the horrible things women had done: 'And yet the Premier wishes to make them members of Parliament!')

Parkes agreed that it was abhorrent to hang a woman; however, it was also abhorrent that a woman could commit such an unwomanly crime, so why shouldn't she suffer the dread sentence of the law? And if the other members thought that the death statutes were wrong, they could remedy the evil by putting forward a bill to abolish capital punishment and he would give it his support. Meanwhile, they could act as citizens and petition the governor about Louisa Collins. Royal instructions decreed that the governor should be hesitant to pardon or reprieve anyone condemned to death unless the Executive Council advised that it was expedient to do so. Nonetheless, in all cases, the final decision was the governor's irrespective of whether the council agreed with it or not.

'I do not know what course could be wrong, or what place could be wrong, if it were possible to save our colony from disgrace, and to save a human life,' countered member Thomas Walker, a close friend of Ninian Melville. 'We are now upon the eve of that period of the year when all humanity indulges in rejoicing, in making merry and in gladness, and we are about to perpetrate an act which, in the opinion of those who do not believe in capital punishment, is nothing short of national murder. Let the woman swing from the gallows and let us behold her as we rise from our Christmas dinners at this season of goodwill towards mankind.' He added that if one iota of good could be achieved by executing the woman, then they should let the death penalty take its course. If it could bring back the murdered husband, then let it be done. But it wouldn't. He suggested that Parkes consider using his large majority to bring in a law to abolish capital punishment.

'Hear! Hear!' shouted other abolitionists.

Walker said that, in the meantime, the law permitted the premier and his cabinet to advise the governor to exercise the prerogative of mercy—as had happened in the case of the Maitland murderesses.

Why withhold similar advice in this instance? Louisa Collins had already suffered considerable punishment in the anticipation of her own death, and she had endured what no other man or woman had endured by being put to trial four times. Moreover, the fact that special arrangements had been made before her fourth trial to change the judge so as to increase the likelihood of a conviction made it all the more reasonable that mercy should be offered her.

Other parliamentary voices were also determined to be heard. Thomas O'Mara, the member for Monaro, disputed Parkes' claim that there was no distinction in law or kind between the treatment of men and women in terms of criminal punishment. He reminded the House that men were still flogged, yet women were not. 'Is there any man who, because flogging is a recognised punishment under our criminal code, would dare to advocate the flogging of a woman?'

'Yes,' said Parkes obstinately. 'Women, unfortunately, are flogged in many countries of Europe, and plenty of men in the world advocate it!'

'Not in New South Wales!' was the appalled response from all over the House.

'I regret exceedingly that this debate has taken place,' declared James Garvan, the member for Eden. An intelligent, thoughtful, principled man, he was well liked in the House and was praised by political commentators as being unafraid to run clear of the ruck. 'If there was a hope that mercy might yet enter into the counsels of ministers in their final decision, this inopportune and early discussion has almost compelled ministers to assume an attitude from which it will be almost impossible for them afterwards to deviate.'

'Hear, hear,' muttered a few voices.

Nonetheless, he could offer some insights from a constitutional perspective. The governor's rights and responsibilities had been reviewed in the aftermath of bushranger Frank Gardiner's release so the governor would abide by whatever decision the executive made. 'Suppose after due consideration the government should decide that the wretched woman ought not to be hanged, would one suppose that the governor would dare to carry out the death sentence? The thing would be impossible. It is not in the power of the governor to enforce the carrying out of the sentence.'

'I am obliged to say that I think the governor could act in direct opposition to the ministry according to the present law!' Parkes countered, knowing that he had personally entreated the governor to do so only two years previously—with some success.

'The ministry has the power to remove the only officer who could carry out the sentence,' was Garvan's simple response.

The colossus, John Neild, with his Garibaldi beard and fiercely curled moustache, could have played the villain in a children's pantomime. Instead, the member for Paddington was one of the few trying to communicate the horror of the Crown's treatment of Louisa's children. 'Almost the chief witnesses for the prosecution at the many trials—witnesses without which her conviction would have been impossible—were her own little children,' he reminded the fathers and grandfathers in the House. 'These ill-educated, uninformed, trembling little creatures were brought up no less than four times, the evidence was practically the same on each occasion, and on the fourth occasion it convicted her—why?—because they had been put through the mill time after time until, unhappily for their mother, they learned their lesson of evidence too well.'

Parkes was affronted. 'That really ought not to be said!'

'I never meant to imply that the officers of the Crown had in any manner tutored the children,' Neild clarified. 'What I desired to convey was that little children could not be brought up time after time to give certain evidence without the matter being impressed on their minds and without the effect of making their evidence gradually more and more important.'

'In what way?' Parkes demanded. 'Against their mother?'

'There is an old saying,' said Neild, 'that if a man told a lie often enough, he would credit his own lie at last.'

'How does that apply to the children?' Parkes asked, refusing to comprehend Neild's meaning.

'It is disingenuous on the honourable gentleman's part to interrupt me in this manner, because he must know the line of argument which I am following—that the more often a story is repeated, the more perfect that story becomes.'

For a short time, the debate descended into bitter sniping, with members accusing Neild of suggesting that the Crown law officers had tutored the children to tell lies. Others grumbled about the introduction of the subject in the first place and the amount of time they had already devoted to discussing it.

'Then do not discuss it!' exclaimed Opposition Leader George Dibbs.

A discussion began about not discussing the subject. Dibbs eventually joined in, using the opportunity to take a swipe at Parkes for making such an impassioned address when he could simply have pointed out the gravity of the question and the fact that the House should not be talking about it.

Parkes, however, was in full flight. He reiterated that the House made the laws and had emphatically declined to abolish capital punishment. He mentioned the case of Mary Ann Brownlow, who had been sentenced to death for the stabbing murder of her adulterous husband while in a fit of jealous rage during her pregnancy, and said that the judge, a man still held in high esteem, had refused to say a word in her favour even though the whole colony had implored him to show mercy. 'That unfortunate woman took her little child and suckled it on the steps of the scaffold, and then walked up and was hanged.'

Cries of 'Shame!' and 'Outrage!' and 'A disgrace of civilisation!' rang around the House for some time.

Digging his heels in, Parkes declared that many women had been hanged in this country, ignoring the fact that the Brownlow case had occurred thirty-five years previously, that no woman had been executed in New South Wales for twenty-eight years and that most laws fell into disuse long before the legislators abolished them. 'The law remains,' he repeated stubbornly. 'Abolish the punishment of death tomorrow if you like, but if you maintain it, let the punishment be justly dealt out to whoever perpetrates the dreadful crime, whether man or woman, rich or poor, favoured by circumstances or utterly unfavoured by circumstances.'

'Why not hang the man who hangs her?' Walker interjected.

Parkes slid past that challenge by saying, 'I did not hear what the honourable member said.'

Thomas Hassall piped up, 'The premier has said that he was in favour of the abolition of capital punishment. Let him close an honoured career by bringing that about.'

'That has nothing to do with this case!' Parkes expostulated.

'It has a great deal to do with this case.' Hassall argued that it would be too late to wait until after the woman was hanged before saying anything about it and that, if she were hanged, it was this parliament that would be responsible. 'I believe that it is the will of parliament and the people that this woman should not be hanged.'

'I believe that the women of the country would vote for her being hanged!' declared Parkes.

'The women of Australia are not so depraved as to desire anything of the sort!' Hassall cried. 'I am astonished at a man like the premier uttering such a slander on the women of Australia.'

'They do not approve of wives poisoning their husbands!' Parkes snapped back.

'I do not think that ten per cent of the women of the colony would sign a petition in favour of hanging this woman,' was Hassall's indignant response.

Ninian Melville took the floor again, saying that, hopefully, his appeal would give rise to a movement outside the House so that the public's opinions could be brought to bear on the executive in the proper way. Then he directed a stream of vitriol at their 'Shylock' premier, ranting about Parkes' willingness to violate the law in other instances, in particular in his treatment of the Chinese.

Melville's diatribe was beginning to alarm some members of the House. One called out, 'That is not the way to gain your object.'

'I am not going to be mealy-mouthed or cowardly in order to gain my object,' Melville declared.

'You will hang her!' cried another.

Eventually, Melville announced that he was withdrawing his amendment to the justice department estimates and sat down.

• • •

Did Melville realise what he had just done? Some of his colleagues were horrified. They knew enough about their premier to recognise how he might react when one of the House gadflies challenged his authority. Parkes the progressive deplored capital punishment; indeed, he was a man who, in his younger days, had seen his nobility in his pursuit of the moral high ground. Parkes the pragmatist, however, had been forced to adopt positions that were at odds with his philosophies. And Parkes the petulant was known to let his vain, overly sensitive nature triumph when his authority was publicly undermined. So when one particular gadfly—a man labelled by the premier himself as 'the veriest charlatan that ever lived'—claimed the moral high ground during a political debate and forced Parkes to retreat to a position he was morally opposed to, it raised the alarming possibility that the premier might so entrench himself that he would refuse to budge even if a lifeline were offered to him, one that might not only save the premier's face—and Louisa Collins' life—but the New South Wales community from the horror of executing another woman.

Chapter 38

> While loathing the crime for which Louisa Collins has been condemned, we regard the punishment of death as a barbarous method of executing justice, and as demoralizing both to the individuals who have to perform the execution, and to the Society by whose sanction the sentence is carried out.
>
> Petition of Women of Victoria

How dare the premier announce to parliament that the females of Australia would vote for Louisa Collins to be hanged! Women in Sydney and Melbourne were incensed. They began preparing petitions to the New South Wales governor, petitions that were to be signed only by women.

The Sydney petition could be signed at the Market Street grocery store of abolitionist and temperance advocate, Henry Prior Palser. Seemingly drafted by his long-term abolitionist ally, Frederick Lee—who would lead the deputation that delivered it—the petition begged for mercy on many of the grounds already argued in parliament and in Lee's correspondence with the press and politicians. It also raised a new subject of concern, an issue that would never have occurred to the men who were largely driving the debate. Not only was it abhorrent to every feeling of humanity that a woman should suffer death by the noose, it was even worse that she should suffer death at the hands of a man.

The women's complaint was a reminder of the many indignities they encountered in their dealings with men, including the sexual foundation underpinning much of the brutality inflicted on them. Who could forget the reminiscences of the loathsome hangman in Charles Dickens' *Barnaby Rudge*? His words intimated that he was revisiting pleasurable sexual conquests when he spoke about killing young women. While the law might see hanging as a gender-blind form of punishment, the reality of its enforcement was a different matter entirely.

The Victorian women's petition—which coincidentally was to be signed in Melbourne's Collins Street—focused on the impact of capital punishment on society as a whole. It also questioned whether death sentences were a greater deterrent than punishments that allowed the possibility of reformation.

The editor of Queensland's *Brisbane Courier* was shocked that the southern women should petition for mercy. He declared that a hasty act, even when the results were terrible, could still appeal to the latent sympathy in our hearts; however, Louisa's actions had drawn nothing from the community's hearts but revulsion and hatred. Her skill and precaution in administering small doses of arsenic, along with the average man's incredulity that such a Lucrezia Borgia could live in Sydney's suburbs, had led the juries to disagree, until unimpeachable evidence at last secured the conviction of the 'most cruel and cold-blooded criminal who has outraged the name of woman'. Yet it was *women* who were agitating for the mitigation of her sentence. Why?

The editor concluded that they and their unsophisticated friends had failed to grasp the true nature of the beast. 'Too often women seem to puzzle our stupid logical male intellects by aberrations of a perversity, charming no doubt, but sometimes a trifle trying,' he declared, dismissing the progressive arguments included in the women's petitions, the same arguments that had already led some of the world's countries to abolish capital punishment and would ultimately drive their own to follow suit.

Some southern women were also horrified at their sisters' appeals for mercy. A Married Woman declared, 'Never was there a case which called for the death sentence to be carried out so completely as this one. Unless such conduct be made an example of, no man's life would be secure if his wife should happen to transfer her affections to another.'

Was she suggesting that any married woman who fell in love with another man was stepping onto a slippery slope that led to homicide?

Other letter-writers—male and female alike—provided similar 'example' arguments. If Louisa was not hanged, society would be giving women a licence to commit murder, to become even greater criminals than men. If Louisa was not hanged, every other instance of capital punishment inflicted on men as well as women would have been unmerciful and unjust.

Of course, the latter argument suggested, by extension, that society should continue to execute people for whatever crimes had historically incurred the death penalty, a notion supporting the abolitionist's contention that capital punishment was unfair rather than offering a solid foundation for the advocates' justifications.

One man declared that Louisa should hang because her deeds were worse than those of Jack the Ripper. 'Hers is a crime not of butchering of the few horrible minutes, but the torturing, hour by hour, day by day, of those who depended on her for loving sustenance instead of the worst of all, slow murder.'

Another argued that she shouldn't hang because women weren't smart enough to know what they were doing. Are you serious? mocked a third. 'What man or woman can be said to be stupid who can plan a murder in such a manner that he or she can subsequently haggle three consecutive juries?'

• • •

'If the champions of Louisa Collins want to obtain a commutation of the death sentence, they would do well to devote their attention to finding solid rather than sentimental grounds,' declared the *Sydney Morning Herald*. The editor—an ardent supporter of the death penalty—said that those begging for mercy had offered three arguments to justify their plea: that the condemned was a woman; that previous juries had been unable to agree upon a verdict; and that it was the Christmas season in the centennial year. He dismissed 'Christmas' as a ridiculous argument, evidently forgetting that Henry Parkes' pleas to Governor Carrington for mercy for the Mount Rennie rapists dwelt at length on the harm to the colony's reputation if the youths were hanged in the lead-up to the centenary celebrations.

Regarding the 'hung jury' argument, the editor said that its force depended entirely on the voting proportions. If a large proportion had voted for a conviction with only a single juror disagreeing, the mandated punishment should be carried out.

No doubt the editor was assuming that there were only one or two hold-outs in an otherwise landslide of guilty votes. The Crown refrained from advising him that, by virtue of his own argument, Louisa should be reprieved because the combined voting numbers in the first two Collins juries had been two-to-one in favour of her acquittal.

As for the 'woman' argument, the *Herald*'s editor suggested that the mercy advocates should reverse the situation and ask if they would be crying out for mercy if Collins had poisoned Louisa. 'If women hold the same rights and privileges as men, and share the same advantages of the law and society alike with them, they should also share the responsibilities that their citizenship places upon them. There is no equality between men and women if there is not an equality of responsibility.'

But that's the point, another letter-writer declared as he offered a counter argument as solid as granite itself. 'Women are not citizens; they have no voice in enacting the laws of the country; they have to obey because they have no share, nor are they consulted, in electing the lawmakers; they have no representation in the parliament of the country, although taxed as if they are citizens. That is taxation without representation, the worst of tyrannies.'

Any politician worth his votes knew that 'taxation without representation' was the bogeyman that had lost Britain its greatest colony: the United States of America. Fortunately, the odd voteless woman signing a mercy petition for a black-hearted female criminal wouldn't be likely to generate a political revolt. Or would it?

Most of the press recognised that New South Wales was at a political crossroad, that the decision made in the next couple of weeks could set the ultimate precedent in the matter of the execution of women. 'If Louisa Collins is not hanged,' declared the *Sydney Morning Herald*, 'then we can hang no woman in time to come, for none could commit a worse crime.'

Chapter 39

It is better that ten guilty persons escape than that one innocent suffer.

William Blackstone, *Commentaries on the Laws of England*

As Sydneysiders pinned mistletoe to doorways and cooked their Christmas feasts, Frederick Lee's thoughts were far from the season's festivities. Louisa's case had been mentioned again in parliament on 20 December, the evening after the acrimonious debate. One of Parkes' supporters had asked the premier if the government would cover the cost of defence counsel if Louisa wanted to appeal to the full court. Parkes replied, 'I can assure the honourable gentleman and the House that I will take it upon myself to extend every possible consideration to this unhappy woman. If it is a question of money to secure counsel for her under any supposable circumstances, certainly counsel shall be paid. In any case whatever, where any attempt may be made to place the conduct of this unhappy woman in a better light, or to serve the ends of justice in her favour, the government will render every conceivable assistance.'

With such a public affirmative, Lee took action. The following morning he engaged solicitors Slattery & Heydon to take on Louisa's appeal. Thomas Slattery was a member of parliament—one of George

Dibbs' Opposition—so he couldn't receive payment from the Crown, although, as he told Lee, he had no desire for such remuneration anyway. Even so, he would require official confirmation of the Crown's offer if he were to engage a barrister to act for Louisa.

Lee wrote to Parkes to advise that Louisa's solicitors were ready to move the Supreme Court to quash her conviction and required the government's authorisation to engage a barrister. Cleverly, he asked that the premier appoint a Queen's Counsel to take charge of the appeal. He justified his request on the grounds that Lusk's experience with the case meant that he should be engaged as a junior barrister, but that bar etiquette was such that Lusk, as a long-standing member of the bar, couldn't be a 'junior' to one more junior than he. Lee's request was approved.

While some newspaper editors muttered that the Crown wouldn't fund such a case if Louisa were a man, the *Sydney Morning Herald* thought it wise that the public's concerns about her case should be openly raised in the full court before irreparable steps were taken. 'It is impossible to calculate the disastrous effect such a blunder might have on the public mind.'

Of course, Frederick Lee was more concerned about the disastrous effect on Louisa herself if she went to the gallows unjustly.

In the meantime, Lee's concerns had grown rather than diminished. During the recent debate about Louisa's case, a parliamentarian had intimated that the Crown had conspired with the judiciary to oust the judge scheduled to preside over her fourth trial and replace him with a more desirable choice. 'The Crown tried at every possible step to convict this woman,' parliamentarian Walker had told the House. 'It had so presupposed her guilt and prejudged her that it moved every machinery within its power in order to get a particular judge, the chief justice, to preside at the trial.'

Surely such a judicial manipulation breached the guidelines of the

Westminster system, the touted separation of powers and independence of the judiciary.

There was more. The premier himself had told parliament that the chief justice explicitly refused to recommend mercy because Louisa had been 'ably defended'. Yet her appeal would show otherwise—and, if his surmises were correct, it would show that the chief justice was well aware of the fact.

• • •

At ten am on Friday 28 December, three sombre-faced judges walked into the Banco courtroom in the Supreme Court building at the corner of Elizabeth and King streets and sat at the bench. A strange hush came over the room: not the usual diminution of sound that accompanied the 'court is in session' announcement, but one broken by squeaks of surprise as each individual face was identified. Among the note-taking pressmen, only the *Echo*'s correspondent would remark that it was 'singular' that the three judges hearing the appeal to quash Louisa's conviction for murdering Collins were the same three judges who had presided over her three trials for murdering Collins.

The recently deceased William Bede Dalley would have frowned at the bench's composition. As attorney-general, he had helped to legislate the Supreme Court Appellate Jurisdiction Act of 1884 and, in doing so, had intended to prevent convicting judges from participating in appeals. He had argued that judges were no more exempt than anyone else from holding wrongful views or from persuading themselves of their own accuracy, and that they would be likely to bring to the appellate courts an 'intellectual interest'—at the very least—in sustaining their judgments. That being the case, the bill stated: 'No Judge of the Supreme Court shall sit on the hearing of an appeal from or on a motion to set aside any judgment, order, decree, ruling or decision made by him.'

Unfortunately, the act covered civil appeals only as there was no criminal appeals court. Common-law doctrine held that the jury's verdict on the facts in a criminal trial was final and sacrosanct. Even though the need for an avenue of criminal appeal had long been recognised, it would be another three decades—the year 1912, in fact—before New South Wales established its own Court of Criminal Appeal.

Louisa's team suppressed any feelings of alarm at the bench's composition. There was nothing they could do to change it and no point in complaining.

Louisa herself wasn't present. She would sit in her cell waiting to hear the results of this last-ditch effort. Her attempt to 'plead the belly' had failed; the authorities had already announced that she wasn't pregnant. Perhaps her eminent Queen's Counsel could find a legal loophole to save her.

• • •

Law reporters from all the major newspapers were in the press gallery. Interest in Louisa's case was so intense that even the *Australian Town and Country Journal* would include a detailed report in words that its readers could easily understand. Its law reporter explained that the application aimed to show that there was something so defective in the trial's proceedings that the conviction was bad and void at law and should accordingly be quashed.

As every lawyer and court reporter knew, if a criminal trial was appropriately conducted, any resulting conviction could not be overturned. Occasionally, though, a mistake of law was made. The defence counsel could point it out during the trial; it was then 'reserved' for later consideration. Alternatively, if something occurred that was not noted at the time but reflected a fatal irregularity, a 'writ of error' motion could be moved. Louisa's counsel would try to use one or both of these avenues to quash her verdict. If he succeeded, she would be set at liberty.

Not that the public wanted her to be set free. Not at all. But many—perhaps most—would rather that she wasn't hanged. All eyes were focused on Queen's Counsel Francis Rogers, the senior barrister chosen to represent Louisa, as he stood up to address the bench.

'I wish to point out to the court that there are two points that I desire to put before the bench,' Rogers began. He explained that his first point related to the admissibility of the evidence regarding Charles Andrews' death, while his second point dealt with a juror's receipt of a telegram without the judge or the defence being informed of its contents. He thought that the telegram issue was a matter on which a writ of error might properly lie. Regarding the Andrews evidence, though, the question of its reception had not been reserved at trial so he felt that the point could not be argued.

Hugh Lusk was sitting beside him at the barristers' table—or perhaps trying to crawl underneath it—shamed by the knowledge that his legal shortcomings might mean the difference between life and death for his client. Further shame was to come: he would be the first barrister struck off the New South Wales roll, albeit for later pecuniary infractions rather than legal misconduct.

'What are you moving for?' asked Justice Windeyer bluntly.

'I am moving on a writ of error to quash the conviction,' Rogers reported. He added that the attorney-general had told him that the court was sitting only to consider the writ of error so he couldn't see how he could argue the first point regarding the admissibility of the Andrews evidence.

Rogers was wily. He wasn't demanding that the bench hear his concerns about the Andrews evidence as he had no legal grounds for raising the subject. Even so, he was hoping to encourage the judges to be less rigid in their application of the law—if they chose to be or if, perhaps, the attorney-general could convince them to be.

'Of course, we are sitting here for any matter that may be legally brought before the court,' said Chief Justice Darley, who, if it had been a civil case, wouldn't have been allowed to sit there at all. 'But there is no doubt that nothing can be legally brought before us now except such matters as can be dealt with on a writ of error.'

Attorney-General Simpson piped up. 'On behalf of the Crown, I am perfectly willing that any point in favour of Louisa Collins should be submitted, and argued if necessary, and decided by your Honours.' The government was desperate to ease the political pressure, especially if it relieved the Executive Council from carrying the burden of this life-or-death decision.

'Why should there be a different course pursued in this case than in any other?' Darley challenged, his hand rigidly clutching the rule book. He had no interest in political machinations.

'I do not see why it should,' the attorney-general agreed. A quick shuffle backwards as he placated the judges, then he gently pushed forward with his own agenda. 'Still, if their Honours think fit to allow any points of law which the prisoner should receive the benefit of, though they might not be legally before the court, the Crown is willing that she should have the benefit of them.'

Louisa's legal team knew they had reached a critical moment in her appeal. The attorney-general—the voice of the executive—had just given his approval for the judiciary to permit the question of the Andrews evidence to be discussed.

The chief justice refused to budge. He stated again that no question had been reserved at trial nor was any question asked to be reserved.

There it was—the admission that Darley must know that Louisa had not been ably defended. If she *had* been ably represented, her counsel would have asked that the point of evidence be reserved for later consideration, allowing that point to now be discussed.

The chief justice opened up slightly, saying that he had taken great precautions to ensure that the Andrews evidence dealt only with his death by poisoning and that he had refused the Crown's attempts to discuss motive. He also reminded Louisa's counsel that the evidence relating to *Collins'* death had been introduced into the *Andrews* trial without the point being reserved in that instance either.

And there it was again. Darley had just told the court that Louisa's counsel had failed to ably defend her a *second* time.

Darley added that, even though the point had not been reserved, the common-law judges had met in the aftermath of the Andrews trial to consider the admissibility question, knowing that Louisa faced another charge. They felt that they needed to decide what course of action the court should take if the same type of evidence was submitted in a future trial.

Frederick Lee hadn't known this. It was a new and startling piece of information. It also proved beyond a shadow of doubt that the chief justice must have realised that Louisa was not ably defended. So why had he said otherwise to the Executive Council?

Windeyer took up the discussion, explaining that the common-law judges had decided that the evidence regarding Andrews' death was just as admissible as in a case of forgery or passing bad money where evidence was offered to show that it had happened before. He added, 'Where a number of persons died by poisoning, you could not shut out from consideration the fact that they all died in the same way, showing that it was not a mere matter of chance, but that the persons died from poison as a matter of design.'

Justice Foster confirmed that he too had no doubts on that point. In fact, he was surprised that the evidence regarding Andrews' death had not been introduced in the first trial.

Accepting defeat, Rogers backed away from the subject. Certainly, the judges were well aware of the importance of the Andrews evidence in convicting Louisa and had already decided that case law supported its admission. Whether Darley's decision to admit the evidence reflected legal brilliance or otherwise would not, unfortunately, be exposed to the harsh light of a legal challenge.

• • •

Louisa had been paying more attention during her trial than her critics had realised. Through her veil of apparent disinterest, she had noticed that a juror was given a telegram without anyone in authority checking what it said. When she eventually told her counsel, he recognised that this was the type of mistake that could be argued in a 'writ of error' motion. If successful, her conviction would be quashed.

Rogers asked the chief justice about his own memory of the telegram incident. Darley reported that he couldn't recollect seeing anything at all—not a telegram nor a juror receiving something that might have been a telegram. However, the Crown prosecutor said that he remembered seeing a juror receive some sort of communication and calling out his answer, 'It is all right.' They all knew that the only way members of the public could inform a sequestered juror about matters of personal importance was via a telegram. So what had this particular telegram communicated?

Darley grumbled, 'Is every trial to be upset because something gets into the hands of a juryman in this way?'

'I may say that I cannot think of anything more dangerous than an unopened telegram going into the hands of a juryman,' countered Rogers. 'I do not say that there was anything in this telegram, but in the case of some great political trial, a communication might be handed to a juryman which would have the greatest possible influence upon him.'

After further fruitless discussion, the court adjourned until two pm so a clerk could make enquiries at the telegraph office. During the break, the juror himself was found. He advised that the telegram was merely a request to know if he needed any clothes in the event of further detention. The telegram confirmed his recollection.

Chief Justice Darley was the first to provide his opinion. He said that to accept a writ of error on the matter of the telegram would require evidence that some mischief had been caused by its introduction and there was no evidence of this. Windeyer said that if they found error in this instance they would be setting a dangerous precedent, that plans could be made to send innocuous communications to jurors in the hope of overturning unwanted verdicts. Foster dismissed any suggestion of irregularity. All three pointed out that, having heard the cases themselves, they also thought that the evidence against Louisa was compelling and that she was guilty of murdering both husbands. With the thump of a gavel, they refused Louisa's application for a writ of error and confirmed her conviction. Her last avenue of judicial appeal was now closed.

'By these proceedings, the administration of justice has been removed above the chance of suspicion,' proclaimed a relieved *Sydney Morning Herald*. 'Any lingering doubt that might have existed in the public mind is thus authoritatively set aside, and the fate of the condemned woman, whatever it may be, is in the hands of the Executive.'

However, the Executive Council, with Parkes as its leader, had already made its decision. That left one person only who still held the prerogative of mercy in his sovereign-empowered hands.

Chapter 40

> The quality of mercy is not strain'd,
> It droppeth as the gentle rain from heaven
> Upon the place beneath. It is twice blest:
> It blesseth him that gives and him that takes.
>
> William Shakespeare, *The Merchant of Venice*

Frederick Lee knew all about the royal prerogative of mercy. Over the past two decades, most of his endeavours as Standing Counsel for Condemned Prisoners had been directed towards obtaining mercy. With no court of criminal appeal and an unrelenting executive, it was the condemned's only hope. Like Louisa, most weren't asking to be freed, only to have their sentences commuted from death to life.

The hard-line conservatives among the press and public regularly asked why mercy was even allowed. What was its benefit to the community as a whole? If crimes like Louisa's were to be stopped, then what was needed was the harsh punishment of all criminals.

In truth, mercy was an essential component of any harsh punishment regime. This royal prerogative also derived from the ancient belief in the divine right of kings and it reinforced sovereignty by placing in the authority's hands the power to decide who should live or die. But the decision to grant mercy wasn't based on the warmth of pity and forgiveness as the power-holders often declared. Rather, it was driven by the cool logic of political calculation. Any decision to grant mercy would be founded upon the perceived benefit to society as a whole and, most importantly, to the power-holders themselves.

Yet, who in this colonial outpost was actually entitled to grant mercy? The royal prerogative had been absorbed into colonial law and had passed into the hands of the Executive Council with the establishment of representative government; however, nobody was quite certain whether the Queen's representative had the final say. Was this one of the powers that had remained reserved to the Crown—that is, to the Queen and her appointee, the governor? The astute felt that the governor *must* retain this prerogative by virtue of his political independence because, surely, such life-or-death decisions should be beyond the reach of political influence.

Frederick Lee knew that Parkes held that very opinion. In 1874, in the discussions about the early release of bushranger Frank Gardiner, Parkes had advised the then governor that he should ask the ministers for their opinions but that the final decision regarding mercy was his. 'In a community so small,' Parkes reminded him, 'the persons entrusted with authority and the relatives and friends of prisoners move closely together. The means of political pressure are easily accessible.' The Secretary of State for the Colonies had later confirmed this 'reserved right' position. Twelve years later, Parkes expressed the same view when he begged Governor Carrington for mercy for the Mount Rennie rapists. And the governor must have thought similarly because he chose to override the decision of the Executive Council and to commute the death sentences of two of the six men.

Had the attitudes of these two pivotal men changed in the meantime? Colonial law hadn't changed. Nor had the royal instructions issued to Carrington when he accepted the governorship, which Parkes had read to parliament during the debate about Louisa's case:

> The Governor shall not pardon or reprieve any such offender unless it shall appear to him expedient to do so, upon receiving the advice of the said Executive Council thereon; but in all such cases he is to decide either to extend or to withhold a pardon or reprieve, according to his own deliberate judgement, whether the members of the Executive Council concur therein or otherwise.

In making these instructions part of the political record, Premier Parkes was telling the people that, by the authority of Her Majesty the Queen, the governor had the right to extend or withhold the hand of mercy as he saw fit. Parkes was also making clear that he was handing the poisoned chalice that was Louisa Collins to the governor, leaving him to decide whether to abide by the council's decision or override it.

• • •

In the meantime, what could Louisa do to influence these decision-makers? To craft her own escape clause, she would have to play the mercy game. She—or someone in a position of authority—would need to concoct a narrative that explained her actions in a way that obscured her culpability. More than that, it needed to mesh with the cogs that turned the wheel of mercy.

Crafting the right narrative was the hard part. 'I am innocent!' wouldn't work. It hadn't before; it wouldn't now. Once the court had judged her, once society had condemned her, any continuing cry of 'innocence' would be little more than a whisper drowned by the clamouring for her blood.

What words might be appropriate? 'I am guilty but . . .' Yes; admitting culpability would help. The public had been bemoaning her failure to confess or show remorse. The press had also been complaining that she continued to behave as if nothing had happened, as if her date with death wasn't looming closer and closer. Saying 'I am guilty' would definitely be a good start; however, she would need an exceptional explanation if she were to have any chance of obscuring her culpability.

'But . . . I did it to protect my children.' It could work, in principle. In reality, her children—the source of the information that convicted her—hadn't shown any evidence of living in fear of a brutal stepfather.

'But . . . I did it to protect myself.' That could work too—if it were true. Instead, the public had read the testimonies of her boarders and children showing that she and her husband had lived on good terms.

'I did it because I was insane.' That wouldn't work. Although some had suggested that she must be mad, any woman who declared *herself* to be mad was unlikely to be mad because, surely, insanity would be normality to the insane. And insanity hadn't saved poor Henry O'Farrell from his own date with the hangman, anyhow.

Perhaps she could try: 'I am just a poor, weak-willed woman who was bereft after our baby died. I turned to drink to drown my sorrows and let the demon invade my soul. I beg everyone's forgiveness and the forgiveness of the Lord and I throw myself on your mercy.' That might do it. It was clear from the children's evidence that she'd lost control of her drinking after her baby died, which suggested she was using alcohol to ease her sorrow. But no one would believe she was weak-willed. They had seen her sitting in the court day after day with rarely a hint of emotion on her face as she listened to her family and friends destroy her character. They had seen her standing in the dock without so much as a tear running down her cheek as the judge sentenced her to the gallows. She would need to show extreme remorse to convince the public she was worthy of mercy. But, in order to do so, she would need to shed the mask of inscrutability that had hidden her emotions, to remove the rod of fortitude that had kept her standing tall throughout each of her four extraordinary trials. She would need to bare her soul. Worse, she would need to become someone other than the person she had always prided herself on being. Could she do so to save her life?

• • •

Louisa defied the watchers by continuing to present an indifferent countenance, by refusing to show that she was disturbed by her predicament. She had deliberately shown no interest in the outcome of the appeal which, in view of the premier's deadly intransigence, seemed to perplex everyone. When they queried why, she had a simple response, 'They will never hang a woman. They will spare my life at the last moment.'

Anyway, how could they think she had killed Mick? 'This man was everything a woman could wish to have,' she wrote to friends and family members. 'He was the apple of my eye. His voice was music to my ear. He was all I wanted in this life. If I was between him and death, do you think I would let him go? Oh, no fear.'

She added that he wasn't always courageous, but she had long accepted that aspect of his character. He wasn't always patient either, although that was partly because people kept throwing things onto their zinc roof, including the poisonous little berries that were everywhere in Botany, that lodged in their spout and washed into their water tank. Not that he'd been killed by those berries, she was quick to add, because she knew what had killed him even though everyone refused to believe her. He feared having his name in the paper so he had slowly poisoned himself.

He couldn't have imagined that his weakness would cause her so much trouble and sorrow or that the consequences of his weakness would send her to her death.

• • •

The authorities read Louisa's statements and correspondence with interest, wondering if she would say anything that might help them to understand why she had killed her husbands. They noticed that she sometimes used extravagant, romantic language, as if she were trying to hide her educational disadvantages. Then she would lapse into her usual more prosaic style as she explained why Collins was the author of his own death. Interspersed throughout were biblical quotes—the ministrations of the gaol's Anglican clergyman, Canon Charles Rich, were having some effect. Yet still there was no confession. Indeed, there was nothing even close to an admission of guilt.

One of her letters was in response to an unkind communication from her mother, yet the tone of her reply was surprisingly affectionate. Even though her mother's actions had forced her into the loveless marriage that began this disastrous journey, she still seemed to hold a deep well of affection for the woman.

Her mother didn't come to see her in the gaol, although some of her children made the journey. Young May wept bitterly throughout the visit and the warders struggled to remove her. Fred also was deeply distressed. The youngest children, Edwin and Charles, weren't brought to the gaol. They had been admitted to the Benevolent Society Asylum after her committal and later discharged to the officer responsible for sending children to foster homes. No doubt it was thought best not to disturb them in such a way.

Canon Rich also read the letters, wondering what insights he might gain into this unusual woman. He had spent many hours in her cell, one or two visits every day since her conviction, hoping that his spiritual consolation might be of help during her final dark days. Initially, she had seemed indifferent to his ministrations, so the authorities placed another female prisoner in her cell in the hope that the woman's sympathetic touch might bring out Louisa's softer side. The strategy worked. Louisa had opened up, becoming more welcoming and attentive. Soon she was praying earnestly with him and humbly accepting his spiritual suggestions.

As their relationship developed, he asked about her cold demeanour during her four trials. She told him that it was 'but a mere shell', that she had felt her position acutely. The more he talked with her, the more he recognised that she was speaking the truth. She wasn't cold and callous as the press had demonised her. Rather, she was the type of person who would prefer to die than let others know she was distressed by a situation. Only a person with exceptionally strong will could maintain that degree of fortitude in such trying circumstances. It was hard not to be intrigued by her, indeed hard not to admire her on some level, whatever the deeds that had led to their encounter. She wasn't an 'educated' woman, of course, although better schooled than most of her class. Nonetheless, she was intelligent and able. In other circumstances, she might have achieved a great deal with her life.

During their conversations, the clergyman also urged her to talk about her world. She spoke bitterly about her neighbours and her eldest son, although she didn't explain the source of their conflict. As she discussed her family life, it became clear that there had been disturbing influences in her home prior to her first husband's death—not that these could be considered mitigating factors for murder.

Over time, Canon Rich began to feel that there was something odd about her, some sort of mental influence or disturbance that operated in such a way, or was deficient in such a way, that led her to act differently to other people. Still, that didn't mean she had committed murder.

As his knowledge and understanding increased, so too did his feeling of sadness at the thought of her future. In his role, he regularly encountered depraved specimens of humanity, but Louisa wasn't one of them. If she could be reprieved to life imprisonment, he would feel the greatest joy.

Besides, her conviction troubled him. His thoughts kept returning to the arsenic-filled tumbler on the bedside table. Among the many letters published in the newspapers was one from a chemical analyst stating that, if Louisa Collins had the cleverness to administer infinitesimal doses of poison, it was hardly likely she would have left behind such strong evidence of her guilt. The issue puzzled him as well. Could she really have been that foolish?

He couldn't stand by and let her hang, he decided. He would join Frederick Lee in his fight for mercy.

Chapter 41

It seems strange in this progressive century that we can find no better use for our criminals than to hang them.

Western Mail

Frederick Lee had been startled by the judges' revelation that they had allowed the Andrews evidence into the Collins trial on the grounds that case law supported it. Windeyer had made it clear that the starting point for the 'similar facts' argument was their acceptance that Andrews had met his death by arsenic poisoning. Evidently, the judges had ignored the fact that the lack of substantial evidence of causation was the stumbling block that had tripped up the Andrews jury. The jurors had been offered motive, means and opportunity, so the 'reasonable doubt' that had hung the jury must have been their lack of certainty that Andrews had been killed by arsenic poisoning in the first place.

If only Lusk had asked to have the admissibility question reserved at trial. Even if the chief justice had refused to do so at the time of the trial, the attorney-general could probably have convinced the appeal judges to allow the point to be discussed on those grounds alone. In that event, how hard would it have been for Louisa's Queen's Counsel to show that the foundation of the 'similar facts' ruling was not facts but conjecture? Since there was not enough arsenic in Andrews' body to kill him or anyone else—or any*thing* else, for that matter—and since there were innocent ways in which those minuscule traces might have entered his body, there was no proof that arsenic had caused his death. Therefore, the judges' foundational statement 'where a number of persons died by poisoning' was as solid as quicksand for the simple reason that there wasn't any proof that a number of persons *had* died by poisoning. If deadly amounts of cyanide or strychnine or oxalic acid had been found in Collins' body and tiny amounts in Andrews', one could more readily accept the common sense reasoning that this was evidence that both men had been poisoned. But arsenic was too commonplace for its mere presence to be considered a sure sign of poisoning.

Still, all was not lost. Lee had found a case that showed the weakness of the Crown's position: *R. v. Hall.* In 1886 in Canterbury, New Zealand, businessman Thomas Hall had been convicted and sentenced to life imprisonment for attempting to murder his wife by antimony poisoning. After the police found a deadly dose of antimony in the exhumed body of Hall's father-in-law, Hall was convicted of murdering him too and was sentenced to death, even though the only real evidence laid against him was his conviction for attempting to kill his wife by the same means. The point was reserved and the Court of Appeal ruled that there was insufficient proof that the two poisonings formed part of the same transaction or were driven by a common design. Accordingly, Hall's murder conviction was quashed.

The Hall case revealed some extraordinary parallels with Louisa's case—not least because it involved deaths by poisoning and an exhumed body. Significantly, the case against Louisa for Andrews' death was much weaker than that against Hall for his father-in-law's death because of the minuscule amount of arsenic found in Andrews' body. Additionally, Louisa's cases couldn't be considered part of the same transaction or common purpose because her motives—if she had killed the two men—were not the same. Most significantly, Hall's counsel had reserved the point at trial whereas Louisa's counsel hadn't. The result? Life for Hall; death for Louisa.

Would the remarkable similarities between the Australian and New Zealand cases be grounds enough for the governor to reconsider Louisa's death sentence? New Zealand cases could not be used as binding precedents by the New South Wales courts; nonetheless, both jurisdictions had their origins and drew their own precedents from British law and the precedents in one jurisdiction could possibly be persuasive in the other. And, irrespective of whether the chief justice had acted wisely in admitting the Andrews evidence, the Hall case made it clear that Louisa's counsel had not acted 'ably' and that the chief justice had not acted justly when he declared that she had been ably defended. Surely, under these circumstances, the governor would agree that Louisa's was a case that merited mercy.

• • •

Late on 3 January, five days before Louisa's planned execution, Frederick Lee, Henry Palser and Canon Rich carried the Sydney women's petition to Government House. As Lee handed the petition to Lord Carrington, he said that the petition had been signed by 584 women who had come forward spontaneously to add their signatures. The petition showed that the women of New South Wales would not 'vote' for Louisa Collins to be hanged as the premier had so peremptorily declared.

Each member of the deputation formally communicated their concerns about Louisa's case. Lee talked about the New Zealand case. Palser expressed the repugnance felt by many members of the community about hanging in general and especially the hanging of a woman. Canon Rich communicated his concerns about the evidence. They added that they were not asking the governor to set her free, merely to reprieve her to life imprisonment.

The governor responded, 'I can assure you, gentlemen, that the petition you have handed in from the women of the colony will receive every possible consideration and my most earnest consideration, but more than that at this present moment it is impossible for me to say.'

• • •

Louisa's case was taking up an increasing amount of Lord Carrington's time. He had convened another meeting of the Executive Council earlier in the day, although the premier himself wasn't in attendance. Among the papers Carrington presented to the council was a body of correspondence from Frederick Lee, along with letters and petitions from others in the community. Some were from well-wishers recognising the difficulty of the governor's decision. A pastor declared that the governor's sorrow was so deeply affecting his own heart that he wanted to offer some words of condolence. He then listed every 'wrath of God' biblical verse he could find to reassure the governor that, if he allowed Louisa to hang, he would be acting in accordance with God's will.

Some writers attempted to persuade the governor to accept their point of view—not always politely—or to suggest that he consider information contained in their missives. One mentioned two cases that offered food for thought: a capitally convicted murderer who was saved when last-minute evidence proved his innocence; and a well-connected wife-killer who was reprieved because of the killer's influential connections. 'Louisa Collins will be hanged,' the letter-writer declared, 'because she was poor and friendless and because a portion of the press in Sydney and Victoria shrieked for her blood.'

The autopsy doctor, Frederick Milford, was among those who expressed concern about the convicting evidence. Having sat through Louisa's trials—and many others during his years as an autopsy doctor—he had noticed that the Crown offered no evidence that directly connected her with the poison. He reminded the governor that the box of Rough on Rats had sat on an open shelf and could have been accessed by one of her children or by Collins himself. He said that this was only his opinion and was unlikely to be of any significance; however, he'd had an exceptional opportunity to watch the case and, as an independent observer, he felt it was his duty to inform the governor of his alarm about this crucial missing link in the chain of evidence.

After discussing the correspondence, the council members decided to adjourn their meeting. They would hold a special meeting within the next few days to continue their deliberations. With sections of the community outraged at the idea of executing a woman, this was too important a decision to be made lightly. And their own political futures might depend upon the outcome.

Chapter 42

> The question we have to ask ourselves is whether, in the interests of justice, in the interests of society, in the protection of life, it is or is not necessary that for the first time in the history of the colony for forty years, a woman should be seen hanged by the hands of a public executioner.
>
> Thomas Chrysostom O'Mara MLA

Free trade versus protectionism. The issue that had troubled New South Wales politics for a quarter-century, that had propelled Parkes into his fourth premiership, had become a metaphor for the Louisa Collins debate. Parkes and his government advocated laissez-faire politics—not just freedom of trade, but freedom of thought and action—and Parkes, a strong supporter of women's rights, believed that the same principle should be applied to the 'woman question'. During the parliamentary debate about Louisa's case, he had said that the world's progress consisted to a large extent of teaching women that they must take responsibility for themselves as intelligent and sentient creatures. Looking at Louisa's situation through the prism of these views, he felt that his attitude shouldn't be hard to understand. 'Believing all that, how could I distinguish between the woman and the man in a diabolical murder?' However, others—including fellow progressives who supported the female suffrage movement—disagreed with him on the grounds that women shouldn't be executed while they lacked the political power to vote for the laws that governed them.

The protectionist opposition welcomed women under its political umbrella, murderesses among them. Importantly, though, its support for the calls for Louisa's reprieve was not founded on a belief that the rights of women should be extended. Far from it, in many cases. Indeed, when the debates about female suffrage began in the 1890s, their leader, George Dibbs, was opposed. The protectionists were largely political conservatives and included some who believed in being tough on crime and who demanded Louisa's execution for the protection of society. Others desired her reprieve because they believed that the fair sex was not equal to men and shouldn't be treated the same way. Women needed to be protected from themselves.

Straddling both sides of the political fence were capital punishment abolitionists, some opposed for philosophical or evidence-based reasons, others for religious reasons—like Quaker Eliza Pottie. Quakers were once persecuted for their beliefs even to the extent of being imprisoned and executed; accordingly, they had long been vocal in their demands for the better treatment of prisoners, with Elizabeth Fry being their most famous advocate (they also supported female ministry). Most importantly, though, they were pacificists. Not only were they against war, they were against capital punishment. So when Eliza advertised for women to attend a meeting at the Temperance Hall to appeal for mercy, she was being driven by these fundamental Quaker beliefs. As it turned out, only a dozen women joined her in what proved to be a prayer meeting. Nonetheless, the women drafted a petition to the governor begging for mercy on the religious grounds that 'blessed are the merciful' and for the simple reason that underpinned most of the calls for mercy: squeamishness. There was something profoundly wrong, something abhorrent, about executing a woman, particularly the mother of young children.

• • •

Opposition leader George Dibbs and his men also called on the public to join them—at the Town Hall, in this instance—to discuss petitioning the governor for mercy. They reminded everyone that the premier himself had suggested that an appeal from the people might help swing the vote.

The majestic venue was crowded, although only a few skirts could be seen. Dibbs himself took the chair. Joining him on the platform were Thomas Walker and Ninian Melville, as well as other politicians and local identities. Dibbs was the first to speak. He deliberately said little, mainly asking the attendees to give the other speakers a quiet hearing.

William Ellard, whose voice was regularly heard in the press begging for tolerance and liberty, told the audience that only a monster would advocate that a woman should be hanged. He moved the first motion: that measures should be taken to obtain a commutation of Louisa Collins' sentence.

Parliamentarian Edward O'Sullivan seconded the motion, advising the attendees that he had no sympathy with crime, nor any desire to divert the course of justice. Rather, he wanted to protest against the barbarous punishment of hanging, particularly of women. Society had already ceased flogging them. 'If it is repugnant to flog a woman, how much worse is it to hang one?' He said that the statute books contained laws that were from the days of barbarism, and that these laws would remain there until the people rose up and compelled the legislators to change them.

Cheers accompanied him back to his seat.

The next speaker, a Mr McDougal, said that his offering was the most tangible ground on which they could prevent the execution of this friendless, penniless woman. 'The woman might not be morally responsible for the crime of which she has been found guilty. Indeed, the commission of the crime itself is prima facie evidence that the woman is insane.'

'Hear, hear!' cried the audience, agreeing that 'bad'—where a woman was concerned—usually meant 'mad'.

When Dibbs put the motion to the audience, many hands were raised in its favour. Groans greeted the ten dissenters. Others failed to raise their hands at all.

Parliamentarian Thomas O'Mara reminded the attendees that the letter of the law might not make a distinction between the sexes, however the spirit of the law certainly did. He moved that the chairman sign a memorial asking for Louisa's reprieve and that a deputation be authorised to take it to the governor.

Thomas Walker seconded the motion, offering his own remarks about the inequality experienced by women socially and politically. He added, 'So why should we, at a time when retribution for crime is called for, then and only then place her on an equality with man and utter a cry for blood and a thirst for death?' As for the 'deterrence' argument used by the hangman's apologists, he asked rhetorically: 'If Louisa is to be the example, how is it that all the examples of hanging have not prevented murder?' In his opinion, the circumstances driving the mercy pleas in Louisa Collins' case were stronger than in all other cases because the critical witnesses were her own children. 'Without the voice of those children, the mother never could have been brought in guilty.'

'Shame!' cried the audience.

'Let us think of these children, who knew not what they were doing, who were coached by the police—' he paused as applause erupted '—who were told, perhaps, what to say.'

The audience applauded loudly.

'Think of the fact that these children will have the stigma resting on their character all their lives that their mother's death was due to them at a time when responsibility had not formed in their minds, and when they knew not what they did. The law goes up only to the foot of the scaffold. We do not cry out against the law. We only ask that it may be tempered with mercy, especially in a year when we are entering into a new epoch, when we have every hope of peace and goodwill towards men. Let mercy reign and stamp the people of New South Wales as the acme of mercy in the nineteenth century.' Prolonged cheering and applause accompanied him back to his chair.

Ninian Melville replaced him, arguing that the evidence might point to Louisa Collins' guilt, but that information might surface in the future that indicated her innocence. 'We will not be able to reopen her grave,' he concluded bluntly.

The resolution to petition the governor was carried unanimously.

• • •

At three pm the following day, George Dibbs and some of his podium companions marched up to Government House carrying their memorial. Accompanying them were representatives of the major newspapers who would report on the results of this critical meeting.

After the governor had joined them, Dibbs read the memorial then said that the deputation fully recognised the difficult position in which his Excellency and the Executive Council stood. He reminded the governor that during his predecessor's term, the council had been required to consider the case of the Maitland murderesses. The executive had decided that the colony would be disgraced if a woman suffered death at the hands of the public executioner while there was the sufficiently severe punishment of life imprisonment. 'We now ask that the same prerogative should be exercised, and that the colony should be saved the degrading spectacle of witnessing a woman hanging from the scaffold.'

'I fully understand and sympathise with the feelings that have brought you here today,' replied Lord Carrington, pulling out a prepared response. He said that all occasions when a governor was asked to extend the prerogative of mercy were painful enough, but that this occasion was ten thousand times worse because the criminal was a woman. 'I do not wish to shrink from the responsibility placed on me, but I am bound to confess, however, that I feel it so deeply that had I known before I left England that such a duty would be cast on me, proud as I was and pleased as I was with the great honour Her Majesty the Queen conferred on me, no power on earth would have induced me to come here. But the duty is cast upon me, and I am responsible for it, and bound in honour to carry it out.'

He said that he had read the newspaper reports of their Town Hall meeting. He also knew that Mr Dibbs, having previously served as premier, was aware of how thoroughly the council considered each case and how hard it tried to find any loophole that might allow mercy to be extended, and he assured them that this particular council had done the same. In fact, the members had just held a special meeting to consider Louisa's case. They had looked over the petitions and memorials and police reports and other correspondence received during the previous few days, including a heartbreaking letter from the condemned woman's mother. 'I am bound to say that the advice has been given me that the sentence of the court should not be interfered with.'

Carrington went on to explain that, as the law stood, the governor did indeed have the right to extend mercy, irrespective of any opinion from the court or advice from the council. On the other hand, the ministers in such a case had the right to resign, and their resignations would be accepted. While the prisoner's life would be spared, the political consequences would be profound. 'It is, therefore, my duty to accept the advice tendered to me by the ministers of the Crown. With deep sorrow, I have to refuse to interfere with the sentence of the court.'

As Dibbs thanked Lord Carrington, he couldn't refrain from reminding him that the prerogative of mercy rested in his hands alone. 'I feel that Your Excellency's bright administration would be tarnished to some extent if mercy was not extended as we have prayed,' he warned. 'I hope that at the eleventh hour, some circumstance might present itself that will cause Your Excellency to change your opinion.'

• • •

The editor of the *Australian Star* was aghast. Political bullying was commonplace in the bearpit of the New South Wales parliament, but this latest example seemed extraordinary. Had Parkes truly intimated to the Queen's representative that his ministry would resign if the governor exercised his rightful prerogative of mercy? This was the premier who had given such an emotive speech to parliament against capital punishment just a short time ago, the same premier who had stated that it was beyond the Executive Council's power to interfere but that the governor was free to reprieve Louisa or to let her sentence stand and his ministers would be content with his decision. 'Insincerity and cowardice, it is well known, are two of Sir Henry Parkes' most prominent vices,' lashed the editor, 'and he has exhibited them very strongly in connection with the unhappy woman now lying under sentence of death in Darlinghurst Gaol.'

The editor compared Parkes' actions with his parliamentary response to the 'Chinese question'. Six months previously, a popular uprising demanding an end to the floods of Chinese landing on colonial shores had led Parkes to disregard the law concerning Chinese immigration, to circumvent the Supreme Court's power, to ram through draconian new laws prohibiting such immigration, and to indemnify the government against its own breaches of the law—the most blatant defiance of the rule of law since the Rum Rebellion of 1808. 'One would be bound to conclude that Parkes deemed the exclusion of a score of Chinese from the province as being of far more importance than the preservation of a human life, or the reproach on our civilisation involved in the hanging of a woman.' Clearly, the editor continued, Parkes' actions in the Louisa Collins case added another atom to the mountain of proof that he was the greatest humbug Australia had ever known. And he recommended that the Legislative Assembly determine whether Parkes' cabinet had truly threatened to resign and, if so, to instantly submit a motion of censure.

While it might previously have seemed as if Parkes was washing his hands of the distasteful dilemma by letting the governor assume responsibility for the onerous decision, it was now clear that Parkes hadn't relinquished his power—not at all. Somehow, he had communicated to his good friend Lord Carrington that the governor could choose to use his prerogative but, if he did so, he would push the colony to the brink of a constitutional crisis. That, of course, was a political albatross that no young governor would want around his neck until the end of his days.

Many were shocked by the governor's capitulation. Was the Queen's representative just a puppet who allowed his strings to be pulled by the premier? One disgusted letter-writer asked what value lay in a royal prerogative if the Executive Council's decision was to be final. If Lord Carrington had been constrained by the ministers' threat of resignation, then the supposed power was only a myth. If that was indeed the case, the sooner the fictitious authority was withdrawn the better because it was misleading to those who might try to petition him on some future occasion.

• • •

Meanwhile, where was the premier? He had been in Sydney at the time of Louisa's appeal on 28 January then had disappeared. Reports surfaced that he and his daughters had caught a boat to Melbourne—not to see the Melbourne Exhibition, as many initially thought, but because it was the shortest journey he could make for an entire change of scenery.

No one was surprised that he wanted a change of scenery. The political atmosphere in New South Wales had long resembled a rumbling thunderstorm. Indeed, the House hadn't even managed to complete its business before Christmas, forcing parliament to return for the summer session during the holiday period. Consequently, many members would be absent and their constituents lacking representation. To make matters worse, the political tension had increased during parliament's brief adjournment. 'An explosion which would scatter business to the winds is not an improbable event,' reported the *Herald*'s correspondent. 'If there is to be an explosion, the sooner it comes the best, so that the air may be cleared. Then, perhaps, the affairs of the country would have some chance of receiving the attention they demand.'

The newspapers reported that Parkes would return around midday on Tuesday, 8 January so as to attend the parliamentary meeting to be held that afternoon.

Midday on Tuesday? George Dibbs and his men knew that this was not good news for Louisa. Parkes would not reach Sydney until a few hours after she was scheduled to be hanged, which meant that he would be travelling on the morning of her execution—and also the day before. There would be no way of communicating with him in the event that there were any new developments in her case.

• • •

Soon, Sydney would hear further evidence of Parkes' willingness to manipulate the law to serve his own ends, although the news wouldn't break until after his return from Melbourne. During the Chinese agitation six months previously, Parkes had strongly urged the colony to maintain the £100 poll tax on any Chinese entering the colony. Yet accompanying him on his journey from Melbourne was a Chinese merchant from South Australia whose tax had been waived by Parkes himself—thus depriving Treasury of a significant piece of revenue. When challenged, Parkes would try to deflect some of the responsibility towards the Leader of the Opposition, claiming that Dibbs had agreed with his action. Outraged, Dibbs responded that he had suggested the passing of a private bill to deal with these special cases. Parkes pleaded that he had misunderstood Dibbs' letter, adding, 'It is but an innocent breaking of the law.'

The *Clarence and Richmond Examiner* thought this the ultimate hypocrisy. 'Is it permissible for offenders against law and order to so plead in extenuation of their crime?' Since the answer was obvious, why should such an excuse be accepted simply because Parkes was the premier? The editor reminded his readers that, during the parliamentary debate about Louisa's case, Parkes had claimed that he could not find a single opening that would allow him to suspend the law to save her life. Yet he could suspend the law to benefit a wealthy Chinaman! 'Louisa Collins may certainly be a depraved specimen of life, but still it is a life which, set in the scale of humanity, is of far more value than a Chinaman's £100.'

Chapter 43

> The ministrations of religion are conducted at breakneck speed to make up for lost time in past life—shut her up with a Bible and a warder and a parson, and it's all right for the next world. So demands justice.
>
> *Australian Star*

Canon Rich had seen the signs of mental strain appearing on Louisa's face as the days turned into weeks. Christmas Day passed, then Boxing Day. Soon, the new year dawned: 1889. Would she live to see another? Before long, he had to tell her that she wouldn't. This was especially troubling considering his own concerns about her case. Still, it was his duty as Louisa's spiritual comforter to help ease her anguish.

'She was for a time a good deal broken down,' he would later report, 'but not in the way you would ordinarily receive the expression "broken down". Rather, it was that she became her natural self and not her artificial self, for I consider—and I have had many opportunities of judging, both before and since her conviction—that she has all along felt her position keenly.'

• • •

Louisa raised her head and straightened her shoulders and tugged on her cloak of fortitude. It was wearing thin now from overuse. Then she reached for a piece of paper.

For weeks she had told herself that they would never hang a woman. Now Canon Rich had made it clear that she was wrong.

She had things to do, decisions to make. Did she want the Geehans to adopt May? James and Mary Ann Geehan, farmers of Wilberforce, were already caring for the child and had asked permission to make the arrangement permanent. She also had to decide how to distribute her possessions. And there was one more thing she had to do.

Dipping her pen into an inkwell, she began a letter to the governor of New South Wales. 'Oh my Lord, pray have mercy and pity on me and spare my life,' she began.

She had two days only to change his mind. If Lord Carrington the son and husband wasn't horrified by the thought of hanging a woman, perhaps Lord Carrington the father might be willing to exercise his royal prerogative.

'I beg and implore you to have mercy on me for my children's sake. I have seven children, the youngest two only seven and five years old. Spare me, oh my Lord, for their sake.'

There was no point raising any of the other concerns about her case. Frederick Lee had already covered them at length.

'If you show your mercy to me by so doing you will spare my poor children the awful disgrace which must ever cling to them to their life's end,' she continued. 'Oh my Lord, my life is in your hands. I must again implore and humbly beg you to spare me my life.'

She handed her petition to the gaol authorities. There was nothing more she could do.

Chapter 44

> The unfortunate woman's crime may be the outcome of an unequal cerebral development which has produced an imbecile mind and an unstable virtue.
>
> P. Besomo, *The Botany Poisoning Case*

Signor Pasquale Besomo knew that he was supremely fitted to assist Lord Carrington in making the right decision. His own special abilities—his scientific skills—had allowed him to see through Louisa Collins' inscrutable exterior to the core of her being.

He had long been interested in her case. Female criminals—particularly poisoners—intrigued him. He had watched her closely during her trials, noting that she was a good-looking woman with a polite and courteous manner. Far from coming across as evil, she was a comely woman indeed. However, his knowledge of physiognomy had allowed him to assess her personality and character. Unfortunately, he couldn't get close enough to her physical being to use most of his phrenological skills, to actually feel her skull or to measure the regions that denoted certain mental characteristics. Even so, he had reached some conclusions that Lord Carrington should find most beneficial.

Her broad, bony, medium-high forehead revealed a capacious memory and an ability to plan and manage, but it also suggested rapaciousness. Her sharp, penetrating eyes reflected a quick perception while their rather large shape suggested a sanguine, optimistic streak; yet their dimensions also spoke of a choleric temperament—a quick temper—which was confirmed by the flush on her high cheekbones. The deep lines that ran down from her nose and turned in at her mouth indicated a greed for power and money. Her lips were voluptuous but, combined with the shape of her chin, demonstrated a secret determination.

These features suggested a character and personality driven by false ambition and moral obliquity, one that was innately crafty and cold-hearted, that endeavoured to gain confidence by flattery then rewarded such confidence with betrayal. Her penetrating eyes were not those of a wise woman, but rather a jealous, suspicious storyteller, or a coquette who clandestinely made mischief. While she could appear mild and docile and pliable to others, this manner was merely the product of artful simulation.

'Had the circumstances of Mrs Collins' life been different,' he wrote in his self-published pamphlet *The Botany Poisoning Case*, 'say in some business that would have kept her mind constantly engaged, having money constantly and liberally passing through her hands, the understanding and watchfulness and self-interest so clearly portrayed in her eyes and eyebrows would, probably, have placed her in some affluence.' He felt that she should have married an ambitious businessman, one she could have helped scale the social and political ladder. Instead, her marriages to unassuming men had contributed to her downfall.

Continuing his assessment, he reported that her hard features were characteristic of famous female poisoners, as was her skull structure. From such a physiognomic and phrenological assessment, he could only conclude that she was suffering from a poisoning monomania—

that is, a psychosis that caused a single-minded obsession. This was a product of her cerebral development, which had led to a predisposition of mind that placed her beyond the pale of ordinary responsibility.

'I have no doubt in my mind of Mrs Collins' obliquity of mind,' he concluded, 'and if she had been set at liberty, we would probably have heard of her having committed similar crimes before she was a year or two older.' Not that such an assessment justified breaking the woman's neck on a scaffold. Rather, she should have the same claim on society's benevolence as the deaf, the blind and the insane. Since she was away from society now, and since there was no possibility of her committing further crimes, he begged the authorities to dispense with the death portion of her sentence. This would allow the true spirit of English law to take force and offer her the benefit of the doubt by virtue of the hereditary tendencies that might have spurred her murderous actions.

He decided against signing his pamphlet 'Professor Besomo' as he sometimes called himself. The title was an affectation, of course, but it impressed the crowds—indeed, helped draw the crowds—when he used his phrenological and physiognomic and mesmeric (hypnosis) skills to entertain. These days, he no longer engaged in palm-reading or fortune-telling. Instead, he devoted himself to science alone, to assessing personality and character, and to curing disease with his homeopathic medicines.

With his published pamphlet in hand, he headed to the Domain to seek signatures for his attached petition to the governor. There, for over a week, he and other like-minded souls talked to the people relaxing and picnicking and wandering through the grassy area lying between the State Library of New South Wales to the west and the eastern ridge on which the Art Gallery of New South Wales now stands. More than a thousand people added their names. At three pm on the day before Louisa's scheduled execution, he led a deputation to Government House to beg for mercy.

• • •

Lord Carrington read Mr Besomo's pamphlet and petition. The pamphlet's description of Louisa Collins wasn't enough to persuade him to commute her sentence, even though it was followed by the details of cases in which the criminal's actions had later been shown to result from deformity or cerebral disorder. As it was, her personality seemed little different to that of many successful businessmen.

The remarks on the final page carried the most weight, though. The petition reminded him—reminded them all—that the principal witness against Louisa was her young daughter. At a future time, the child's mind might become seriously disturbed when she realised, if she hadn't already, that her own testimony was instrumental in causing her mother's death. Moreover, warned Besomo, if the governor failed to commute the woman's sentence, he risked having the whole world point the finger of scorn and disgrace at their colony for allowing *a mother* to be hanged on the evidence of *her own child.*

Chapter 45

When in doubt, don't.

English proverb

William Clarke, the Minister for Justice, was worried. In a letter published in the *Daily Telegraph* that morning, one day before the scheduled execution, barrister Archibald Nugent Robertson had written that he hoped the community wouldn't think him filled with maudlin sympathy for a criminal when he suggested that there were grounds for Louisa's reprieve even at the last moment. But the question of the admissibility of the Andrews evidence had not been satisfactorily settled, and many evils would ensue if the correctness of the court's decision was challenged at a later date.

Robertson quoted the rule governing the admissibility of such evidence and made the same point that Lee and others had made: that the Collins evidence was admissible in the Andrews trial, however the Andrews evidence was not admissible in the Collins trial because there was no way of proving that Andrews had died from arsenic poisoning. That being the case, the chief justice ought to have withdrawn this evidence from the consideration of the jury, which had undoubtedly been heavily influenced by it. While the law prevented the point from being argued before the full court, this did not debar it from the governor's consideration.

The Minister for Justice accepted that the opinion of this respected barrister carried considerable weight. He would need to discuss the matter with the chief justice.

Then a package arrived from Louisa's solicitors containing letters and newspaper cuttings that raised questions about the poison found in the two bodies. One letter was from a chemist who reported that bismuth—one of the medical preparations given to both husbands—sometimes contained arsenic, so it might have been the doctors themselves who had administered the arsenic. 'Even the best maker of the solution (Schacht) distinctly specifies on the label that the preparation is guaranteed perfectly free from corrosive sublimates,' the chemist reported, 'so the inference to be drawn from such an advertisement is that other preparations of bismuth are liable to contain poison.'

The letter directed the authorities to two respected medical texts. The first, the *Note-Book of Materia Medica, Pharmacology and Therapeutics* by R.E. Scoresby-Jackson, reported that there had been fatal cases connected with bismuth's use, though the deaths had not been caused by the bismuth itself but rather by arsenic impurity. Alfred Swaine Taylor's *The Principles and Practice of Medical Jurisprudence* made a similar claim. Taylor also noted that he had found comparatively large proportions of arsenic in bismuth samples obtained from three respectable retail druggists, with only two specimens out of five being free from arsenic impurity. That being the case, chemists needed to be especially careful in reaching their conclusions when they found traces of arsenic in those who had ingested medical bismuth.

Could such an impurity explain the minuscule trace of arsenic in Andrews' body? If so, it would upset the 'double murder' argument that was largely responsible for Louisa's conviction.

Clarke gathered up the correspondence and set out to obtain the advice of the medical authorities.

• • •

Medical practitioners knew that adulterations causing illness and death were regularly reported in the newspapers and journals. In one case, a Londoner kept falling ill after eating Gloucester cheese. Tests showed that the cheese contained red lead. But how had it got there? The man questioned the cheesemaker, who said that he had mixed the innocuous dye annatto in the cheese to give it a more intense colour. When the dye-maker was tracked down, he admitted that he had added vermilion, a compound of mercury, to improve the colour of that particular batch of annatto. When the druggist who had produced the vermilion was questioned, he revealed that he had added the less expensive red lead to his vermilion to increase his profit, thinking that it would only be used for the production of house paint.

The cheese-eater survived this cascade of adulterations; however, others were not so lucky. Arsenic was often the culprit. In 1858, a British confectioner killed two dozen and caused sickness in hundreds after he used what he thought was plaster of Paris in place of the more expensive sugar. Coloured confectionery—green, most often, but sometimes red and yellow—was also responsible for many arsenic-induced illnesses and deaths. And so much arsenic was added to British wine in the early 1800s that one writer estimated it was enough to kill over three million people annually. Under the circumstances, how many people wouldn't have tiny traces of arsenic in their system?

• • •

When Clarke spoke to the government's medical adviser, the man suggested that they question Hamlet, the government analyst. Hamlet reiterated his comments from the trial that arsenic had once been common in bismuth, as mentioned in the cited sources, but that it was now rare to find such an impurity. Moreover, the brand used by the pharmacist in question was renowned for its purity. That being the case, it was highly unlikely that the bismuth was responsible for the two men's deaths.

The Minister for Justice asked Hamlet to put his comments in writing so he could apprise the governor. Then he took Robertson's letter to the chief justice.

• • •

William Bede Dalley had been wise to argue that a convicting judge should not be allowed to sit on an appeal—or, for that matter, to be the first port of call when questions were asked about his rulings. Not surprisingly, the chief justice dismissed Robertson's concerns.

Others, however, agreed with Robertson. There wasn't enough rat poison in Andrews' body to kill a mouse, so where was the 'proof' that arsenic had killed him? It was merely a matter of opinion—and belated opinion at that. Evidently, the chief justice was determined that nothing would overturn Louisa's conviction. Was a 'spirit of unreasoning vengeance' driving the judiciary as well as the government in the pursuit of the death penalty for Louisa?

Letter-writer William Hogan wasn't going to let the chief justice's decision stand uncontested. He informed Lord Carrington that he had served as an adviser to the governor's predecessors and that, if he were asked to do so in this instance, he would suggest that the authorities reprieve Louisa for a week. During that period, the defence would prepare a short precis of the four trials and of the chief justice's summation, covering his references to the Andrews evidence. The chief justice would also provide his own reasons for his summation while the attorney-general would remark on the legality or otherwise of the Andrews evidence. This material would then be sent by telegram to the Secretary of State in London to allow England's great luminaries to consider the case. If they ruled that the chief justice was correct, the law could take its course. However, if they decided otherwise, Lord Carrington could refuse to sign the death warrant on those just grounds. Louisa Collins would be respited and incarcerated for life, the possibility of a constitutional crisis would be averted, and the governor would have the gratification of establishing a point of law that seemed to have been misunderstood.

Could this be the lifeline the community needed?

Chapter 46

> Properly carried out, execution is a painless extinction of life; but, apparently recognising this, the law, from the date of the sentence to its being carried into effect, interposes a period of not less than three weeks . . . in which, under the guise of preparing for another world, the prisoner may undergo a sufficiency of mental torture to make up for the absence of bodily torture.
>
> *Australian Star*

While only a small detail, it made the abolitionists feel worse about the coming barbarity: Louisa was to be the first woman executed at Darlinghurst Gaol.[8] Lots of men had been slain, of course—indeed, there would be an average of one per year over its seventy-two-year history—but no women . . . until now. As the date for this first female execution drew near, the public wanted to know more about the death penalty. Was hanging painful?

Once, no one had cared whether executions were painful or not. Pain was something that everyone had to endure. The ability to withstand pain, or at least rise above it, was seen as evidence of physical and moral fortitude. Thus, the physical and psychological pain suffered by those who died on the gallows was considered part of the punishment ritual, a sign of God's retribution, of the eternal fires of hell. After the benefits of ether were discovered, pain came to be seen as an evil needing to be overcome. By extension, society came to believe that the evilness of pain also needed to be eliminated from the law's violence so it could appear cool and rational—humane—in contrast to the hot-headed viciousness and cruelty of the law-breaker. People needed to believe that the ultimate punishment was instantaneous and painless rather than a form of judicial torture.

The *Australian Star* endeavoured to quell concern by providing a simple answer to the 'pain' question. If Louisa's neck broke and her spinal cord ruptured, death would be immediate and effectively pain-free. If, however, her execution was bungled and she strangled to death, it wouldn't be painless. Not that the *Star* mentioned Louisa personally; rather, the word 'it' was used liberally as if she were an animal being butchered. The article also failed to mention that Louisa would be hooded and pinioned to ensure that the spectators couldn't see her facial contortions or her hands clawing at her neck.

The *Star* also mentioned the French custom of reprieving prisoners when the rope broke, which allowed them to discuss their experiences. Most said that they hadn't experienced any pain at all. One man mentioned seeing a bright light then blackness while another recalled that the sensations were rather more pleasurable than otherwise.

It wouldn't be public of course. The salaciousness and savagery of the mobs drawn to public executions—the 'hanging sports' as they were called—had helped to drive the spectacle indoors. Nonetheless, concerns had been expressed about the dangers of private hangings, including the potential for governmental abuse. The uncondemned might find themselves swinging, perhaps for reasons of expediency, while the moneyed and powerful might escape their legally mandated fate. Thus, the pressmen's pens served as the community's eyes, reflecting the public's right to see for themselves that the death ordered in their name, the death ordered for their protection, had taken place in an orderly and efficient manner. Unfortunately, it was a 'right' the pressmen rarely wanted. Few volunteered for such a duty.

Others would join the pressmen at the gallows site, including Darlinghurst's gaolkeeper, chaplain and surgeon. Female warders would attend Louisa; however, the women's petition had failed to sway the authorities in terms of the hangman himself. Frederick Lee had told the governor, as he handed over the women's petition, 'If a woman ever has to be hanged, another woman should be deposed to perform the ceremony. It is a most repulsive idea that a man should perform such an office on a woman.' Of course, to most people, the idea of having a woman act as the hangman was even more repulsive. More to the point, how many would volunteer? Any woman who did so would become a social pariah. Instead, the state hangman, Robert Howard—'Nosey Bob'—would preside.

His was a sad story. He had once been a Sydney cabman until a horse kicked him in the face and smashed his nose, leaving the 'noseless' man unable to find any work. Desperation led him to take the unwanted job of serving as the colony's first salaried hangman. As he soon discovered, the judge who sentenced a prisoner to death was revered, but he who carried out the decree was despised. Worse, those who demanded the blood of convicted criminals were among the most vocal complainants when he spent time among them, when he travelled on public transport or sat in public bars—his second home in the days before an execution.

Nonetheless, he took pride in his work. 'He has just the same eye for a neck that a painter has for a pretty scene,' remarked an interviewer, having noticed Nosey Bob eyeing the throat of a new acquaintance as if he were thinking about the size of the required knot.

After an execution, he would rub his hands and ask the gentlemen of the press to bear witness that the criminal had been executed in a prompt and workmanlike manner—if there wasn't a bungle. In recent years, there had been too many bungles for the pressmen's liking, another reason why there were few volunteers to attend the spectacle. Hopefully, Louisa's would be a 'workmanlike' turning off rather than a horror to be imprinted on their minds forever.

• • •

Would she confess? It was part of the hanging ritual, the 'dying confession' that offered truth and clarity, that proved the wisdom of the community's judgement and condemnation. Not that a 'dying confession' had the same impact now that executions were hidden from the public. Still, there were practical reasons in Louisa's case. There was too much reasonable doubt: about the execution, the conviction, even whether she was guilty or not. A confession would ease the minds of the populace.

Most thought it unlikely that she would confess. 'In view of her extraordinary manner, it is quite possible that she will meet her fate with her lips sealed and with a cool indifference,' declared Victoria's *Gippsland Times*.

Sydney was not alone in its fascination with Louisa's case. With the benefits of the instant telegraph service, all of Australia was waiting to hear what would happen as the gallows clock continued its unrelenting countdown.

Part 4
RETRIBUTION

Thou shalt not kill.

Exodus 20:13

Chapter 47

Suffer the children.

Matthew 19:14

The thud, thud of a workman's hammer rang out across the gaol yard. Preparations for an execution began a few days beforehand to allow the executioner time to practise with his ropes and weights. Now, with only one day to go, the atmosphere was tense, as it always was before an execution. Many of the workers and inmates took a moment to say a quick prayer or to lift their faces to the sun, as if the closer they were to the spectre of death, the more intensely they valued their own existence, pitiful though it might be.

The tension, though, was worse than usual, worse than ever before. Some of the female warders—toughened by life even before they took charge of Sydney's wickedest women—were sobbing wrecks. Louisa had been incarcerated in the gaol for five months so they all knew her. In the past few weeks, in the closeness of her special cell, the relationships between warder and prisoner had deepened. These weren't friendships, exactly, but more a feeling of mutual dependency and respect. Still, through this enforced contact they had come to know Louisa better. She was no thieving, cursing, drunken whore. Rather, she was an attractive, middle-aged woman who was courteous and respectful, reserved but not unfriendly. She was an enigma, true, but no monster—not from what they could see. Yet on the morrow they would have to walk beside her to the gallows and watch her hang by the neck until she was dead.

Unless the governor decided to reprieve her. Would he? Surely there was still time.

• • •

There were many knocks on the door of Government House that Monday, but one pair of visitors was greeted with astonishment and consternation. Two fair-haired children stood there. They said that their names were May Andrews and Fred Andrews and that they were Louisa Collins' children. They wanted to talk to the governor, to ask him to reprieve their mother. Could they see him, please?

Who had sent them? they were asked.

Could they have been dispatched by their mother in a desperate ploy to tug at the governor's heartstrings? Even worse, it might be a piece of despicable underhandedness on the part of the political opposition.

The children replied that no one had told them to come. They had made the decision by themselves.

Mrs Collins' young children? These were the last faces Lord Carrington wanted to see. He told his private secretary that he couldn't speak to them.

His secretary returned to the room where the children were waiting. 'I am sorry you have come,' he said. 'It costs me a severe struggle to have to tell you. While His Excellency is anxious to do everything in his power for your unfortunate mother, he must carry out the law. Nothing can be done on behalf of your mother.' Then he escorted the sobbing children to the door.

• • •

The look in Canon Rich's eyes said it all. Her plea to the governor had failed.

Louisa pushed aside the horror. What now? She asked to see May one last time. She wanted to explain to her daughter that she was to be adopted by the Geehans; she wanted to reassure her, somehow, about her future.

May was a bright child, one who waited and watched and took her cues from those around her. But she was only a child. She'd had no comprehension of the devastating consequences of her testimony—not at the time, anyway. Of course, she knew now that her mother was to die, although she perhaps didn't fully comprehend the role she had played. What would life hold for her when that knowledge struck her like a lightning bolt?

May wasn't alone when she arrived at the cell door. Her brothers Fred and Herbert accompanied her. Had Herbert come from Newcastle to make peace with his mother on her 'deathbed' or to demand answers to those unanswerable questions?

There was one beloved face missing: Arthur, her favourite, to whom she had left all her trinkets; Arthur, whose words had also condemned her to death.

Soon, too soon, her children left the cell, their bewildered faces turning back for one final glimpse. And the remnants of her fortitude finally crumbled around her. She wept.

Chapter 48

> There is nothing more abhorrent to my sense of feeling than the strangling of a woman. A woman! from whose breast the nurture of life is drawn by the human frailty; a woman! who presides over the paths of our little children; a woman! who is the very centre of everything that is gentle and lovable in social life.
>
> Sir Henry Parkes

As night's gloom started to dissipate around four-thirty on Tuesday, 8 January 1889, they began to gather outside the gaol, the crowds who refused to abide by the law's decision to exclude them from these judicial sacrifices. Rattling the gaol gates, they tried to get inside. For once, these barriers were locked and barred against them.

Drunks walking home from an evening's dissipation joined the revellers. Thirsty wretches tarried as well, awaiting the hour when the first public houses would open. By the time the sun peeped over the horizon, a hundred people were lounging against the gaol walls or scampering up nearby trees in the forlorn hope of seeing over them. The police were already on duty—the masses thronged every time a felon was to be dispatched—and used their might to return the oglers to terra firma.

'A woman is going to be hung,' the spectators muttered to each other with glee. It hadn't happened before in their lifetime—not in Sydney anyway—so this execution had a particular appeal. 'A *woman* is going to be hung!'

Women and children were among those who joined the burgeoning crowd. By nine am, some two thousand people were gathered outside the gaol walls, waiting for a sign that another wretch had been slain.

• • •

Louisa had been sleeping soundly, unaware that the ghouls were flocking. She awoke around seven to a fresh but brilliantly sunny morning with not a wisp of a cloud to mar its splendour. It was almost an insult, somehow. When even the elements refused to mourn her fate, there could be no reprieve.

At eight o'clock, the warders told her it was time. She was to be moved to the condemned cell, situated only twenty or thirty feet from the gallows. There she would await her final summons.

Meanwhile, a deathly silence hung over the gaol, broken only by the sobs of sympathetic women. All of the inmates had been ordered to cease their work and return to their cells. The gaol would remain locked down until after the execution was over.

An eerie emptiness surrounded the little troupe as it began the long walk across the courtyards, past the governor's imposing mansion, past beds of bright, summer flowers. Louisa's step was steady and firm, as if she were making her way to her Sunday church pew rather than to the hangman's altar.

• • •

Around twenty to nine, the gate to Darlinghurst Courthouse opened. Only those with special permits were allowed through. The Minister for

Justice had decreed that the first execution of a woman at Darlinghurst Gaol was to be a strictly private event and that the well-endowed and well-connected would not be granted approval to attend. He wanted no prurient eyes watching this disturbing scene.

Warders guided the select few through the subterranean tunnel that connected the courthouse with the gaol: a surreal experience, as if they too were to meet the ferryman. It was a relief to reach the gaol-side door and to climb the sunlit stairs. When they reached the gaol's inner courtyard, they were told to halt and wait. Others soon joined them there, including Inspector Hyem, the police's representative.

Soon after nine a warder stationed on a balcony adjacent to the condemned cell called out, 'All right.' The waiting men proceeded to a courtyard—an exercise yard—in front of a triangular first-floor gallery that faced the north-eastern gaol wall.

The men saw a stoutly built platform. A massive beam sat on two solid uprights about eight or ten feet above the platform, all painted a forbidding black. Hanging from the beam was a rope ending in the distinctive menacing loop.

Those who had attended previous executions knew that Nosey Bob would have greased the rope above and below the loop's knot to allow the knot to slide freely when the noose was tightened around Louisa's neck. Currently, the noose was resting on a piece of carpet lying over the top of a chair sitting to one side of the scaffold. The chair was there to hold Louisa in the event that she collapsed before the deed could be carried out.

In the centre of the gallows was a trapdoor consisting of two flaps that met in the middle. They were kept in position by a bolt, a drawbar attached to the underside of the trapdoor. The flaps had hinges on their outer edges and were opened by pulling a lever located on top of the platform. When the lever was pulled and the bolt withdrawn, the weight of Louisa's body would force the flaps to swing down and away from each other. Heavy weights prevented the flaps from swinging back again.

Underneath the gallery on the courtyard level was an open door. As soon as the bolt was withdrawn, the spectators would be able to see Louisa's body falling through the trap and hanging underneath.

To ensure that the trapdoor did not open prematurely, Nosey Bob had placed a small iron pin in the bolt lever. The pin would need to be removed before the lever could be pulled.

The spectators knew that the executioner would have tested the 'drop' to ensure that it worked smoothly. He would have pre-stretched the rope, most likely by soaking it in water and leaving it overnight with a bag of sand hanging from it, one that weighed the same as Louisa's eleven stone three pounds (seventy-one kilograms). It was critical to calculate the length of slack rope required to do a satisfactory job.

In the past, a 'short drop' of only a couple of feet had been used, with the result that most prisoners had choked to death. The recently implemented 'long drop' aimed at a speedier demise. By dislocating the uppermost cervical vertebrae and thereby separating the spinal cord from the brain stem, it caused a quick and painless death. If the long drop was too long, however, death would result from decapitation rather than dislocation.

Over time, scientific calculations and experiments had helped hangmen determine the correct position for the knot's placement and the appropriate rope-length to pound-weight ratio so as to avoid both decapitation and strangulation. The optimal combination meant that, when the trapdoors were opened, the body would fall with the force of gravity, with the head's movement limited by the constraint of the noose. When the rope reached its maximum length, the amount of energy generated by the correct calculation of body-weight and rope-length would cause the rope to jerk up again. If the knot was properly positioned under the left side of the jaw, the rope's jerk would throw the head backwards and snap the neck, ensuring a quick, pain-free death. Not that all capital punishment advocates wanted the 'ultimate deterrent' to be such an easy demise. Rather, they had to make allowances for the suffering endured by those forced to spend interminable minutes watching a fellow human choking to death.

Nosey Bob had decided that Louisa's drop-length would be five feet six inches, his calculation based partly on her weight, but also on her gender. If he'd been hanging a man of the same weight, he would have allowed a longer drop; however, he recognised that a woman's neck lacked the same musculature as a man's and that her tissues had likely been softened by prison discipline and dietary restrictions. Worryingly, as he hadn't executed a woman before, the allowances he had made might not be accurate.

At six minutes past nine, the spectators heard Canon Rich's solemn tones as he began to recite the Anglican service for the burial of the dead: 'Man that is born of woman hath but a short time to live . . .'

• • •

Canon Rich's hopes of a reprieve hadn't been realised. He had stayed with Louisa until late the previous evening, praying with her and offering every ounce of spiritual comfort he could summon. He had joined her on her walk to the condemned cell, where they knelt together and continued their prayers. There had been no word from the governor. Louisa was going to hang.

He tentatively broached the subject of a confession. She sidestepped his urgings by claiming to have confessed all her sins to Almighty God and to have begged for his forgiveness.

Was this a tacit admission? He had long realised that she of all people was unlikely to confess to a mere mortal. A confession to God was probably all that could be hoped for.

Nosey Bob came in and pinioned her, attempting to soothe her as if she were a plump turkey sensing its imminent demise. She stood there passive yet uncowed, seemingly a willing participant in the coming sacrifice.

As they prepared to leave the cell accompanied by two sobbing female warders, Canon Rich realised that his strong-nerved charge was bearing up far better than the warders assigned the responsibility of carrying out the law's fatal decree.

Chapter 49

What says the law? You will not kill. How does it say it? By killing!

Victor Hugo, *Les Misérables*

Dressed in his white robes of office, Canon Rich appeared on the balcony that led from the condemned cells to the gallows platform. The spectators could hear him reading aloud as he began his funereal march, stepping slowly but surely towards the gallows.

Behind the clergyman, Louisa came into view. She was dressed in a long, loose prison gown of dark, reddish-brown wincey, drawn in slightly at the waist. A piece of common cord, cheaper even than a clothesline, bound her arms above her elbows so tightly that she couldn't move them forwards or backwards. Her hands lay listlessly at her side, not even clutching her gown. Her head was bent forward, drooping onto her chest, and her shoulders were stooped. For a woman who had kept her chin high throughout the nightmare of four trials, it was a sign of her deep despair. She hadn't been vanquished, though. Apart from a slight shuffle in her gait, she moved with a firm step.

A female warder walked on either side of her, there to provide a helpful arm as much as a hindrance to any attempt to flee. But Louisa, dry-eyed, disdained the support offered by these weeping women.

She glanced down at the pressmen. They noticed that her face seemed gaunt, her expression haggard. The contrast from a month earlier was shocking. The mental agony she had endured had clearly crushed the resolute spirit manifested at her various trials. Still, traces of colour remained on her cheekbones, evidence that she still retained some of her stoutheartedness.

Canon Rich stepped onto the gallows platform and stood to one side of the trapdoor. He fell silent.

Louisa's gaze was still fixed on the ground as she neared the platform. Suddenly, she looked up, and appeared to falter. Then she continued walking. The warders stepped to one side. She alone took the two steps up to the gallows platform.

As she stepped beneath the beam, Canon Rich pronounced the closing words of the burial service. 'I am the resurrection and the life; he that believeth in me, though he were dead, yet shall he live.'

Her voice low but clear, Louisa responded, 'Amen.'

The clergyman whispered a few final words to her. She inclined her head slightly but said nothing further. Not a sob passed her lips nor a tear fell from her eye.

Canon Rich stepped away from the trapdoor. The assistant hangman passed Nosey Bob the white cap and he pulled it over Louisa's head and face. Bending her head, she managed to raise her right hand high enough to pull down one of the cap's lower corners. Her face was now invisible.

The hangman slipped the rope over her head and positioned the knot carefully under her left ear. He pulled the noose tight with a couple of hard jerks so the knot was close to the angle of her jawbone. The shock of feeling the noose's coarse embrace caused her body to slump. Even so, she managed to remain standing.

The executioner stepped away from the trapdoor and motioned to his assistant that it was time. The assistant pulled the lever that would withdraw the bolt and allow the trap to open. Nothing happened. He tugged again. Still nothing.

Louisa stood there waiting, blinded by the hood, unaware of what was going on.

The executioner glared at his assistant and sent more silent but now peremptory signals. The assistant prodded and tugged to no avail.

A look of alarm crossed the executioner's face. He stepped onto the trap and pulled the noose tighter around Louisa's neck. Realising the foolishness of his action—what if the pin suddenly gave way?—he took a hasty step off the trap. The last thing he needed was for drama to turn into farce.

When it was clear that the assistant's endeavours were not working, the executioner cried out for someone to find a hammer.

The spectators were too far below the gallows platform to see exactly what was happening, but they could see the assistant struggling to release the lever. What was the problem?

Louisa remained standing alone in the centre of the trap, her fortitude surely weakened by the shock of the delay, although she still wasn't trembling. Truly, the woman had exceptional courage.

Then she staggered slightly.

Loud gasps greeted her movement. What if she fainted and fell across the trap? What if her courage failed and she attempted to flee? The noose would jerk her back, causing her to tumble to the ground. It might even strangle her.

A male warder rushed forward with a wooden mallet and hit the pin. Nothing. He pounded again . . . and again. Each blow sent a jolt through the spectators.

At the sound of the thumps, a roar arose from the crowd lining the gaol walls. 'She is off!'

Louisa heard the crowd announce her demise. Her strength of will began to dissolve. She began to tremble.

Again the warder pounded . . . and again.

How long had it been? Half a minute? A minute? More? The horror seemed interminable.

Without warning, Louisa dropped through the trapdoor like a sack of potatoes. Through the opening in the scaffold base, the spectators could see her body continue dropping until the rope stretched to its fullest then jerk up again.

A gush of blood spurted from her neck. It looked as if her head was being severed from her body. Still, the spectators watched, unable to drag their eyes away. Could this hanging fiasco get any worse?

Blood ran down her prison dress, dripping into the pit below. Her head lolled. Her hands remained loose by her sides. She showed no sign of pain or suffering. She was unconscious at least, unaware of this next torment. But was she dead?

All eyes remained frozen on the horrible sight. The spectators could see that the noose, tightened an extra notch or two by the distressed hangman, had ripped her neck open. The noose knot partly filled the gap, but it didn't hide the sight of her severed windpipe. Her head remained attached to her body only by her vertebrae. She couldn't be alive, surely, not with such an injury. Still they watched. She didn't move, not a muscle quiver. Her hands began to turn purple. The deed was done.

'There at the end of a hideous cord,' wrote the sickened *Australian Star* reporter, 'dangles a mutilated corpse, all that remains of one that was a woman, a wife, a mother—but a murderess—and now—aye, God rest even her soul—the law is satisfied; she is dead.'

• • •

The doctor examined Louisa and pronounced her dead but her body was not removed. It dangled for twenty minutes in accordance with the regulations. All the while, a thin stream of blood trickled down the front of her dress.

By ten am, the body was on its way to the gaol mortuary, where it was placed on a table. The spectators had been unable to see Louisa's hood-covered face and could only imagine how her terror must have contorted her features. Surprisingly, when the hood was removed, the reporters could see that her features were unaltered. Indeed, her face bore the same stolid expression she had worn during her many trials, apart from the closed eyes and purple lips and traces of blood oozing from her nose and mouth.

After her body had been examined, the female warders washed and dressed it and placed it in a coffin, leaving the lid off so the inquest jury could see her remains for themselves. 'Death by hanging' was their unsurprising verdict.

• • •

The authorities had planned to bury Louisa that afternoon; however, the hanging debacle necessitated an investigation, which delayed their plans. At eight o'clock the following morning, her coffin was taken from the gaol's deadhouse to Redfern station and loaded onto a train destined for Rookwood cemetery. An anonymous gentleman had purchased a grave in its Church of England section rather than leave her to be buried in the gaol's unconsecrated ground. There, without any of the remorseless publicity of the past six months, she was buried. No family or friends were present to mourn her departure.

Chapter 50

> The semi-savages who insisted that Louisa Collins' blood was shed have had their wishes fulfilled to the very letter, and they should now feel as content as the ancient Romans did after a holiday spent in the Coliseum.
>
> *Australian Star*

'The scene was a disgrace to humanity' was the community's disgusted opinion of the botched execution, even among those who had demanded Louisa's death. The press wrote that the public was prepared to allow a criminal's life to be taken when it was justly forfeited, but it was not prepared to allow even the worst of criminals to be tortured. And, without a doubt, Louisa Collins had been cruelly tortured when she stood on the gallows awaiting death.

How could such a thing happen? The machinery was simple. The hangman had ample time to practise. Indeed, why were so many executions bungled? No one could forget the Mount Rennie fiasco of two years previously when three of the four youths had taken interminable minutes to die.

Sheriff Cowper tried to minimise the extent of the delay, saying that it was only of a few seconds' duration and that, since death was instantaneous, it was a successful execution. Few were fooled.

Most of the press recognised that the impact of such brutality would be to intensify the feelings against capital punishment, in particular against the execution of women. 'It is evident that a strong feeling must inevitably grow which will sound the death-knell of execution by hanging.'

• • •

Sir Henry Parkes wouldn't lead the abolitionist charge. The day after Louisa's execution, the death-knell tolled for his government. 'Their light goes out like that of a tallow candle,' wrote the disenchanted *Daily Telegraph*, 'leaving nothing to mark the place where it was but a disagreeable political smell.'

It wasn't Louisa's execution that toppled the government, although it added significantly to the political tensions of the moment. In truth, what happened was little short of farcical. The trail leading up to that strange day included corruption charges against a government-appointed railway commissioner; a government inquiry that exonerated the appointee; Parkes' promise to stand by the man; a declaration in the House that the correspondence supposedly clearing the man actually substantiated the charges; and a demand that Parkes respond. Far from supporting his appointee as promised, Parkes said arrogantly and dismissively, 'I have nothing to say.'

Only half the Assembly was present that evening. The summer session had commenced before the end of the Christmas break and, unusually, the numbers were evenly divided. Parliamentarian John Want moved for an adjournment in order to deal with the correspondence relating to the corruption charges. Seven of Parkes' supporters crossed the floor on the grounds that the premier's response was a 'treasonous betrayal of political trust'. The motion passed by thirty-seven votes to twenty-three. Effectively, it became a motion of censure, leaving Parkes little choice but to resign. Parkes' government wasn't defeated on a noble issue like the morality or efficacy of capital punishment, or even on a formal motion of censure. It was merely a motion 'that this House do now adjourn'.

As the public looked on, perplexed, the *Sydney Morning Herald* asked if, perhaps, Parkes had intended such a result—because, otherwise, his actions were impossible to explain. Had the House's obstructiveness and the challenges facing him on more serious political issues beaten him down until, in a fit of pique, he had abdicated the throne?

While Louisa's case was not the trigger for the government's downfall, it was at least symbolic, according to those who had little love for the premier or his politics. 'The hideous spectacle of the execution of Louisa Collins was a fitting termination to their career in office,' declared the *Clarence and Richmond Examiner*. 'The manner in which this last victim to our sanguinary criminal code met her fate is symbolical of the manner in which the octopus of Parkesism has strangled the energies and progress of this unfortunate country.'

• • •

The government's fall became the new topic of conversation, eclipsing any further discussion of capital punishment in general. Regarding Louisa's case, though, one letter-writer made a helpful suggestion. He said that those who had demanded mercy should turn their philanthropic minds towards helping the innocents who had suffered the most from her crimes—her children. Of course, the same could be said for the 'hang her' advocates, those determined that the children should lose the single parent that did remain.

The fate of most of Louisa's children is known. May's adoptive father, James Geehan of Wilberforce, was perhaps the 'Windsor gentleman' said to be employing Arthur and Fred at the time of Louisa's death. These two boys, along with their elder brother Herbert, all married and had families of their own; however, Reuben and Edwin slipped into the mists of history. Louisa's youngest surviving son, Charles, was sent to live with John Gilby and later Samuel Grimson, both of Crookwell, New South Wales, but his whereabouts in adulthood is not known.

As for May, she was described as being 'pretty and intelligent' by the *Windsor and Richmond Gazette* when it praised the Geehans for their kindness in adopting her. May called herself Mabel thereafter. A feisty girl, she was in 1894 assaulted by a woman for having slapped the woman's sister for impudence. Within the next few years, she moved to the Newcastle district, presumably to be closer to her siblings. She was a resident of West Wallsend in 1898 when she married railway fettler John McGuiness. She named the eldest of her three children Alice Louisa, although this child and another died in infancy. May herself died of heart failure in 1911, a week before her thirty-fourth birthday.

Louisa's offspring failed to pass on to their own families the details of their parents' fates. This particular skeleton was not pulled from history's closet until a century later, when Louisa's descendants began tracing their family histories. By then, enough time had passed for them to treasure the infamy rather than feel personally tainted—or publicly condemned—by the disgrace.

Part 5
JUSTIFICATION

If Louisa Collins is the sister of anyone, she is probably the sister of the celebrated 'Jack the Ripper'.

William Johnston Allen

Chapter 51

There are strings in the human heart that had better not be vibrated.

Charles Dickens, *Barnaby Rudge*

Louisa, the stout-hearted, the defiantly inscrutable, refused to appease society's concerns by confessing her guilt or publicly professing her innocence. It falls to history's detectives to reassess the evidence in order to determine the truth about this celebrated historical case.

The question of causation is pivotal: how did Andrews die? While the chemical evidence conclusively shows that Collins died of arsenic poisoning, it is inconclusive in terms of Andrews' death. Nonetheless, the similarities between their illnesses are glaring: the vomiting and diarrhoea, suggesting that their bodies were attempting to expel substances that acted as irritants; the failure of the prescribed medicines to ameliorate their symptoms or slow down their deterioration; the evidence of arsenic, an irritant, in their remains.

There are other less obvious but no less significant similarities, including the fact that both men vomited green matter; industry once used arsenic to produce green dyes. Both men included 'shoulder pain' in their short list of symptoms—not foot pain or knee pain or wrist pain but shoulder pain—and arsenic poisoning can cause joint pain. Also, Andrews complained of a severe burning in his stomach and bowel, which resembles the 'bowels of fire' mentioned by other victims of arsenic poisoning. And the region of Andrews' torso covering his stomach and gut—that is, the region that would have suffered most from short-term arsenic poisoning—was surprisingly well preserved, which is worth noting because the exhumed remains of Styrian arsenic-eaters showed considerably less decomposition than other corpses from the same period. Thus, while it is impossible to state with one hundred per cent certainty that Andrews died of arsenic poisoning, the body of evidence supports the conclusion 'beyond reasonable doubt'. Moreover, this was the verdict of the treating doctors and other expert medical practitioners once they had assessed all the evidence for themselves.

So how did arsenic enter Andrews' body? Although Andrews might have been exposed to tiny amounts of arsenic while working as a wool-washer, evidence now shows that this type of exposure does not cause fatal arsenic poisoning. The authors of an article published in *The Lancet* in 1899 could find no cases of arsenic poisoning resulting from contact with items made from the wool of arsenic-dipped sheep. The arsenic bonded so tightly to the wool that even carding and combing failed to release it.[9]

Importantly, though, Andrews was not working in the month before his death because his employer's business had closed. Therefore, workplace absorption could not have been responsible for the arsenic traces found in his stomach remains. His continued vomiting and purging throughout his illness suggests that he received a moderate dose of arsenic around ten days before his death and another dose or doses in the days following. As his body had expelled most of the arsenic prior to his death, the last dose was probably administered a few days beforehand.

Since there is no evidence that Andrews accidentally ingested or absorbed the arsenic and no evidence of suicidal intent, it is clear that he was murdered. This brings us to the question of culpability, not only in terms of Andrews' death but in relation to Collins' as well. Putting Louisa aside for the moment, there are others who need to be considered as possible perpetrators.

A suggestion at the time was that Collins was responsible for both Andrews' death and his own; however, this is highly unlikely. Andrews' unemployment meant that Collins no longer had ready access to the house, let alone to the family's food and beverages, during the critical ingestion period. And Collins' 'suicide' seems improbable; humans do not put themselves through an extended period of torture when they are intent on killing themselves. Indeed, James Whorton, Professor Emeritus of the History of Medicine at the University of Washington, Seattle, came across no instances of suicide by slow arsenic poisoning during his extensive research for his book, *The Arsenic Century*.[10]

Another suggestion was that Collins was responsible for Andrews' death and Louisa for Collins' death. To posit that there were two murderers, both working independently of each other using the same modus operandi without recognising what the other was doing, beggars belief. Moreover, if Collins and Louisa had acted together to kill Andrews, Collins would have had to be remarkably obtuse not to recognise that he was suffering from the same symptoms. Under the circumstances, the only logical conclusion is that Collins was not responsible for either death.

Could someone else in the house have been responsible? Louisa's son Arthur, for instance? While there was no love lost between him and Collins, he had no reason to kill his own father. Nor did his younger siblings, who were barely into double digits at that time, or his older siblings, who were not even in Sydney when Collins died.

If we apply Ockham's Razor to the question of culpability—that is, 'Of two (or more) competing theories, the simplest explanation is to be preferred'—the 'simplest explanation' is that Louisa caused the deaths of her two husbands as she alone had means and opportunity for both deaths and a recognisable motive for one. If we accept this 'simplest explanation' for the sake of argument and attempt to find supportive evidence by focusing on Louisa's remarks and behaviour, the case against her becomes much stronger.

Louisa showed an extraordinary callousness in her attitude and behaviour towards Andrews during his illness and afterwards. Most notably, this is seen in her failure to follow the basic mourning tradition of straightening his body before racing off to obtain his insurance money, and in permitting Collins to move into her marriage bed less than a week after Andrews' death. Moreover, she showed guile when she attempted to justify her abandonment of Andrews' body by saying that the insurance doctor might have needed to see it.

Her callousness can also be seen in her behaviour towards Collins. She left his body unattended for hours with the front door wide open and showed no grief or concern when she discovered that the police had removed his body during that period. She behaved in a conniving manner when she attempted to obtain his death certificate by telling the doctor that the police were meeting her at his surgery. Additionally, she showed overt displays of affection towards Collins on the morning of his death after she had sent a message requesting Senior Constable Sherwood to visit her—an obvious move to divert suspicion.

And what about 'Mick's milk': the jug of condensed milk that sat on the kitchen bench? She stopped her children from pouring the milk into their tea, and even refused to let her son drink his tea after he'd already added the milk to his mug. Significantly, the deadly beverage on Mick's bedside table comprised condensed milk laced with arsenic.

The most eloquent evidence of her guilt, though, is her silence. She failed to protest her innocence on the occasions when she could and should have done so. After Senior Constable Sherwood told her she was to come with him to the Darlinghurst police station, she did not ask why or declare her innocence, but assumed she wouldn't be returning. When he charged her with Collins' murder, she didn't say that she hadn't done it as most people would do, innocent or guilty alike. Most significantly, she did not make a 'dock statement' in any of her four trials. Surely, anyone who was unjustly accused would vociferously protest his or her innocence to the court, particularly when facing a death sentence. Her failure to do so would have been noted by the judges and, no doubt, contributed to their certainty, as mentioned in the appeal, that she was guilty of both deaths. She didn't even cry, 'I am innocent!' after being sentenced to death or when she begged the governor for mercy for the sake of her children.

When the body of evidence is examined in its entirety, it is clear that Louisa was responsible for dosing her two husbands with arsenic and watching them die the most agonising of deaths. If she hadn't been caught, it is feasible that she would have killed again—perhaps not even intentionally. Keeping arsenic-laced milk in an unmonitored jug on the kitchen bench was a recipe for disaster if ever there was one.

But why did she murder her husbands?

Her motive for killing Andrews is obvious: lust and greed. Needless to say, most greedy, lustful people do not commit murder. Something has to happen to trigger a murderous response, something that creates a problem for which killing seems the optimal solution. The trigger in the Andrews murder was probably his sudden unemployment. With limited opportunities for romance, Louisa found herself at a crossroad. She must have known that her Romeo would soon tire of her if the situation didn't change. One option was to abandon her family and run away with him; however, Collins was too lazy to be a good provider and her situation would have been dire if he'd later abandoned her. There was another option: Andrews' insurance money, the ropes of gold that might tie Collins permanently to her side.

Killing Andrews rewarded her with love and money; however, there was no such payout for killing Collins. The lack of an obvious motive for killing her second husband handicapped the prosecution in the first two trials, although the issue was largely ignored in the third Collins trial because of the 'double murder' scenario presented. Nonetheless, in order to understand her actions, it is essential to determine her motive for killing Collins.

Studies reveal that women who kill their husbands are usually reacting in self-defence to ongoing violence. Louisa, however, was not the victim of physical assaults in either of her marriages. She wasn't revenging herself on an unfaithful husband or, in the case of Collins, killing him to make room for another. Moreover, unless there was an insurance policy that never surfaced, she did not gain any financial benefit from the second killing. Perhaps Besomo and Canon Rich were correct in saying that she was suffering from a neurological or psychological disturbance, although the rewards for killing Andrews would suggest that a more pragmatic reason acted as a trigger in the second killing as well.

One type of husband-killer is the 'black widow': a female killer—sometimes a serial killer—who murders family members, usually by slow doses of poison and primarily for financial gain. All the 'black widow' boxes are ticked for Andrews' death, but few for Collins' death. Still, the driving force appears to be similar. Louisa's drama began with the illicit thrill of an affair. Then came Andrews' unemployment, followed by the killing, which empowered her both financially and emotionally, probably for the first time in her life. In the aftermath, she faced a new set of problems. Collins' laziness created difficulties when the insurance money began to run out. Another trigger seemingly followed: the baby's death in April 1888. Louisa began to drink heavily. Collins snapped at her and tried to stop her drinking. And Louisa decided to make use of those deadly crystals again.

The prosecution stumbled when attempting to provide a motive for the Collins killing because the only motive it could establish—Collins' desire to stop Louisa drinking—seemed too weak a trigger in a relationship that otherwise seemed loving. Since Louisa's day, the guilt/innocence pendulum has swung both ways. Some writers have concluded that she was innocent because of the problems with the evidence and the lack of a motive for killing Collins. Others have assumed guilt without attempting to explain motivation. A few have proclaimed guilt while providing a motive unsupported by the evidence—for example, a reaction to marital abuse. With the benefit of today's medical wisdom, we could also propose that postnatal depression might have triggered her actions; however, as this trigger would relate only to the Collins killing, and as serial killers are usually driven by similar underlying motivations, this seems an unlikely explanation.

As it turns out, when the evidence is exhaustively examined, a similar underlying motivation can be glimpsed in the Collins killing. It is clear from Louisa's actions, conversations and communications that she loathed Andrews yet loved Collins. In fact, she loved Collins so much that she killed to get him. So how would she react if Collins threatened to leave her? Collins was much younger than most contemporary records suggested. Louisa reported that he was aged twenty-nine at the time of his death; however, Collins, by his own more reliable admission, said that he was only twenty-three when they married. Clearly, Collins was little more than a boy—and a lazy one at that. When his beloved son died, he found himself with a lush of a wife who was nearly twice his age, an empty purse, and a bevy of disliked stepchildren to support. What did the relationship hold for him?

That Collins was feeling unhappy about life in general is suggested by his taciturn manner even in the early days of his illness, which contrasted strongly with his garrulity at the dance held shortly after Andrews' death. That he was less enamoured of Louisa is also suggested by his irritated attitude towards her while on his deathbed.

So, when Collins told Louisa that he would stop her drinking—as the children testified—it seems likely that an 'or else' was sooner or later attached. What form could that 'or else' have taken? He could have threatened to beat her into submission but, according to the children's testimonies, that wasn't the nature of their relationship. Otherwise, Collins had few sources of leverage. He had no money, no assets, no skills; in fact, he had nothing to offer except himself. So, the only 'or else' he could have threatened her with was to take himself away—to abandon her.

For Louisa, this 'or else' would have transformed an impotent demand for her to stop drinking into a life-changing threat to their relationship—one she had killed to gain. Additionally, it would have served as a challenge to her authority.

In many abusive marriages, the husbands see their wives as 'possessions'. Some kill fleeing wives partly to stop anyone else having them but, primarily, as the ultimate expression of their power and control. In the Collins household, Louisa 'wore the pants'. After their marriage, she not only acted as the couple's voice, she retained control of all of their money, which was at odds with custom in her patriarchal society (and could even be seen as a 'castrating' move). Seemingly, she wanted to maintain the power and authority that her first killing had bequeathed her, particularly over her young, lazy, perhaps not-too-smart but much-loved husband. A threat that he would leave, with everything such a threat encompassed, would have served as a powerful trigger for one who had already killed to gain him.

Thus, the only motive that accounts for all the evidence is that Louisa killed Collins because she 'loved too much'—if such a possessive, controlling attitude could be considered 'love'. She killed to get him and she killed to 'keep' him. As she said in one of her letters, 'It was not money I wanted from Collins, it was himself.' Lust and greed had metamorphosed into wrath with devastating consequences for those around her.

Louisa seems to have given Collins low doses of arsenic until the Friday before his death, when the doctor said that he would recover if carefully looked after. Collins' rapid decline over the next twenty-four hours, along with the large quantity of arsenic found in his body, suggests that she upped the dose after the doctor's visit. Ironically, it was Collins' rapid deterioration that most alarmed the doctors when they visited on the Saturday evening and led them to report the case to the police.

It is also possible that Louisa dosed him in front of her neighbours shortly before the doctors arrived on the Saturday night before his death, as he convulsed soon after she gave him a newly concocted drink. Such brazenness would suggest that this type of empowerment excited her, evoking the same type of illicit thrill that her affair had once generated.

The police found no evidence of Rough on Rats in the house despite an extensive search. It seems likely that the box was in Louisa's purse during her many attempts to leave the house after Collins' death, and that she eventually disposed of it when she visited Dr Marshall the following day.

A critical mistake, however, was Louisa's failure to discard the contents of the arsenic-filled tumbler. It seems a strange error for such a clever woman, particularly when she knew the police were involved and that tests had already been undertaken. Or was this not *her* failing?

The arsenic in the tumbler can only have been introduced in one of two ways. Either, the person responsible for poisoning Collins put it there or someone tampered with the tumbler's contents after it was collected by Constable Jeffes. While the tumbler evidence is beset with problems, to argue deliberate tampering wanders into conspiracy theory territory. Using Ockham's Razor again, the simplest or most likely explanation is that Louisa was responsible for the arsenic in the tumbler but, in the stress of the moment, she forgot to get rid of its contents, only realising her omission when Jeffes picked up the tumbler with a view to taking it away.

As for the discrepancy between Jeffes' and Hamlet's testimonies regarding the quantity of the liquid, the simplest and most likely explanation is that some of the contents of the unsealed tumbler spilt in the time between collection and testing. It must be remembered that Jeffes carried the unsealed container when he walked the few hundred yards from the Collins house to the police station, and that he later took the container all the way into the city. Nonetheless, the fact that no one could account for the spill raises concern about the use of this evidence to convict her.

If Louisa was tried today for Collins' death, the tumbler evidence would not be admissible because the chain of custody was not intact. Even if the constable and government analyst massaged their testimonies so they both testified to, say, a 'half-filled' glass of milky liquid, the tumbler itself had been left unsealed and unsecured for two days. By contrast, the autopsy doctors carefully sealed and secured their own specimen jars, indicating that the court of the day expected such a level of care with potentially critical evidence.

Other pieces of evidence would also be inadmissible. For example, May's statement that she had seen Rough on Rats in the house prior to Andrews' death would be problematic, partly because she revealed a faulty memory during the first trial about events that had happened only a month previously, which should have raised doubts about her likely accuracy when recollecting events that had happened nearly two years previously.

Finally, the evidence regarding Andrews' death would be inadmissible because of the inability to establish Andrews' cause of death with certainty, making this 'similar facts' evidence more prejudicial than probative. That being the case, if Louisa was brought to trial today for Collins' murder, it is unlikely that she would have been convicted. Still, current procedure is of little relevance when exploring the reliability of a historical verdict. The question needing to be asked is whether she should have been convicted under the rules in force at the time of her own trial.

It seems unlikely that the Crown would have broken the usual two-trial convention and proceeded with a third Collins trial if the prosecutor hadn't made the decision to include the critical Andrews 'similar facts' evidence. The ruling of the New Zealand Supreme Court suggests that the chief justice should not have allowed its admission; however, Lusk's failings as Louisa's counsel meant that the New South Wales courts were unable to answer the admissibility question.

They were, however, able to address the same type of question in an 1893 appeal. The judge presiding over the trial of baby-farmer murderers John and Sarah Makin had admitted 'similar facts' evidence regarding the deaths of other babies on the grounds of 'commonsense' rather than a legally binding authority. One of the appeal judges, Justice Innes—the same judge who allowed the Collins 'similar facts' evidence to be introduced into the Andrews trial (which was acceptable then and would be today)—argued that the 'commonsense' approach was unsafe and prejudicial except in cases where there was a large body of independent evidence to support the case; otherwise, an accused person might be tried and convicted of an offence not because of evidence connected with the offence, but because of evidence that the accused had committed other similar offences. However, Innes' concerns—which reflected the type of concerns expressed by others about the admission of the Andrews evidence to secure Louisa's conviction—were dismissed by the two other judges presiding over the Makin appeal, who happened to be two of the judges who presided over Louisa's appeal. Consequently, what the three appeal judges—or any others from the then Supreme Court—would have decided if Louisa's Queen's Counsel had been able to raise the 'similar facts' question is still open to doubt.

Accordingly, we must turn to the opinions of those well versed in colonial law to determine how the courts should have treated Louisa's case. For the many reasons mentioned above—the four trials, the problems with the tumbler evidence, the manipulation of the bench, and so on—along with the extremely prejudicial remarks made by the final prosecutor in his closing address, Judge Gregory D. Woods, who wrote *A History of Criminal Law in New South Wales*, declares that her case was 'a legal disgrace'.[11] There can be no doubt whatsoever that a 'spirit of vengeance' drove both the Crown and the judiciary in its pursuit of her conviction and execution.

• • •

Should Louisa have been executed?

Ignoring the big-picture question of the morality and efficacy of capital punishment, we are still left with all the evidentiary and procedural problems identified by Louisa's supporters and other members of the populace. Most serious of all was the psychological damage inflicted on a child by the knowledge that her words had killed her mother. If ever there was a case that demanded the hand of mercy, Louisa's was it. Instead, the hand of wrath prevailed.

So why were these problems ignored? Why was she hanged?

Of the two dozen New South Wales women deposed for homicide between 1880 and 1900, nine were convicted; yet Louisa was the only woman to be sent to the gallows—and it wasn't because she was a suspected double murderer. Baby farmer Sarah Makin, for example, had her 1893 death sentence commuted although she and her executed husband were considered responsible for killing a dozen infants for financial gain. Rather, the driving force in Louisa's case seems to have been the social and political environment of her time.

Louisa broke not only the written criminal law but the unwritten social law. She breached society's expectations of 'womanly' behaviour when it was particularly unwise to do so. Moreover, the face she presented to the world was cold and unemotional—'unwomanly'. This was a time when society believed that external appearance denoted internal nature, that crime was most often a male behavioural trait, therefore, an unwomanly woman—that is, a more manly woman—was more likely to be criminal by nature.

This, also, was a time when women were becoming more assertive in demanding equality in employment, educational opportunities and voting rights, so the question of gender inequality was topical. One gender inequality that favoured women was the application of capital punishment. Men were executed; women were not. The Mount Rennie executions two years previously had shone a spotlight on this form of gender inequality. Four youths had been executed for a 'single' crime, one considered much less heinous than murder. As one newspaper argued, if men were to be hanged to protect women, then women should also be hanged to protect men.

It was time to set an example, time to show the public that society was not as unequal as the reformers might claim—and, conversely, that society was making efforts to increase women's autonomy. By a bizarre piece of logical illogic, it was time to hang a woman. The cold-hearted killer of one husband (if not two), a killer who had failed to endear herself to the public and had offered no mitigating explanation, was the ideal choice. Louisa Collins was to be hanged, not only because of what she had done but because a female sacrifice was needed. She was the perfect scapegoat.

Yet even though Louisa breached society's womanly rules, she was not completely unwomanly. She was an attractive, soberly dressed mother of seven children. Thus, while the 'hang her' advocates used womanhood as one of their supportive arguments, the 'mercy' advocates were able to do so as well. A tug-of-war began with Louisa in the middle: Louisa the stereotype rather than Louisa the person.

Capital punishment would always be a politically divisive subject; however, when Ninian Melville introduced Louisa's case into parliament, he forced the members of this especially adversarial House to take sides along party lines. It became another contentious issue confronting parliament. Parkes reacted by, ostensibly, taking the decision-making power away from his cabinet and passing it to the one person who could rise above the maelstrom of New South Wales politics—the governor.

Lord Carrington was an intelligent man with progressive views. He would have seen the myriad problems in the material submitted with the mercy pleas. His words rejecting these mercy pleas suggest that his response would have been different if he had truly enjoyed unfettered authority, but Parkes' government had made it clear that to pursue such a course would be political suicide. Carrington had little choice but to toe Parkes' line. His shame at doing so, though, is evident in his refusal to see Louisa's children.

Ultimately, Louisa was hanged because Parkes was determined to get his own way and was willing to push New South Wales towards a constitutional crisis to achieve it. Yet Parkes was a social progressive who deplored capital punishment and favoured women's rights, so why was he determined to hang Louisa? He justified his government's decision on the grounds that capital punishment was 'the law', that the law was gender-blind, and that women had the same rights and responsibilities as men so should be treated similarly when they broke the same law. On the surface, this seems a valid 'progressive' argument. Nonetheless,

Parkes was soon reminded that the law was not gender-blind and that women had no vote so, clearly, they hadn't the same rights and responsibilities as men. Moreover, as everyone knew, Parkes had himself breached the law six months previously when he responded to public concerns about Chinese immigration. Accordingly, his 'it's the law' argument lacked any moral authority. Even Parkes must have been aware, at some level, of his hypocrisy, especially as the press was keen to point it out. That being the case, it seems surprising that he didn't dismiss all the rhetoric and embrace the opportunity to grant her a reprieve, particularly in view of his statement to parliament that his government would render every conceivable assistance that would serve the ends of justice in her favour.

The explanation for Parkes' wrathfulness seems to lie in the community's long-held and widely embraced views about women. Parkes and his brethren still maintained a patriarchal and patronising attitude to women. While the conservatives were determined to control and silence women for fear that those who had money, knowledge and power would destroy the fabric of society, the progressives were at least willing to allow women a say in their own future so long as the decision was made by men in a timeframe that suited their own agenda.

These men had a primal attitude to power. They saw it as a dichotomy—either they had it or fought to gain it, or they *chose* to support someone else who had it. They did not share power or accept its imposition lightly. This type of attitude was carried into their strongest relationships with women. Marriage was never intended to be a power-sharing arrangement. The word 'obey' made that clear—to everyone.

Then along came a 'black widow' who dished out love and arsenic and nearly got away with killing two husbands.

While husband-killing was no longer 'petit treason' in the eyes of the law, the notion that this act reflected a profound betrayal of trust and a serious social threat still permeated the community consciousness, as the contemporary articles and correspondence about Louisa's case reveal. Since husband-killing had long been considered nearly as heinous as killing a king, a woman who could kill *two* husbands, two 'petit kings', must therefore be the personification of evil, a destroyer not just of souls but of society and its core values.

Additionally, Louisa inflicted on her two husbands a humiliating death. Dying in battle was noble. Being poisoned by one's wife? Effectively, she didn't just kill them; she castrated them. And impotence for a man is one of the greatest fears of all.

Fear unbinds the ropes that cage superstition. To Parkes, Louisa was a reminder that, while everyman's home was his castle, Eve still lurked in the dungeon. He stated his attitude clearly when he said, 'At all times, and under all circumstances, when woman once forgets the character of her sex, there is no barrier to the lengths she will go to in crime.' Clearly, a message needed to be sent to those lurking Eves.

Evil women were no longer burnt at the stake. The gallows would have to do.

Epilogue

> A popular writer has said we may begin to believe in modern civilisation when it abolishes the hissing of actresses and the hanging of women.
>
> *South Australian Advertiser*

'It is forty years since a woman was hanged in New South Wales,' wrote the disgusted *Clarence and Richmond Examiner* in the aftermath of Louisa's bungled execution, 'and I am inclined to think that it will be forty years before another is executed. The probability is that Louisa Collins is the last woman who will be subjected to that punishment.'

Prophetic words indeed. Despite more prolific killers facing the courts in the decades to come, Louisa was the last woman to die on a New South Wales scaffold. The name 'Louisa Collins' had come to represent the barbarity of capital punishment—for women at least—in the same way that, a century later, the name of an equally inscrutable woman, Lindy Chamberlain, would warn of the danger that would be inherent in its reintroduction.

The horror of Louisa's execution failed to deter some other Australian colonies. Five more women were later executed, including four in Victoria, the colony most strident in its demands for Louisa's blood. Victoria also had pride of place in executing the last woman in Australia—Jean Lee in 1951—and the last man—Ronald Ryan—as recently as 1967.

Even so, New South Wales was the last state to abolish capital punishment, in 1985, for all that the law had lain dormant for half a century.[12] Federally, it was struck from the statutes in 1973. The reasons for its abolition included those raised by the people who had called for Louisa's reprieve, along with statistical evidence showing that harsh punishments failed to deter crime and that, conversely, murder rates were higher in states and countries that actively pursued the death penalty. The evidence also showed that the executed were mostly the poor and marginalised. Then—and now—they were the people like Louisa who couldn't afford skilled legal representation and hadn't the ear of the moneyed or the powerful, such as Sir Henry Parkes.

In 1888, this political Methuselah, who would become Australia's most famous and revered nineteenth-century politician, was in his fourth of five terms as premier. In his next term, he would play a pivotal role in the drive for federation and in the early introduction of female suffrage. He was also a man before his time in his attitude to capital punishment. Thus, it seems ironic that he, of all people, should pass into history as the man responsible for the last execution of a woman in New South Wales. The Parkes who decried capital punishment in 1852 would have been horrified at such an ignominious legacy.

Louisa's name, too, will forever be inscribed in Australian history books—along with her notorious nickname, Lucrezia Borgia. Unlike her unjustly accused predecessor, however, she was indeed a femme fatale, a poisoner of lives and souls.

Yet Louisa's story is more than just the tale of a 'black widow' serial killer. This figure of well-deserved infamy also provoked public concern and outrage at a time of social and feminist upheaval. New South Wales feminists such as Rose Scott and Louisa Lawson

(Henry Lawson's mother) sometimes lent their voices to the mercy pleas when female murderers were facing the wrath of the law; however, they kept ominously silent in Louisa's case. Without mitigating circumstances to justify her actions or an appealing persona to engage the community, the case of a drunken adulteress who murdered two husbands could not be used to further the feminist cause. These feminist leaders recognised the need to engage with rather than alienate the establishment if they wanted to improve the status of women. They recognised that Louisa's portrait on the banner of feminism would have shouted of revolutionary ideals, of the desire to improve the status of women at the expense, indeed the destruction, of men. While Louisa Collins as a woman was politically problematic, Louisa Collins as a metaphor was politically toxic.

Following her execution, Louisa became a juicy tale to be drawn from the archives when other husband-killers graced the courts and a cry of warning against the dangers and horrors of capital punishment. Today, she remains a figure of interest, largely because of her historical importance but also because the question 'did she?' has continued to be asked, because her motive could not be determined. Now that the matter of her guilt has been established, we can reassure ourselves that, while her conviction and execution were legally and morally questionable and her death a sacrifice to appease society's pro- and anti-feminist concerns, she at least wasn't an innocent who was condemned unjustly.

But what of Louisa herself? Wherein lay the seeds of her downfall? Female serial killers usually remain undetected for longer than their male counterparts because women are less likely to kill so they are trusted more than men. Moreover, female serial killers generally target those in their care while hiding behind a benevolent mask. As it happens, Louisa's crimes were discovered because she made a mistake. Some might argue that her biggest mistake was in forgetting to dispose of the contents of the arsenic-laced tumbler. In truth, it was her decision to take her second husband to the same Elizabeth Street surgery that had treated her first husband. Thanks to a chance meeting between two brothers-in-law, a chance comment, Louisa's web of deceit and duplicity began to unravel.

The only question remaining to be answered was why she would make such a fatal mistake. Was it a witting or unwitting decision to engage with the doctors, to draw them into her cat-and-mouse game, to see if she could outwit them? Or was it an unspoken plea for them to stop her? Whatever the reasons for all of her actions, her failure to publicly protest her innocence suggests an integrity of sorts, a refusal to deny what she had done. On the other hand, her failure to confess suggests a refusal to admit what she had become.

Louisa Collins, the woman, will always remain an enigma, an intriguing mystery that cannot be solved. Louisa Collins, the murderer, however, has achieved a notoriety that will never be eclipsed. She was the first female serial killer in Australia, appearing on Sydney's criminal stage in the same year that Jack the Ripper launched himself onto the world stage. And she was the last woman executed in New South Wales, her gruesome death on the gallows a Calvary that warns against the sacrifice of human life in the name of justice and the greater good.

Author's Note

Six court hearings; hundreds of pages of depositions and court transcripts; a hundred thousand words of testimony: for a writer of historical true-crime thrillers, this amount of original source material makes Louisa Collins' case a dream story.

While my account of her trials and tribulations is non-fiction, it reads in part like fiction because the characters are allowed to live their own stories. To write history in this way, I require information from the characters themselves or from others who were engaging with them at the time. Most of the characters testified in court on multiple occasions, some as many as six times, providing the detailed description and dialogue I need to bring such a story to life.

I did not make up the dialogue in this book. One of the reasons I write true crime stories is because the witnesses, during their testimonies, quote the words they spoke at the time of the events in question and the words others said in response. Thus, the dialogue comes straight from the mouths of the characters themselves.

Sometimes I use the description and dialogue recorded in the court cases to recount the events at the time they occurred. In other parts of the book, I use the dialogue as part of the developing court case. Dividing the information in this way lends drama and tension to the tale.

In terms of Louisa herself, to gain an understanding of her character I used only the original records rather than any of the sensationalist accounts of her story that have been published in books and newspapers during the last half century. The authors of these accounts have sometimes depicted Louisa as a highly strung woman who wails and shouts hysterically and flings herself from the room in a fit of pique. Nothing could be further from the truth. What the original records make clear is that Louisa was extraordinarily calm and emotionally cold even under the most trying of circumstances. She occasionally wept during extremely emotional times (after her first husband died, when her second husband was dying and then dead, and when her daughter 'betrayed' her in court) and alcohol stimulated an aura of excitement in her, but that was all. Otherwise, she was the opposite of the overwrought woman imagined by other authors. And, like Lindy Chamberlain a century later, her emotional coldness was one of the reasons for her conviction.

Louisa Collins' story is not just the tale of the woman herself. It takes us on a journey through a time when society was beginning to recognise that women had a right to social autonomy and a political voice—but that, nonetheless, their desire for autonomy could not be expressed in the serial killing of two husbands.

I hope you enjoy reading Louisa's story as much as I enjoyed writing it.

• • •

A book such as *Black Widow* could not be written without the help of others. I wish to express my heartfelt thanks to the following: to Louisa's descendant Joy Harper, who reminded me at a talk I gave some years ago about Louisa's fascinating story and who provided a wealth of birth, marriage and death certificates and other information about the family; to Emeritus Professor of Law Bruce Kercher, who listened to my concerns about Louisa's case, realised that some of the law and evidence questions I was troubled about would be best answered by an expert on colonial criminal law, and reached out to the perfect person; to District Court judge Gregory Woods, the author of *A History of Criminal Law in New South Wales*, who read the manuscript in twenty-four hours and agreed with my conclusions and who also provided two critical pieces of information that helped me to answer the question as to whether Louisa was guilty (her failure to make a dock statement in any of her four trials was a strong suggestion of her guilt) and why she was executed (partly because killing a husband had been considered 'petit treason' under the common law); to James Whorton, Professor Emeritus at the University of Washington School of Medicine and the author of *The Arsenic Century*, who answered the critical question as to whether a person was likely to kill themselves slowly by arsenic poisoning; to Deborah Beck, author of *Hope in Hell*, who took me around Darlinghurst Gaol and showed me the important sites so I could picture the scene; to Inspector Ann Brown of the Sheriff's Office who escorted me through Darlinghurst Courthouse; to my literary agent Tara Wynne, publisher Rebecca Kaiser, editor Angela Handley and copyeditor Ali Lavau for their continued support and much appreciated suggestions to improve the manuscript; and to my ever-helpful readers, Kate Wingrove, Keith Johnson and Mike Elliott. And last, but never least, I wish to thank my beloved family: my husband, Allan Ashmore, offspring Camillie and Jaiden Ashmore, and mother Jill Baxter, who are with me at every stage of the researching/writing journey—whether they want to be or not.

Notes

1 A 'grain' represents the weight of an average grain of wheat; that is, around 65 milligrams or 0.0002 ounces.

2 Many publications claim that Louisa was born at the Belltrees property in the Scone district of New South Wales; however, this is not necessarily correct. Louisa was born on 11 August 1847, nine years prior to the commencement of the civil registration of births, deaths and marriages in New South Wales, so birth certificates did not exist at that time. All that survives is her baptism entry, which records that she was born on 11 August 1847 and baptised three months later on 7 November, at which time her family was residing in the Township of Scone. While her parents had once resided at Belltrees—they were living there in May 1845 when their eldest two daughters were baptised—they left Belltrees at some point in the thirty months between May 1845 and November 1847 never to return.

In later records, Louisa and her husband sometimes noted that she was born at Belltrees and sometimes Scone (or elsewhere); however, this information is hearsay as we cannot remember our own births. No direct evidence of her birthplace has survived, so we must resort to probability. There is only a 10 per cent chance that her parents were still residing at Belltrees at the time of Louisa's birth. Whatever the case, the Hall family had left there by the time she was three months old and had settled at the Thornthwaite estate near Dartbrook before she was two. They continued to move around the Hunter Valley district in the years that followed.

3 Louisa's parents, Henry and Catherine Hall (née Ring), were married on 17 August 1842 and had the following children:

- Elizabeth, born 22 March 1843; parents residing at Belltrees (father a labourer) when baptised on 5 May 1845.
- Margaret, born 28 April 1844; baptised same day as sister Elizabeth.
- Charlotte, born 12 September 1845; parents residing in the Township of Scone (father a labourer) when baptised on 7 November 1847.
- Louisa, born 11 August 1847; baptised same day as sister Charlotte.

- Samuel, born 15 July 1849; parents residing at Thornthwaite near Dartbrook (father a shepherd) when baptised on 23 July 1849.
- Sarah, born 2 January 1852; parents residing at Thornthwaite (father a shepherd) when baptised on 12 July 1852.
- Ann, born 27 May 1855; parents residing at Sandy Creek near Kayuga (father a shepherd) when baptised on 29 August 1855.
- Richard, born 18 November 1857; parents residing at Mr Cox's Well station (near Muswellbrook) when baptised on 13 April 1858.
- Maria, born 29 May 1862 at Hall's Creek (father a shepherd).

Henry Hall died in November 1880 at Owen's Gap, Scone. His widow died on 28 May 1904 at the Newington Asylum on the Parramatta River.

4 Charles and Louisa had the following children:
- Herbert, born 1 June 1867 at Merriwa; died 26 December 1935 at Newcastle Hospital.
- Ernest, born around March 1869 at Merriwa; died 27 October 1872 at Muswellbrook.
- Reuben, born 27 August 1871 at Muswellbrook.
- Arthur, born 15 October 1873 at Hunter Terrace, Muswellbrook; died 14 June 1919 at Sydney Hospital.
- Frederick William, born 25 August 1875 at Forbes Street, Muswellbrook; died 26 January 1962 at Royal Newcastle Hospital.
- May, born 16 October 1877 at Bridge Street, Muswellbrook; died 10 October 1911, Killingworth.
- Edwin, born 1880.
- David, born 2 October 1881 at Botany; died 13 October 1881 at Botany.
- Charles, born 29 May 1883 at Botany.

5 The baby was registered as 'William Collins' in his birth certificate but as 'John Collins' in his death certificate.

6 Sometimes her nickname was spelt Lucrezia Borgia and sometimes the press and public anglicised it to Lucretia.

7 A 'larrikin' in the late 1800s was the equivalent of today's gang banger.

8 Ten women were executed in New South Wales between 1788 and 1888, seven for murder. Only four executions took place after the major changes to the criminal laws in the 1830s, all for husband-killing. In 1842, Lucretia Dunckley and her 'fancy man' died on the Berrima Gaol gallows for the axe-murder of Lucretia's husband. Another love-triangle murder, a poisoning, sent Mary Thornton and her lover to the Newcastle gallows in 1844. Mary Ann Brownlow, the infant-suckler, was the next—in 1855. Ellen Monks was executed in 1860; she had used a hammer to bludgeon her constantly drunk husband then had ensured his death by burning his body. Meanwhile, all female child-killers (mostly convicted of infanticide) escaped death along with husband-killers Mary Ann Perry (1859) and the Maitland murderesses, Mary Ann Burton and Sarah Keep (1885).

9 James Whorton, *The Arsenic Century*, p. 315.
10 Correspondence with Professor Emeritus James Whorton, 31 July 2012.
11 Conversations and correspondence with Judge Gregory D. Woods, July 2014.
12 Queensland was the first state to abolish the death penalty—in 1922. It was followed by Tasmania in 1968, Northern Territory in 1973, Victoria in 1975, Tasmania in 1976, the Australian Capital Territory in 1983, Western Australia in 1984 and New South Wales in 1985.

Bibliography

Primary sources

MITCHELL LIBRARY, SYDNEY, NSW

Benevolent Society, Index to Admissions and Discharges: Edwin & Charles Andrews, 1888 [Z D566; Reel CY1804]

Benevolent Society, Inmate Journals: Edwin & Charles Andrews, 1888 [A 7237 date 27 July 1888; Reel CY1970]

Benevolent Society, Register of Admissions and Discharges, Edwin & Charles Andrews, 1888 [Z D578; Reel CY1816]

Grevilles Post Office Directory, Muswellbrook, 1872, pp. 369–72

NSW Parliamentary Debates (Hansard), 1888, pp. 1319–43, 1386

NSW Police Gazette, 1888, pp. 235 & 244

Sands Sydney Directories, Botany, 1887, p. 184; 1888, p. 174

NEWSPAPERS (NSW UNLESS OTHERWISE STATED)

Argus (Vic)
Australian Star
Australian Town and Country Journal
Barrier Miner
Bathurst Free Press
Brisbane Courier (Qld)
Bulletin
Clarence and Richmond Examiner
Daily Telegraph
Echo
Evening News
Freeman's Journal
Gippsland Times (Vic)
Illustrated Australian News
Kiama Independent
Maitland Mercury

Singleton Argus
South Australian Advertiser (SA)
Sydney Mail
Sydney Morning Herald
The Newsletter
Traralgon Record (Vic)
Tribune
Windsor and Richmond Gazette

REGISTRY OF BIRTHS, DEATHS & MARRIAGES, SYDNEY, NSW
Original certificates
Andrews, Arthur: Birth 1873 [73/14890]
Andrews, Charles: Marriage to Louisa Hall, 1865 [65/1940]
Hall, Louisa: Marriage to Charles Andrews, 1865 [65/1940] (partial entry only)

Transcriptions by Joy Murrin
Andrews, Arthur: Birth (certificate listed above); Marriage 1896 [96/26257]; Death 1919 [19/5087/31437]
Andrews, Charles: Birth 1883 [83/9462]
Andrews, Charles: Death 1887 [87/4915]
Andrews, David: Birth 1881 [81/8395]; Death 1881 [81/4148]
Andrews, Ernest: Birth c. 1869 (no certificate); Death 1872 [72/5398]
Andrews, Frederick William: Birth 1875 [75/15591]; Marriage 1903 [03/6088]; Death 1962 [62/5962]
Andrews, Herbert: Birth 1867 [67/8316]; Marriage 1894 [94/3253]; Death 1935 [35/24209]
Andrews, May: Birth 1877 [77/16403]; (as Mabel) Marriage 1898 [98/7969]; Death 1911 [11/16783]
Andrews, Reuben: Birth 1871 [71/13888]
Andrews/Collins (née Hall), Louisa: Marriage to Michael Peter Collins, 1887 [87/3316]; Death 1889 [89/44]
Collins, John: Birth (William) 1887 [in file *Regina v. Collins* 9/6758]; Death 1888 [88/5715]
Collins, Michael Peter: Death 1888 [88/5843]
Hall, Maria (Louisa's sister): Birth 1862 [62/13399]
Martin, Thomas Morgan: Birth of son Charles, 1887 [86/81]
McGuiness, Alice Louisa: Birth 1903 [03/7912]
McGuiness, Edward: Birth 1907 [07/19184]
McGuiness, Thelma: Birth 1908 [08/9440]

SCONE AND UPPER HUNTER HISTORICAL SOCIETY
Hall, Louisa: Marriage to Charles Andrews, 1865, Holy Trinity, Merriwa [Microfilm LH14]

Hall, Richard: Baptism, 1858 (born 1857), Rowan Parish, County Durham [Microfilm LH14]

STATE RECORDS OF NSW

Attorney-General, Index to Registers of Letters received: Louisa Collins, 1888 [X2051 pp. 102, 105], 1889 [X2052 p. 90]

Colonial Secretary In-Letters: Agnes Shiell, 16 April 1889 [5/5930 No. 89/4438]

Colonial Secretary In-Letters: Petition from F Lees, 1889 [5/2561 No. 89/90; Reel 2604]

Colonial Secretary In-Letters: Petition from women of Victoria, 1889 [5/2561 No. 89/89; Reel 2604]

Colonial Secretary In-Letters: Water Police, 27 July 1888 (regarding Louisa's youngest sons) [1/2715 No. 88/9300]

Colonial Secretary, Letters sent to Judicial Establishments, Sheriff and Coroner 1888–1889: Louisa Collins [4/3771, 14 December 1888; Reel 644]

Colonial Secretary, Register of Governor's minutes and memoranda received 1881–1900: Louisa Collins [4/6987 No. 19599]

Crown Solicitor, Index of committals from Magistrates Court to Sydney Criminal Court, 1877–1902: Louisa Collins, 1888 [3/1029 1888 Nos 12, 13]

Darlinghurst Gaol Correspondence Register [5/1846 1888 Nos 1591, 1599, 1849, 1943, 2096, 2245, 2623, 2634, 2663, 2665, 2675, 2693, 2710, 2733, 2767 & 1889 Nos 14, 27, 32, 34, 35, 40, 46, 49, 54, 59, 62, 76, 100]

Darlinghurst Gaol Death Book: Louisa Collins, 1889 [COD 1884 Year 1889 No. 2]

Darlinghurst Gaol Entrance Book: Louisa Collins, 13 July 1888, 18 July 1888 [5/1929 1888 Nos 5456, 5588]

Darlinghurst Gaol Photographs: Louisa Collins, 1888 [3/6050 p. 84, No. 4335]

Deceased Estate File, Charles Andrews [20/7024 Z12086]

Executive Council Minutes 1888 [4/1580 p. 368 A, 13 December 1888, Minute No. 58].

Executive Council Minutes 1889 [4/1581 p. 1 A, 3 January 1889 Minute No. 1, p. 26 A, 4 January 1889, Minute No. 2]

Police Service Registers: George Henry Hyem (No. 1866), George Jeffes (No. 4109) [8/3251; Reel 3043]

Police Service Registers: George Henry Hyem (No. 1866), George Jeffes (No. 4109), Abraham Robert Sherwood (No. 4501) [8/3252; Reel 3043]

Probate: Charles Andrews [17/2183 No. 14439] and Deceased Estate File [20/7024 Z12086]

State Children's Relief Board—Dependent Children's Registers: Charles Andrews [11/22097 No. 5; Fiche 7028]

Registers of Baptisms, Marriages and Burials

Baptism: Ann Hall, 1855 (born 1855) [Vol. 42 No. 1840; Reel 5014]

Baptism: Charlotte Hall, 1847 (born 1845) [Vol. 32 No. 2605; Reel 5009]

Baptism: Elizabeth Hall, 1845 (born 1843) [Vol. 30 No. 3020; Reel 5008]

Baptism: Louisa Hall, 1847 (born 1847) [Vol. 32 No. 2606; Reel 5009]
Baptism: Margaret Hall, 1845 (born 1844) [Vol. 30 No. 3021; Reel 5008]
Baptism: Samuel Hall, 1849 (born 1849) [SRNSW Vol. 34 No. 3201; Reel 5011]
Baptism: Sarah Hall, 1852 (born 1852) [Vol. 38 No. 3273; Reel 5012]
Marriage: Henry Hall & Catherine Ring, 1842 [Vol. 26 No. 500; Reel 5007]
Sheriff: Certificates of Execution: Louisa Collins [SRNSW ref: X945 No. 31; COD 530]
Supreme Court, Notebook of Justice Foster: *Regina v. Louisa Collins*, 6–9 August 1888 [2/4249 pp. 63–147]
Supreme Court, Notebook of Justice Windeyer: *Regina vs Louisa Collins*, 5–8 November 1888 [2/7403 pp. 1–91]
Supreme Court, Notebook of Justice Innes: *Regina vs Louisa Collins*, 19–22 November 1888 [2/4552 pp. 61–133]
Supreme Court, Notebook of Chief Justice Darley: *Regina vs Louisa Collins*, 6–9 Dec 1888 [2/2873 pp. 44–172, 2/2874 pp. 1–38]
Supreme Court, Regina vs Louisa Collins, 1888 [9/6758] (a box of material relating to Louisa's case, including the depositions from the two inquests)

Secondary sources

Australian Dictionary of Biography Online (website), <http://adb.anu.edu.au>
Australian Legal Information Institute (website), <www.austlii.edu.au>
Barr, Jane, '*The influence of Saint Jerome on medieval attitudes to women*', in Janet M. Soskice (ed.), *After Eve*, Collins Marshall Pickering, London, 1990, Ch. 6, <www.womenpriests.org/theology/barr.asp>
Beck, Deborah, *Hope in Hell: A history of Darlinghurst Gaol and the National Art School*, Allen & Unwin, Sydney, 2005
Bennett, J.M., *A History of the New South Wales Bar*, Law Book Company, Sydney, 1969
——*A History of the Supreme Court of New South Wales*, Law Book Company, Sydney, 1974
——*Portraits of the Chief Justices of New South Wales 1824–1977*, John Ferguson, Sydney, 1977
Ben-Ze'ev, Aaron & Goussinsky, Ruhama, *In the Name of Love: Romantic idealogy and its victims*, Oxford University Press, Oxford, 2008
Besomo, P., *The Botany Poisoning Case*, Sydney, 1888 [Mitchell Library, self-published]
Birch, Helen (ed.), *Moving Targets: Women, murder and representation*, University of California Press, Berkeley, 1993
Burney, Ian, *Poison, Detection, and the Victorian Imagination*, Manchester University Press, Manchester, 2006
Carney, Gerard, *Separation of Powers in the Westminster System*, Paper presented to the Australasian Study of Parliament Group (Queensland Chapter), Parliament

House, Brisbane, 13 September 1993, <www.parliament.qld.gov.au/aspg/papers/930913.pdf>

Cass, Kathryn, *The Last Woman Hanged in NSW: The extraordinary case of Louisa Collins*, City of Botany, Sydney, 2009

Clark, Andrew Inglis, *Studies in Australian Constitutional Law*, Charles F. Maxwell, Melbourne, 1901, <http://setis.library.usyd.edu.au/ozlit/pdf/fed0010.pdf>

Clark, David, 'The struggle for judicial independence: The amotion and suspension of Supreme Court judges in 19th century Australia', *Macquarie Law Journal*, Vol. 12 (2013), pp. 21–59, <www.law.mq.edu.au/public/download.jsp?id=131963>

Clune, D. & Turner, K., *The Governors of New South Wales 1788–2010*, Federation Press, Sydney, 2009

Cushing, Nancy, 'Woman as murderer: The defence of Louisa Collins', *Journal of Interdisciplinary Gender Studies*, Vol. 1, No. 2 (1996), pp. 147–57

Davis, Carol Ann, *Women Who Kill: Profiles of female serial killers*, Allison & Busby, London, 2001

Davison, G., McCarty, J.W. & McLeary, A. (eds), *Australians 1888*, Fairfax, Syme & Weldon, Sydney, 1987

Dictionary of Sydney (website), entries on 'Darlinghurst courthouse' and 'Prisons in 1920', *Dictionary of Sydney*, <http://dictionaryofsydney.org>

Duff, Charles, *A Handbook on Hanging* [1961], New York Review of Books Classics, New York, 2011

Edwards, Susan, *Women on Trial: A study of the female suspect, defendant and offender in the criminal law and criminal justice system*, Manchester University Press, Manchester, 1984

Farrell, A.L., Keppel, R.D. & Titterington, V.B., 'Lethal ladies: Revisiting what we know about female serial killers', *Homicide Studies*, Vol. 15 (2011), pp. 228–52, <http://hsx.sagepub.com/content/15/3/228>

Fox, J.A. & Levin, J., 'Multiple homicide: Patterns of serial and mass murder', *Crime and Justice*, Vol. 23 (1998), pp. 407–55

Frei, A., Vollm, B., Graf, M. & Dittmann, V., 'Female serial killing: Review and case report', *Criminal Behaviour and Mental Health*, Vol. 16 (2006), pp. 167–76, <http://www.ncbi.nlm.nih.gov/pubmed/16838388>

Ghirardo, Diane Yvonne, 'Lucrezia Borgia as entrepreneur', *Renaissance Quarterly*, Vol. 61, No. 1 (2008), pp. 53–91, <www.jstor.org/stable/10.1353/ren.2008.0029>

Greenwood, Kerry (ed.), *The Thing She Loves: Why women kill*, Allen & Unwin, Sydney, 1996

Helfield, Randa, 'Female poisoners of the nineteenth century: A study of gender bias in the application of the law', *Osgoode Hall Law Journal*, Vol. 28, No. 1 (1990), <http://digitalcommons.osgoode.yorku.ca/ohlj/vol28/iss1/2/>

Higby, Gregory, 'Chemistry and the 19th century American pharmacist', *Bulletin for the History of Chemistry*, Vol. 28, No. 1 (2003), <www.scs.illinois.edu/~mainzv/HIST/bulletin_open_access/v28-1/v28-1%20p9-17.pdf>

Hillgarth, J.N., 'The image of Alexander VI and Cesare Borgia in the sixteenth and seventeenth centuries', *Journal of the Warburg and Courtauld Institutes*, Vol. 59 (1996), pp. 119–29, <www.jstor.org/stable/751400>

History of Judicial Hanging in Britain 1735–1964 (website), <www.capitalpunishmentuk.org/hanging1.html>

Holledge, James, *Australia's Wicked Women*, Horwitz, Sydney, 1963

Judicial Commission of New South Wales, Criminal Trial Courts Bench Book: Tendency, coincidence and background evidence, <www.judcom.nsw.gov.au/publications/benchbks/criminal/tendency_and_coincidence_evidence.html/?searchterm=tendency>

Kaladelfos, Amanda, 'The politics of punishment: Rape and the death penalty in colonial Australia, 1841–1901', *History Australia*, Vol. 9, No. 1 (2012), pp. 155–75, <www98.griffith.edu.au/dspace/bitstream/handle/10072/53294/87128_1.pdf?sequence=1>

Kaufman-Osborn, Timothy, *From Noose to Needle: Capital punishment and the late liberal state*, University of Michigan Press, Michigan, 2002

Kukulies-Smith, W. & Priest, S., '"No hope of mercy" for the Borgia of Botany Bay: Louisa May Collins, the last woman executed in New South Wales, 1889', *Canberra Law Review*, Vol. 10, No. 2 (2011), pp. 144–58

Lee, Carol Ann, *A Fine Day for a Hanging: The real Ruth Ellis story*, Edinburgh Mainstream Publishing, Edinburgh, 2012

Lennan, J. & Williams, G., 'The death penalty in Australian law', *Sydney Law Review*, Vol. 34 (2012), pp. 659–94

Ludlow, Christa, 'The Reader Investigates: Images of crime in the colonial city', *Continuum: Journal of Media and Cultural Studies*, Vol. 7, No. 2 (1994), pp. 254–68, <http://www.austlit.edu.au/austlit/page/C786822>

Lumb, R.D., *The Constitutions of the Australian States*, University of Queensland Press, St Lucia, 1991

McDermid, Val, *Forensics: The anatomy of crime*, Profile Books, London, 2014

McGowen, Randall, 'A powerful sympathy: Terror, the prison and humanitarian reform in early nineteenth century Britain', *Journal of British Studies*, Vol. 25, No. 3 (1986), pp. 312–34, <www.jstor.org/stable/175466>

——'Civilizing Punishment: The end of the public execution in England', *Journal of British Studies*, Vol. 33, No. 3 (1994), pp. 257–82, <www.jstor.org/stable/176073>

——'"He Beareth Not the Sword in Vain": Religion and the criminal law in eighteenth-century England', *Eighteenth-Century Studies*, Vol. 21, No. 2 (1987–88), pp. 192–211, <www.jstor.org/stable/2739104>

——'The Body and Punishment in Eighteenth-Century England', *The Journal of Modern History*, Vol. 59, No. 4 (1987), pp. 651–79, <www.jstor.org/stable/1879947>

McQueen, Rob, 'Of wigs and gowns: A short history of legal and judicial dress in Australia', *Law in Context*, Vol. 16, No. 1 (1999), pp. 31–58 <http://search.informit.com.au.ezproxy.une.edu.au/fullText;dn=20012467;res=AGISPT>

Martens, Jeremy, '"Disturbing and Most Poisonous Agitations": Henry Parkes, populism and the usurpation of law in New South Wales, 1888', in Peter Limb (ed.), *Orb and Sceptre: Studies on British imperialism and its legacies, in honour of Norman Etherington*, Monash University ePress, Melbourne, 2008

Martin, A.W., *Henry Parkes: A biography*, Melbourne University Press, Melbourne, 1980

NSW Capital Convictions Database, 1788–1954 (website), <http://research.forbessociety.org.au>

Overington, Caroline, *Last Woman Hanged: The terrible, true story of Louisa Collins*, HarperCollins, Sydney, 2014

Öztürk, Anil, 'The Christian men's oldest prejudice: Misogyny, hate or fear', <https://www.academia.edu/2030628/The_Christian_Mens_Oldest_Prejudice_Misogyny_Hate_Or_Fear>

Parliament of New South Wales (website), <www.parliament.nsw.gov.au/prod/parlment/members.nsf/V3ListFormerMembers>

Pearson, Patricia, *When She Was Bad: Violent women and the myth of innocence*, Random House, Toronto, 1997

Perri, F.S. & Lichtenwald, T.G., 'The last frontier: Myths and the female psychopathic killer', *The Forensic Examiner*, Summer (2010), pp. 50–67, <www.all-about-forensic-psychology.com/support-files/female-psychopathic-killers.pdf>

Polk, Kenneth, 'Homicide: Women as offenders', in Patricia Easteal and Sandra McKillip (eds), *Women and the Law*, Australian Institute of Criminology, Canberra, 1993, pp. 149–62, <http://aic.gov.au/media_library/publications/proceedings/16/polk.pdf>

Potas, I. & Walker, J., 'Capital punishment', *Trends & Issues in Crime and Criminal Justice*, No. 3 (1987), <www.aic.gov.au/media_library/publications/tandi/ti03.pdf>

Reid, Joan A., 'Crime and Personality: Personality theory and criminality examined', *Student Pulse*, Vol. 3, No. 1 (2011), <www.studentpulse.com/pdf-files/359-1396165294-6601.pdf>

R. v. Collins [1888] NSWSupC 2, Decisions of the Superior Courts of New South Wales, 1788–1899, <www.law.mq.edu.au/research/colonial_case_law/nsw/cases/case_index/1888/r_v_collins/>

R. v. Makin and Wife, *The Weekly Notes*, Vol. VII (July 1890–July 1891), pp. 129–41

Shipman, Marlin, *'The Penalty is Death': US newspaper coverage of women's executions*, University of Missouri Press, Columbia, 2002

Springfield medicine chest (website), <www.nma.gov.au/__data/assets/pdf_file/0012/3027/FriendsJun07-Springfield-medicine-chest.pdf>

Strange, Carolyn, *Qualities of Mercy: Justice, punishment and discretion*, University of British Columbia Press, Vancouver, 1996

Taylor, S., Lambeth, D., Green, G., Bone, R. & Cahillane, M., 'Cluster analysis examination of serial killer profiling categories: A bottom-up approach', *Journal of Investigative Psychology and Offender Profiling*, Vol. 9 (2012), pp. 30–51

Tobin, Paul N., 'The position of women: The teachings of the theologians', *The Rejection of Pascal's Wager*, <www.rejectionofpascalswager.net/womenfathers.html>

Travers, Robert, *Henry Parkes: Father of Federation*, Kangaroo Press, Sydney, 2000

University of Sydney (website), <http://sydney.edu.au/about/profile/history/origins.shtml>

Whorton, James, *The Arsenic Century: How Victorian Britain was poisoned at home, work and play*, Oxford University Press, Oxford, 2010

Woods, G.D., *A History of Criminal Law in New South Wales: The colonial period, 1788–1900*, Federation Press, Sydney, 2002

Zedner, Lucia, *Women, Crime and Custody in Victorian England*, Clarendon Press, Oxford, 1991

Index